Shakespeare Dwelling

Shakespeare Dwelling

Designs for the Theater of Life

JULIA REINHARD LUPTON

The University of Chicago Press ❋ *Chicago and London*

The University of Chicago Press, Chicago 60637
The University of Chicago Press, Ltd., London

Published 2018
Printed in the United States of America

27 26 25 24 23 22 21 20 19 18   1 2 3 4 5

ISBN-13: 978-0-226-26601-5 (cloth)
ISBN-13: 978-0-226-54091-7 (paper)
ISBN-13: 978-0-226-26615-2 (e-book)
DOI: https://doi.org/10.7208/chicago/9780226266152.001.0001

The University of Chicago Press gratefully acknowledges the generous support of the University of California, Irvine, toward the publication of this book.

Library of Congress Cataloging-in-Publication Data

Names: Lupton, Julia Reinhard, 1963– author.
Title: Shakespeare dwelling : designs for the theater of life / Julia Reinhard Lupton.
Description: Chicago ; London : The University of Chicago Press, 2018. | Includes bibliographical references and index.
Identifiers: LCCN 2017038263 | ISBN 9780226266015 (cloth : alk. paper) | ISBN 9780226540917 (pbk. : alk. paper) | ISBN 9780226266152 (e-book)
Subjects: LCSH: Shakespeare, William, 1564–1616—Criticism and interpretation.
Classification: LCC PR2976 .L8258 2018 | DDC 822.3/3—dc23
LC record available at https://lccn.loc.gov/2017038263

∞ This paper meets the requirements of ANSI/NISO Z39.48–1992 (Permanence of Paper).

For Ellen Lupton, my design teacher
and Colby Gordon, my design friend

Contents

Introduction

Entries into Dwelling

Give place to me that I may dwell.
«ISAIAH 49:20»

As lovers together desireth to dwell,
So husbandry loveth good huswifery well.
«THOMAS TUSSER, *Five Hundred Points of Good Husbandry*[1]»

Scapes

In Act 3, scene 3 of *The Winter's Tale*, the Old Shepherd discovers the baby Perdita abandoned on the stormy seacoast of Bohemia:

> Good luck, an't be thy will, what have we here! Mercy on's, a bairn! A very pretty bairn—a boy, or a child, I wonder? A pretty one, a very pretty one—sure some scape; though I am not bookish, yet I can read waiting-gentlewoman in the scape. This has been some stair-work, some trunk-work, some behind-door work; they were warmer

1. Thomas Tusser, *Five Hundred Points of Good Husbandry*, 227.

> that got this than the poor thing is here. I'll take it up for pity; yet I'll tarry till my son come; he hallooed but even now. (3.3.67–75)[2]

The shepherd "reads" in the "scape" a whole narrative of courtly intrigue: a lady-in-waiting must have engaged in secret intercourse in the leftover spaces of the nearby palace, leading to her eventual abandonment of her baby. "Scape" is an elision of "escape": we would now say "escapade."[3] Yet "scape" begins to sound like "landscape" as the Shepherd imagines in that trembling bundle of baby and blanket the tale of an infant bred in the hidden hallways of the court and exposed on the stormy margin between forest and sea. According to the *OED*, "scape" only separated from "landscape" in the eighteenth century; derived from the Dutch "landschap" and taking its bearings from shaping, not escaping, "landscape" was often spelled "landskip" during Shakespeare's lifetime, and he never used the word himself. Yet the interest in scapes—both adventures and environments—is central to the late plays in particular, and a recurrent problematic throughout Shakespearean drama. From *A Midsummer Night's Dream* to *The Tempest*, settings composed of built and unbuilt elements host dramatic actions that in turn remap the potentialities of locale.

If the Shepherd gets the story wrong, it is because he mistakes romance for realism. Yet romance itself is a great incubator of landscape thinking. Consider, for example, Giorgione's enigmatic *Tempesta*, which houses a naked nursing mother, both abandoned and potentially abandoning, in the sequestered middle foreground of a scene that includes sylvan, urban, antiquarian, watery, and climatological vistas.[4] Like Shakespeare's romances, Giorgione's painting hosts allegorical, vernacular, and environmental sensibilities in one experimental space.

2. Citations from *The Winter's Tale* taken from the Oxford edition, ed. Stephen Orgel.

3. "scape, n. 1," *OED Online* (Oxford University Press, March 2016), accessed May 5, 2016.

4. For a recent Lucretian reading of Giorgione's painting, see S. Campbell, "Giorgione's Tempest."

FIGURE 1. Giorgione da Castelfranco (1477–after 1510), *The Tempest* (ca. 1508). Gallerie dell'Accademia. Photograph: HIP / Art Resources, New York.

The first references to the painting appear in an inventory from 1530: "'El paesetto in tela cun la tempesta, cun la cingana et soldato' (the little landscape on canvas with the storm, with the gypsy and soldier)," redescribed in another inventory thirty years later as "'una cingana, un pastor in un paeseto con un ponte' (a gypsy, a shepherd in a little landscape with a bridge)."[5] Like Shakespeare's Old Shepherd, these descriptions discover esca-

5. Ibid., 305.

pades in landscapes, inviting the viewer to imagine narrative connections among the contiguous regions of the image. If narrative possibilities animate Giorgione's scene, the image *as landscape* (*paesetto* or *paesaggio*, literally "little village" or "a bit of countryside") also presents itself as something other than the scenes of action it hosts.[6] The painting both builds perspectival space through the visual streaming of the river and aggregates a series of contiguous environments, like a map or tapestry. In Giorgione's *paesetto*, urban settlement and architectural excrescence coexist with climate, bank, and tree.

In the tempestuous *paesaggio* monitored by Shakespeare's Shepherd, animal actors join human ones in a perfect storm of creaturely partnerships and antagonisms.[7] In the Oxford edition, Stephen Orgel indicates that the sound of dogs and horns precedes the famous bear's entry:

> [*Storm, with a sound of dogs barking and hunting horns*]
> Antigonus: A savage clamour!
> Well may I get aboard!—This is the chase;
> I am gone forever! (3.3.55–57)

The bear is chased onto stage not by its own hunger but by the movement of animals and aristocrats in the biopageant of the hunt. Their clamor also scatters the shepherds' flock: "Would any but these boiled-brains of two-and-twenty hunt this weather?" complains the Shepherd; "They have scared away two of my best sheep" (3.3.62–64). The largely bare space of the stage relies on offstage sounds "within" to build landscape and soundscape as a continuous theatrical experience.[8]

In contemporary design and media theory, "scape" attaches it-

6. The Italian *paesetto* or *paesaggio* was first attached to pictures, usually Flemish scenes purchased by Italian collectors "primarily for their depiction of scenery rather than for the human or religious events they described" (Cosgrove, *Social Formation and Symbolic Landscapes*, 22–23).

7. Cf. Lowell Duckert on the bear's "queer" and "transspecies" connections in "Exit, Pursued by a Polar Bear (More To Follow)."

8. On the many affordances of sounds and speech occurring "within" (backstage, or in the doorways of the tiring house), see Ichikawa, *The Shakespearean Stage Space*, 29–51.

self to a range of phenomena that combine an attention to spatial organization and connectedness with an alertness to possibilities for human activity. Seascape and cityscape entered the language in the late eighteenth and nineteenth centuries to describe regions of vitality not fully captured by the more generic "landscape." In the late twentieth century, we began seeing hybrids that combine the sense of geographical setting communicated by older "scapes" with new information flows; thus Arjun Appadurai carves the social imaginary into *ethnoscapes*, *mediascapes*, *technoscapes*, *financescapes*, and *ideoscapes*. "The suffix -scape," he writes, "allows us to point to the fluid, irregular shapes of these landscapes" while also indicating that "these are not objectively given relations that look the same from every angle of vision."[9] Architect and marketing consultant Anna Klingmann uses the word "brandscape" to describe the organization of post-Fordist space by communicative processes, from signage and logos to the quasi-theatrical staging of consumer experience using sound, light, temperature, and smell.[10] Meanwhile, landscape architecture, which once played maintenance crew to the more august profession of architecture proper, has become an advocate for the environmental bases and systems-sensitive character of all building projects.[11] Finally, anthropologist Tim Ingold has developed the term "taskscape" to describe the way in which human actors cultivate their environments as scenes of action.[12]

Shakespeare Dwelling concerns the ways in which Shakespeare's plays enlist setting as a player on the stage, itself a taskscape and mediascape. I build the concept of dwelling from mixed materials that include phenomenology, modern design theory, Renaissance husbandry and housekeeping, and scripture and theology. "Dwell" comes from the Old English *dwellan*, "to lead astray, hinder, de-

9. Appadurai, "Modernity at Large," 421.

10. Klingmann, *Brandscapes*.

11. See, e.g., Balmori, *A Landscape Manifesto*; Poletto and Pasquero, *Systemic Architecture*; Waldheim, ed., *Landscape Urbanism Reader*; and Swaffield, ed., *Theory in Landscape Architecture*.

12. Ingold, "The Temporality of the Landscape."

lay . . . to be delayed, tarry, stay," and it derives its later, largely affirmative sense of remaining in place from this earlier, darker sense of being stopped in one's tracks.[13] In the Hebrew Bible, dwelling (*yashab* and *shoken*) covers sojourning and tent living as well as permanent residence.[14] God's directive that the Israelites "make me a sanctuary; that I may dwell among them" (Exod. 25:8; KJV) is the first of many biblical building plans that concern the crafting of sacred space, with major implications for ecclesiastical architecture most certainly, but also for the political-theological aspirations of a range of lightly built dwellings, from the tents of the Israelites to the house-churches of early Christianity to Thoreau's cabin in the woods.[15] One of God's names is *Ha Makom*, "the place," suggesting both particular sites and the world itself, as God's creation and the dwelling place of all living things. In the Hebrew Bible, God's dwelling, creaturely dwelling, and the relations between them are conceived architecturally (as *mishkan* and temple),[16] territorially (as the Land of Israel),[17] cosmically (as the heavens and as the world of creation),[18] and covenantally, as wherever Jews gather and live according to the laws of the Torah. In Christianity, God and man come to dwell in each other through the intimate exchanges of the Eucharist, which is

13. This discussion of etymology and definition is from the *OED*.

14. Strong's Concordance 7931 (*shakan*) and 3427 (*yashab*), accessed through Biblegateway.com. On *yashab* as dwelling, see "Dwell/Dwelling Place," in Keri Wyatt Kent, *Deeper into the Word*, n.p. (digital).

15. Selections from Thoreau are included in Andrew Ballantyne and Chris Smith's *Architecture Theory*, 150–56. See also Rykwert, *On Adam's House in Paradise*, 17.

16. In Exodus, God enjoins the Israelites in the desert to "make me a Sanctuary, that I may dwell among them" (Exod. 25:8); this traveling *mishkan* or ark of the covenant, both realized as a physical object and designed for desert transport, later becomes the core of the Temple at Jerusalem, constructed as "an house for my dwelling" (2 Sam. 7:5).

17. See Isaiah, "Surely a people shall dwell in Zion" (30:19), and Ezekiel, "And ye shall dwell in the land that I gave your fathers, and ye shall be my people, and I will be your God" (36:28). "The land" (*ha'aretz*) usually refers to Israel considered as a territory.

18. "The mountains tremble for him, and the hills melt, and the earth is burnt at his sight, yea the world, and all that dwell therein" (Nah. 1:5). The heavens are also God's "dwelling place" (1 Kings 8:43), and he is said to "dwell in the dark cloud" (2 Chron. 2:3) and to "dwell on high" (Ps. 113:5).

enjoyed in community: "He that eateth my flesh, and drinketh my blood, dwelleth in me, and I in him" (John 6:56).

In modern philosophy, the word "dwelling" is strongly associated with Heidegger and his 1951 essay "Building Dwelling Thinking [*Bauen Wohnen Denken*]." Heidegger attributes to preindustrial forms of building the capacity to create "clearings" (*Lichtungen*) in which the mutual appearing of persons, things, and environments can take place. "Genuine buildings," he writes, "give form to dwelling in its presencing and house this presence."[19] Although Heidegger's essay may appear locked in nostalgia for the farmhouses of the Schwarzwald, his phenomenological attention to the continuum between building and dwelling, that is, between architecture and the forms of life that edifices cultivate, has influenced postmodern thinking about how design might better support and reflect social and environmental processes.[20] A performative element animates Heidegger's account of dwelling, insofar as authentic acts of building bid whoever and whatever is assembled within their boundaries to appear or manifest themselves. Bert States's phenomenology of theater draws on Heidegger in order to define the stage as "a place of disclosure, not a place of reference."[21]

In *Shakespeare Dwelling*, I supplement Heidegger with Hannah Arendt, who aimed to restore action as the domain proper to both politics and drama, but did so by calling our attention to action's dependences on work (human making) and labor (the routines of meeting daily needs). Whereas action orients us to each other as speaking subjects, work fashions a durable world of objects while labor manages our constitutive exposure to biological and climactic pressures. Although Shakespearean drama largely consists of human action in Arendt's sense of substantial speech, *Shakespeare Dwelling* addresses those moments in which the plays frame the conditions of action in object worlds and

19. Heidegger, "Building Dwelling Thinking," 156.

20. See Scharr, *Heidegger for Architects*.

21. States, *Great Reckonings in Little Rooms*, 4.

built environments. How does action in response to other human beings (love, courtship, and valediction; praise and blame; rivalry, diplomacy, and murder) also imply reliance on the settings in which daily living unfolds? Through what avenues does sheltering seep into Shakespeare's play worlds, coming to appear for us in theater's phenomenological "space of disclosure"?

In its attention to the scapes of dwelling, this book constitutes my dialogue and settlement with the recent wave of writings attuned to object worlds, including Jane Bennett's Deleuzian-Spinozist political ecology, the object-oriented ontology pioneered by Graham Harman and Timothy Morton, and Bruno Latour's "post-phenomenological" actor-network theory, as well as the "universe of things" and "democracy of objects" explored in the speculative realism espoused by Steven Shaviro and Levi Bryant.[22] This body of work imagines an expanded *demos* shaped by the active participation of objects, a political sphere that houses humans alongside power grids and slime mold. Opposing any political project centered exclusively on the desires and agency of human forces, this critical field emphasizes the agential quality of objects and environments, the vital properties inhering in nonhuman objects that manifest as what political philosopher Jane Bennett calls the "vibrant matter" of a "political ecology of things."[23] From this perspective, undue attention to the category of the human appears politically suspicious, evidence of a stubborn refusal to imagine a world not designed for *us*. Thus, Levi Bryant strives to envision "an object for-*itself*," a "subjectless object" that would break us out of an "anthropocentric universe" in which "all of being is subordinated to [human] forces," while Bruno Latour offers actor-network theory as an effort to "redistribute the capacity of speech between humans and nonhumans" instead of making the phenomena of language and agency the "privilege of a human mind surrounded by mute

22. Jane Bennett, *Vibrant Matter*; Latour, *Reassembling the Social*; Harmon, *Tool-Being and The Quadruple Object*; Morton, *Ecology without Nature and Hyperobjects*; Shaviro, *The Universe of Things*; and Bryant, *The Democracy of Objects*.

23. Bennett, *Vibrant Matter*.

things."[24] With a nod to Quentin Meillassoux's critique of neo-Kantianism, Timothy Morton dismisses anthropocentrism as a species of "correlationism," the incorrect assumption that "things can only exist in relation to (human) minds or language."[25] Likewise, Bennett's political ecologies are premised on a "dogged resistance to anthropocentrism" that, for her, speaks to narcissistic "fantasies of a human uniqueness in the eyes of God." For Bennett and Morton, the hubris of human supremacy has initiated "earth-destroying" processes that include global warming, factory farming, and petrocapitalism.[26]

This ecological and posthuman turn has transformed Renaissance and early modern studies, drawing forth a multiverse of work that takes objects, animals, and environments as crucial components of new scholarly programs. In *The Accommodated Animal*, Laurie Shannon recovers the creaturely capacities of animal life from religious topoi of creation and man's governance in order to critique the "negative exceptionalism" of human supremacy.[27] Binding Jane Bennett's Deleuzian ecologies to queer theory, Drew Daniel attends to the strange materiality of black bile in *The Melancholy Assemblage*, exploring the tentative collectivities formed by "affinity groups" of pain and shame from *Hamlet* and Dürer to Benjamin.[28] Jonathan Gil Harris's landmark book, *Untimely Matter in the Time of Shakespeare*, as well as his collaboration with Natasha Korda, *Staged Properties in Early Modern English Drama*, and his now-iconic essay "Shakespeare's Hair" are major efforts toward placing objects in Renaissance drama and life.[29] Even thorny theological issues have been posed

24. Bryant, *The Democracy of Objects*, 19; Latour, *Pandora's Hope*, 141–42.

25. Morton, "Here Comes Everything," 164. For Quentin Meillassoux's resistance to the linguistic turn, see especially *After Finitude*.

26. Bennett, *Vibrant Matter*, xvi, ix. See Timothy Morton's *Hyperobjects* for an object-oriented account of environmental catastrophe as the inevitable fallout of a human-centered politics and ontology.

27. Shannon, *The Accommodated Animal*, 20.

28. Daniel, *The Melancholy Assemblage*.

29. Harris, *Untimely Matter*; Harris and Korda, ed., *Staged Properties in Early Modern English Drama*; and Harris, "Shakespeare's Hair."

as questions that concern objects and environments, as in Julian Yates's account of the Catholic underground and the exchange of oranges; or Alexandra Walsham's treatment of Reformed England's lingering landscapes of pagan enchantment; or Luke Wilson's work on the aspergillum, or "holy water sprinkle," the liturgical tool used by priests to bless their congregations.[30] Moving from physical to psychic space and back again, Mimi Yiu bids us to consider interiority at the juncture of religion, theater, and architecture.[31] The object adjuncts to sovereign power come forward in Aaron Kunin's masterful analysis of Tamburlaine's human footstools.[32] From Vin Nardizzi's performative forests to the oceanic tides of Steve Mentz's shipwreck ecologies to the "green" Shakespeares outlined by Robert Watson, Bruce Smith, and the *Ecocritical Shakespeare* volume, the pull of environments has rendered the nonhuman world a serious object of literary inquiry.[33]

Shakespeare Dwelling seizes upon current interest in objects and environments with readings of plays that draw their life from the ensemble work of hospitality, household service, and religious observance, and this book considers the object world as an incubator of politics rather than an abject outside excluded from a properly human polis. Shakespearean scenes of dwelling refuse to decouple the *vita activa* from the care of objects, including puddings and marzipan, daggers and torches, candles and votive offerings, coffins and jewels, beds and blankets. Where object-oriented and ecologically minded criticism participates in the posthuman turn, however, the phenomenological orientation of *Shakespeare Dwelling*, grounded in the work of Arendt and Heidegger, spotlights the mutual appearing of persons and things in the dramaturgy of dwelling. Arendt might seem a strange pairing

30. Yates, "Towards a Theory of Agentive Drift," 47; Yates, "What Are 'Things' Saying in Renaissance Studies?"; Walsham, *The Reformation of the Landscape*; Luke Wilson, "The Fate of the Second Bird."

31. Yiu, *Architectural Involutions*.

32. Aaron Kunin, "Marlowe's Footstools"; see also Julia Reinhard Lupton, "Soft Res Publica" and Cohen and Yates, ed., *Object Oriented Environs*.

33. Watson, *Back to Nature*; Bruckner and Brayton, eds., *Ecocritical Shakespeare*; Vin Nardizzi, *Wooden O's*; Steve Mentz, *Shipwreck Modernity*; B. Smith, *The Key of Green*.

with the object-driven projects discussed earlier, given their wariness of the anthropocentrism that motivates humanism and the humanities. After all, in *The Human Condition*, Arendt appears to assign the capacity for politics, history, and drama to the category of the human, since the "element of action" and "initiative" that she calls "natality" remains "inherent in all human activities," strictly separating the political sphere from the *oikos*.[34] And yet, building out an argument begun in *Thinking with Shakespeare*, I contend that Arendt's philosophy is premised upon the entanglement of the artifactual world built by work and labor and the scenes of speaking and appearing that comprise the political realm.[35] *Thinking with Shakespeare* began to link up persons and things through the discourse of virtue, which gestures toward the excellences cultivated by civic humanism as well as the unique capacities of animals, objects, and environments. *Shakespeare Dwelling* tracks the resonances between the deep history of object worlds and contemporary user-oriented design theory, particularly the ecological anthropology pioneered by James Gibson and Tim Ingold, as a point of entry into Renaissance environments. Just as my association between the Shepherd's "scape" and landscape only becomes effective in the later evolution of the language, so too the project of *Shakespeare Dwelling* is not strictly historical, since I allow the issues and ideas animating current thinking about design to infuse my reading of Shakespearean locales and the creatures that populate them. Moreover, taking my lead from Jan Kott's *Shakespeare Our Contemporary*, a masterpiece of criticism marked by a distinctively urban and dramaturgical sensibility, I approach Shakespeare's plays as works that continue to participate in spatial and social thinking, in a manner that often prefers modernist minimalism to historical dress.[36]

For the purposes of this book, then, dwelling can be defined as *a phenomenological approach to the interfaces among poetics, design,*

34. Arendt, *The Human Condition*, 9.
35. Lupton, *Thinking with Shakespeare.*
36. Kott, *Shakespeare Our Contemporary.*

and environment. If dwelling were only a design orientation, it would be called architecture. If dwelling were only poetic, it would simply be a theme for literary analysis. If dwelling were only considered environmentally, it would be object-oriented, posthuman, or ecocritical. Instead, the dwelling perspective addresses the action-possibilities of place implied in works of human making, whether they are plays, novels, floor plans, cookbooks, landscape paintings, or acts of benediction. In pressing the plays for their insights into what Arendt called "the human condition," I track exchanges among action, work, and labor as the fundamental forms through which human beings make themselves and their worlds appear. In this respect, *Shakespeare Dwelling* clears space for object-conscious but subject-centered humanities. The careful attention to object worlds found in the work of Kunin, Yates, and a host of other fellow travelers has directed me to self-disclosing acts of speech in which the fluid movement among persons and environments is also made manifest. The dwelling perspective acknowledges human beings as creatures who rely on things for their survival, and who express those dependencies by facing each other in intersubjective acts of avowal, care, and blessing as well as conflict, curse, betrayal, and revolt.

In the sections that follow, I lay out three entries into dwelling and suggest their relevance to Shakespeare studies. The first section below drafts an approach to dwelling in Arendt. The second section suggests an alliance between architecture, landscape, and humanism. The third section maps the affordance theory of James J. Gibson and contemporary design. *Shakespeare Dwelling* concerns the destiny of things and the capacities of place in the scenes of human action that remain at the center of Shakespeare's dramatic poetry.

Arendt's Interests

In *The Human Condition*, Arendt declares the link between acting and action that makes drama the most political of the fine arts:

> The specific revelatory quality of action and speech, the implicit manifestation of the agent and speaker, is so indissolubly tied to the living flux of acting and speaking that it can be represented and "reified" only through a kind of repetition, the imitation or *mimēsis*, which, according to Aristotle prevails in all arts but is actually appropriate only to the *drama*, whose very name (from the Greek verb *dran*, "to act") indicates that playacting actually is an imitation of acting.[37]

In both political action and acting upon the stage, the person who risks public speech manifests and even gives birth to an involuntary image of self in relation to interlocutors and witnesses endowed with the unpredictable capacity to react to the "who" that appears before them. The self-disclosure that occurs when one actor speaks to another convenes what Paul Kottman calls "a politics of the scene," a contingent public space where the consequences of deeds cannot be calculated in advance.[38] Such action seems very far from dwelling, which belongs rather to the exertions of labor that Arendt works hard to separate from the operations proper to the polis. Whereas action engages persons as speaking beings, work centers on the durability of objects and labor is beholden to the needs of life managed in the household. Indeed, at times the authenticity of Arendt's public sphere seems to depend on its strict segregation from the rhythms of dwelling. In *The Human Condition*, Arendt decries the catastrophic collapse of *oikos* and polis that produced the modern state as a giant household glorifying *Homo faber* and *animal laborans* at the expense of the *bios politikos*, life in its symbolically expressed and civically organized dimensions. If a genuine politics for Arendt involves the adventure of human speech, modern consumer society and the state forms designed to promote its interests center too exclusively on the needs of life, at the expense of the good life of classical citizenship.

37. Arendt, *The Human Condition*, 187.
38. Kottman, *A Politics of the Scene*.

This at least is the main line of *The Human Condition*, posed as a response to both the Marxist romance of the worker and the capitalist cult of consumption in the postwar period. Yet, simply by bringing work and labor into contact with action as joint conditions of the human, Arendt suggests their significance for the mise-en-scène of existence. Patchen Markell counters what he calls Arendt's "territorial" desire to divide action, work, and labor with a second, "relational" impulse, in which artifactuality, caught between work as making and work as work of art, acts as a Möbius strip connecting the three forms of activity. Arendt's project, Markell argues, ultimately delivers "a rich, non-reductive understanding of work and its objects, and of their significance *for* action and politics . . . it tries to reintegrate human activity understood instrumentally and human activity understood as meaningful performance."[39] In related work, Bonnie Honig calls work "the spine and soul of *The Human Condition*."[40] In her phenomenology of action, Arendt speaks of the Greek *daemon* as the involuntary manifestation behind the shoulder of the speaker of who he or she is by dint of what she or he has said and done, a phantasmatic element of agency visible not to the actor but to those who watch and listen.[41] Bearing traces of the laboring life and the acts of workmanship that support action in the polis, the flash of self-disclosure named by the *daemon* might also accompany the things and efforts excluded by action in Arendt's stricter, "territorial" analysis of the *vita activa*. Because work, in its alliance with art, is a form of speaking and witnessing and hence of action, work cannot be associated with the creation of utilitarian objects alone. And because labor expends its energies with the things created by work, it is also caught up in the world

39. Markell, "Arendt's Work." Susan Bernstein compares dwelling in Heidegger and Arendt in *Housing Problems*, 133–34.

40. Honig, *Public Things*, 41.

41. I have argued elsewhere that insofar as the Greek *daemon* itself derives from prephilosophical rites and beliefs surrounding animal life, the Arendtian *daemon* belongs to the forms of human being cultivated by the *bios politikos* without being identical to it. See Lupton, "The Taming of the Shrew; or, Arendt in Italy."

of action, even if in classical drama, and classical politics, it only appears intermittently. "Action and speaking," Arendt writes, are "outward manifestations of human life."[42] Action, through which "men exist not merely like other living or inanimate things but make their experience explicitly," may separate men from the realm of "inarticulate things," but nevertheless remains inseparable from the routines of living beings caught up in relations of sustenance and care.[43] In this respect, the *bios* that is "a kind of praxis" remains for Arendt part of an integrated vitality that never fully disentangles the political action of human actors from the object environments that support human copresence.

We see the outlines of this integration in, for example, Arendt's brief analysis of war monuments:

> The monuments to the "Unknown Soldier" after World War I bear testimony to the still existing need for glorification, for finding a "who," an identifiable somebody whom four years of mass slaughter should have revealed. The frustration of this wish and the unwillingness to resign oneself to the brutal fact that the agent of war was actually nobody inspired the erection of monuments to the "unknown," to all those whom the war had failed to make known and had robbed thereby, not of their achievement, but of their human dignity.[44]

Although Arendt's emphasis here is on human action as self-disclosure and the truncation of that action in a world war administered technologically, her attention alights for a moment on the built environment. These monuments, often attached to existing assemblages of commemorative statuary, aimed to grant a "whoness" to the masses of unidentified fallen soldiers of the war. In Arendt's evaluation, however, these monuments end up revealing something else: the way in which the war in general, by treating both soldiers and civilians anonymously, had robbed people of their dignity in a manner that mounted an attack on personhood as such, in consonance with her account of the camps

42. Arendt, *Human Condition*, 95.
43. Ibid., 198.
44. Ibid., 181.

in *The Origins of Totalitarianism*. If the casualties of the war had been reduced to whatness by the indiscriminate character of killing, it is by way of another kind of whatness, the war monument, that Arendt makes her analysis. The monuments "bear testimony," both entering into public space and revealing something unintended about the quality of the commemorated actions and by extension about their own status as assemblages. These monuments *act in public*, involuntarily manifesting the war's violation of the possibilities of appearing as such.

As Markell and Honig argue, work and labor can become occasions for public action in Arendt. Works of art record action, which is itself ephemeral; and they also provide occasions for the kinds of judgment that can lead to action.[45] But labor in its quotidian character of meeting needs can also lead to action. The following passage in *The Human Condition* manifests the mutual dependence among labor, work, and action in the mixed terrain of the *vita activa*:

> Action and speech go between men, as they are directed toward them, and they retain their agent-revealing capacity even if their content is exclusively "objective," concerned with the matter of the world of things in which men move, which physically lies between them and out of which arise their specific, objective, worldly interests. These interests constitute, in the word's most literal significance, something which *inter-est*, which lies between people and therefore can relate and bind them together. Most action and speech is concerned with this in-between, which varies with each group of people, so that most words and deeds are *about* some worldly objective reality in addition to being a disclosure of the acting and speaking agent. Since this disclosure of the subject is an integral part of all, even the most "objective" intercourse, the physical, worldly, in-between along with its interests is overlaid, and, as it were, overgrown with an altogether different in-between which consists of words and deeds

45. On aesthetic judgment and political action in Arendt, see Victoria Kahn, who argues that "Arendt's defense of a Kantian idea of culture is thus at the same time a defense of the realm of politics"; "Political Theology and Liberal Culture," 40.

> and owes its origin exclusively to men's acting and speaking directly *to* one another.[46]

Arendt's dramatic understanding of human action is in full evidence here. Action consists of substantial exchanges among people, verbal efforts contingent enough that their outcomes cannot be gauged in advance, and which thus have the capacity to affect the existing network of human relationships. Yet the passage also acknowledges the fact that speech often takes on its public character in the process of attending to practical affairs, and thus can occur anywhere that people gather to get things done.

"The things of the world," Arendt writes, are "interests," literally "something which *inter-est*, which lies between people and therefore can relate and bind them together."[47] On this point, compare Arendt to Latour on what he calls a *Dingpolitik*:

> It's clear that each object—each issue—generates a different pattern of emotions and disruptions, of disagreements and agreements. There might be no continuity, no coherence in our opinions, but there is a hidden continuity and a hidden coherence in what we are attached to. Each object gathers around itself a different assembly of relevant parties. Each object triggers new occasions to passionately differ and dispute. Each object may also offer new ways of achieving closure without having to agree on much else. In other words, objects—taken as so many issues—bind all of us in ways that map out a public space profoundly different from what is usually recognized under the label of "the political."[48]

The placement of "the political" in quotation marks might be taken as a dismissive reference to Arendt, much like the frequent

46. Arendt, *Human Condition*, 182–83.

47. Compare Sianne Ngai, who cites Isabelle Stengers: "In science, for Stengers, 'interesting' is what links or reticulates actors; it is not just an adjective but a verb for the action of association," and these associations include nonhuman as well as human actors. *Our Aesthetic Categories*, 112.

48. Latour, "From Realpolitik to Dingpolitik," 5.

derogations of Arendt that appear in the Italian autonomist and biopolitical writers.[49] Yet if we read Arendt through the relational rather than the territorial framework proffered by Markell, we can begin to reconcile Latour's gathering with Arendt's willingness to entertain a political discourse that grows out of a world of things. In Arendt's political phenomenology, we gather around things like tables with the help of things like chairs in order to discuss things like the price of wheat, matters of "inter-est" that *exist between* those who speak while they work. Earlier Arendt cited Latin usage: "Thus the language of the Romans, perhaps the most political people we have ever known, used the words 'to live' and 'to be among men' (*inter homines esse*) or 'to die' and 'to cease to be among men' (*inter homines esse desinere*) as synonyms."[50] To be among men is also to deal in things: with their manufacture and their trade, their distribution and their use, their maintenance and their disposal. Things gather us, and in this gathering, we begin to speak.

In *Lear*, the word "interest" binds together affect and action in a scene oriented by objects. The king addresses his youngest daughter in the final movement of act 1's fateful love test:

> Now, our joy,
> Although our last and least, to whose young love
> The vines of France and milk of Burgundy
> Strive to be interessed . . . (1.1.79–82)[51]

The image "interesses" amorous embrace, sovereign rivalry, dynastic union, and georgic cultivation. Lear speaks these words, moreover, while overseeing a map, at once a made thing and a conceptual representation of territory. The map may lie atop a table, another made thing that models the ideal flatness of land conceived as itself a kind of *tabula* capable of redrawing and division. Around this double thing (map-table) the whole court is

49. On the negative yet productive place of Arendt in Italian thought, see my essay, "The Taming of the Shrew; Or, Arendt in Italy."

50. Arendt, *Human Condition*, 7–8.

51. *King Lear*, ed. Claire McEachern.

anxiously convened to witness a public action. The play is an astounding exploration of the tensions between abstract and lived space, in which the map's symbolic presentation of land as divisible and measurable extension becomes the vastness of the heath and then the strange flatland of Dover.

This set of interests will continue to reconfigure throughout the play: the throne of state becomes the seat of torture that serves to constrain Gloucester for his blinding. Gloucester is brutalized by way of the chair, but the chair too is brutalized, turned against its proper functions, opening up the prospect of a heritable world unmade by violent repurposing.[52] The weaponization of the chair resembles the deodand that Jane Bennett recovers from English law in order to recapture some of the agency of objects:

> The idea of agency as a continuum seems also to be present in the notion of "deodand, a figure of English law from about 1200 until its abolishment in 1846. In cases of accidental death or serious injury to a human, the evil thing involved—the knife that pierced the flesh or the carriage that trampled the leg—became deodand or "that which must be given to God." . . . In what can be seen as recognition of its peculiar kind of culpability, the deodand had to be surrendered to the Crown in order to be used (or sold) to compensate for the harm done by its movement or presence.[53]

The chair that supports the blinding of Gloucester is not a direct instrument in the way that a knife might be, nor is it destroyed or disabled as a result of its usage; the chair is in another sense, however, given to God, rendered up for redemption through reuse. When the chair returns to the stage in act 4, scene 7, it has become a chair of ease, precursor of the wheelchair, which bears the sleeping King Lear into the camp of Cordelia near Dover:

52. Compare Elaine Scarry, who writes that "the room, both in its structure and its content, is converted into a weapon, deconverted, undone. Made to participate in the annihilation of the prisoners, made to demonstrate that everything is a weapon, the objects themselves, and with them the fact of civilization, are annihilated: there is no wall, no window, no door, no bathtub, no refrigerator, no chair, no bed" (*The Body in Pain*, 41).

53. Bennett, "Thing Power," 355. See Peter Stallybrass, "The Mystery of Walking," for a moving account of assisted living in the play.

"*Enter* LEAR *in a chair carried by* SERVANTS" (SD, 4.7). By the end of the scene, he accepts Cordelia's invitation to walk with him: "Will't please your Highness walk?" In this powerful exit-image, chair, daughter, father, and servants are bound together by a comportment of care that belongs to the homely scenography of dwelling. Politics for Arendt, *like* drama and *as* drama, may consist of substantial speech, but burgeons out of engagement with things and the forms of conservation that their management requires.

Heidegger's Landscape Architecture

Renaissance guides to husbandry and housekeeping do not contribute to architecture per se; rather, they address the layout and organization of buildings insofar as they serve the needs of dwelling within an environs reticulated by artisanal and agricultural enterprises. Barnaby Googe's *Four Books of Husbandry*, composed as a humanist dialogue between a retired statesman and his guest from court, includes a walk through the host's estate. The proprietor explains the disposition of courtyards, buildings, gardens, and groves as a sequence of services designed in response to the climate and lay of the land, including air and light flows. Because no site is devoid of defects, the builder must "supply the defect of nature with art and industrie."[54] The visitor praises his host for having placed the house "commodiously and handsomely," since it "receiveth the Sunne in winter, and the shadowe in Sommer," while the "fayre Porche . . . keepeth away the wind and the rayne from the doore."[55] "Commodious" and "handsome" derive aesthetic value from practical achievement, with "handsome" retaining some of its original sense of ready-to-hand.

Googe's book reveals the topographical orientation of vernacular and premodern architectural traditions, a place-based

54. Googe, *Four Books of Husbandry*, 9.
55. Ibid.

attitude reclaimed in the dwelling perspective that characterizes a strand of postmodern design.[56] Architect and theorist Christian Norberg-Schulz defines dwelling as "the establishment of a meaningful relationship between man and a given environment"; his highly influential phenomenological approach to architecture gave voice to the place-conscious ethos of architects and planners seeking alternatives to mid-century modernism's postplace stance. Norberg-Schulz is of course drawing on Heidegger's essay "Building Dwelling Thinking," first delivered as a lecture to a group of architects, engineers, and philosophers, who had assembled in Darmstadt in 1951 to consider the postwar *Wohnungsfrage* (housing problem), the task of rebuilding bombed cities and accommodating refugees from the East.[57] Heidegger begins his piece by declaring that he will not attempt to give "rules for building," thus distinguishing his project from the main line of architectural theory that stretches from Vitruvius's *De Architectura* (first century BCE) to Le Corbusier's *The Radiant City* (1935). Instead, Heidegger will focus on the originary unity between building and dwelling: "Building as dwelling, that is, as being on the earth . . . remains for man's everyday experience that which is from the outset 'habitual'—we inhabit it, as our language says so beautifully: it is the *Gewohnte*."[58] Following Heidegger, I take dwelling to be the lived dimension of architecture, including the many laboring processes by which inhabitants meet the needs of life along with the tools that support those efforts. The building-dwelling continuum thus frames for humanistic inquiry as well as for design practice the range of phenomena that connect human activity to the spaces in which people assemble.

Heidegger's most extended example of a building is neither a domestic house nor a public plaza, but rather a bridge. The

56. Postplace "anywhere" character of International Style; Corbusier exhibition on importance of place in his architecture.

57. Heidegger, "Building Dwelling Thinking." On the essay's postwar context, see Adam Scharr, *Heidegger for Architects*.

58. Heidegger, "Building Dwelling Thinking," 145.

bridge, he argues, brings together a site (*Statte*) *and* constitutes it as a location (*Ort*), a meaningful place that exists in space (*Raum*). Heidegger writes that the bridge

> does not just connect the banks that are already there. The banks emerge as banks only as the bridge crosses the stream. The bridge designedly causes them to lie across from each other. One side is set off against the other by the bridge. Nor do the banks stretch along the streams as indifferent border strips of the dry land. With the banks, the bridge brings to the stream the one and the other expanse of the landscape lying behind them. It brings stream and bank and land into each other's neighborhood. The bridge *gathers* the earth as landscape around the stream.[59]

Heidegger understands space not as measurable extension, but as the assemblage of regions, landmarks, and pathways that orient human movement, a congeries brought into existence by structures like bridges.[60] "The bridge gathers the earth as landscape around the stream": the word "gathering" here links the bridge as a *gebautes Ding* (built thing) to the discourse of things that Heidegger had initiated in his 1950 lecture "The Thing" and that continues to constellate his consideration of dwelling.[61] Rather than focusing on the substantial character of the thing, Heidegger identifies it with an act of gathering that flows in two distinct directions, one environmental and one social. On the one hand, the thing gathers what Heidegger calls the fourfold, *das Geviert*, which includes earth, sky, mortals, and the divinities. *Earth* and *sky* encompass the environmental features of land and climate, *mortals* concerns human existence, and *divinities* suggests forms of creativity and alterity not fully accommodated by either the natural world or human sociability. The very figure of the fourfold suggests the outline of a rudimentary house, one crafted not out of straw, wood, or brick but out of those habits and routines

59. Ibid., 150.

60. On paths and landmarks as orienting human movement, see Lynch, *The Image of the City*.

61. Heidegger, "The Thing."

that nest architecture in a cat's cradle of social and environmental metabolisms. Dwelling, Heidegger writes, "preserves the fourfold by bringing the presencing of the fourfold into things," an active "staying with things" that involves care and acknowledgment by those who live with them.[62]

"Thing" also has a more directly political meaning in Heidegger:

> The Roman word *res* designates that which concerns somebody, an affair, a contested matter, a case at law. . . . Only because *causa*, almost synonymously with *res*, means the case, can the word *causa* later come to mean cause, in the sense of the causality of an effect. The Old German word *thing* or *dinc*, with its meaning of a gathering specifically for the purposes of dealing with a case or matter, is suited as no other to translate properly the Roman word *res*, that which is pertinent, which has a bearing.[63]

Like Arendt's interests, the Heideggerian thing serves as a source for assembly and discourse: the thing as *res* is not only an object or artifact, but a cause, an issue, an affair, and thus an occasion for political speech. Heidegger seizes upon the old German *dinc*, which moves the sense of *thing* from an object of contention to the contention itself. In this respect, Heidegger has proven useful for later object-rich theories of political action. The association of thing with "cause" is developed in Bruno Latour's account of objects as actants, as possessing a middle-voice form of agency within heterogeneous networks. Moreover, in his call to move from "matters of fact" to "matters of concern," Latour mobilizes the link between the thing as a gathering of mixed social and environmental features (*assemblage*) and the thing as a gathering of persons for deliberation (*assembly*).[64]

62. Heidegger, "Building Dwelling Thinking," 149. Compare Ian Baucom's temporal discussion of "extra-historical" (natural history), "infra-historical" (human history), and "super-historical" (theological time): Heidegger's fourfold could be conceived as a spatialization of these temporal orders, in and as the setting of human existence ("History 4," 123).

63. Heidegger, "The Thing," 173.

64. Latour, "Making Things Public," 32.

In the preface to *Genius Loci*, Norberg-Schulz identifies the title term of his text with the Heideggerian project of dwelling:

> A place is a space with a distinctive character. Since ancient times, the *genius loci*, or "spirit of place," has been recognized as the concrete reality man has to face and come to terms with in his daily life. Architecture means to visualize the genius loci, and the task of the architect is to create meaningful places, whereby he helps man dwell.[65]

He defines "character" in architecture:

> On the one hand it denotes a general comprehensive atmosphere, and on the other the concrete form and substance of the space-defining elements. . . . We have pointed out that different actions demand places with a different character. A dwelling has to be "protective," an office "practical," a ball-room "festive," and a church "solemn." . . . Landscapes also possess character, some of which are of a particular "natural kind." Thus we talk about "barren" and "fertile," "smiling" and "threatening" landscapes.[66]

The idea that buildings might possess character is not too troubling, since the qualities of human action supported by a particular establishment might indeed reflect a particular mood (the "festive" ballroom of *Romeo and Juliet*, the subject of chapter 1). But the project becomes more uncertain when it wanders into landscapes of a "natural kind." "Barren" and "fertile" (Lear's heath, Caliban's island) hover between objective descriptions and more ethos-laden characterizations, but the image of the "smiling" landscape may seem to cross into a suspect anthropomorphism.

In classical rhetorical theory, however, the image of the "smiling" or "laughing" meadow (*pratum ridet*) is commonly given as an example of metaphor. Hans Blumenberg makes the following commentary:

> To use Quintilian's much-belabored example, it is a disaster for the smooth flow of information when an intention that is initially fixed on a meadow makes the leap—in a manner that surprises because

65. Norberg-Schulz, *Genius Loci*, 5.
66. Norberg-Schulz, "The Phenomenon of Place."

> it goes beyond the range of typical expectations—to the predicate: this meadow laughs, *pratum ridet*. . . . Metaphor captures what is not present in the qualities of a meadow when viewed objectively but is also not the subjective and phantastic addition made by an observer who, only for himself, could find the contours of a human face in the surface of the meadow. . . . Not only has what laughing means for us been "carried over," in the past, to a meadow, but this meaning of "laugh" was also enriched and "fulfilled" by the fact that it could reappear in the life world.[67]

What makes a meadow laugh? Grasses mixed with wildflowers gently moving in the breeze? Sunlight warming the colors and releasing fragrances into the air? A welcoming openness met by the comforting enclosure of a grove or fence? Although none of these is excluded from the phrase, they are also in no way necessitated by the image, which barely rises to the status of image at all. Blumenberg sees the smiling meadow not as a projection onto nature of our own experience with smiling, but rather as a genuine exchange that completes the meaning of laugh itself in a "life world" premised on the engagement between human language and environment. This enriching fulfillment may be an effect of language, but it is not simply a projection; smiling reappears as real and transformed, something other than our own grimace in flowers. The word "intention" here implies the phenomenological sense of a fundamental orientation in perception that is subjectively located, but that takes its bearings from the environment and remains submerged in motivated acts of dwelling.

The *genius loci* is Norberg-Schulz's way of naming this objective appearing of the landscape as character. And it is, as he notes in passing, a concept from classical religion that borders on the *daemon*: "It is not necessary in our context to go into the history of the concept of *genius* and its relationship to the *daemon* of the Greeks. It suffices to point out that ancient man experienced his environment as consisting of definite characters. In particular he recognized that it is of the greatest existential importance

67. Blumenberg, *Shipwreck with Spectator*, 83–84.

to come to terms with the *genius* of the locality where his life takes place."[68] "Coming to terms with" implies active forms of acknowledgment that could take on the features of drama. Although Norberg-Schulz largely emphasizes a pastoral and lyric alignment between people and places, he also takes note of the emerging ecological crisis: "pollution and environmental chaos have suddenly appeared as a frightening *nemesis*."[69] Environmental degradation, coupled with the modernist depersonalization of the built environment, creates new scenes of action for architecture and design. The dwelling perspective grants an autopoetic autonomy to the landscape while acknowledging the architect's fundamental service to the human needs of dwelling. Serving those needs means bringing dwellers into a relationship with the setting as "character," involving recognition that the landscape possesses some of the features of personhood (rights? ethos? soul?) without being personified (possessed of consciousness, say, or capable of speech).

This is a fundamentally Heideggerian problematic. Heidegger writes of the bridge that it "gathers the earth *as landscape* around the stream" (emphasis added). Heidegger's use of the word *Landschaft* shifts here between the sense of a physical terrain brought into a new state of organization by the bridge and the pictorial sense of a vista. Before the bridge entered the scene, the river and its surrounds certainly existed, but in retrospect the area will appear to have lacked a certain differentiation, spreading indefinitely as unmarked space, and thus fundamentally disorienting, because un-oriented, for a human traveler. Not unlike the smiling meadow of Quintilian and Norberg-Schulz, the passage risks overly subjectivizing the land-building relationship by giving too much constitutive power to buildings: "The location is not already there before the bridge is. Before the bridge stands, there are of course many spots along the stream that can be occupied by something. One of them proves to be a location, and does so

68. Norberg-Schulz, *Genius Loci*, 18.
69. Ibid., 370.

because of the bridge."[70] By making location the retroactive effect of building, Heidegger might be seen to make the landscape overly dependent on human actors, at the expense of the self-organizing existence of the earth itself.

We can, however, discern a more complex relationship between human and environment in Heidegger's text. Thus he speaks of the stream, banks, and river "being brought into each other's neighborhood [*in die wechselseitige Nachbarschaft*]" by the bridge, a formulation that draws on "neighborhood" as a simultaneously geographical and social category, a form of lived space that Heidegger had used earlier in the essay: "The Nachbar is the *Nachgebur*, the *Nachgebauer*, the near-dweller, he who dwells nearby."[71] If this sounds again like brute anthropomorphosis, we can also hear a sociality or *Nachbarshaft* that obtains among the landscape elements themselves, brought into a new relationship with each other as an effect of human intervention most surely, but *not* as a projection of the human mind. After all, the bridge will alter the habitats of fish, birds, and squirrels by resettling shelters, sight lines, and microclimates around the arc made by wood and stone. When Heidegger writes that the banks are brought into relationship *as banks* by the bridge, we might discern here nonhuman forms of communication that exist as part of the informational complexity of the environment, and not simply as a pictorial effect. The bridge, writes Heidegger, "gathers the fourfold in *such* a way that it *allows* a site for it."[72] Note that in the grammar of this sentence, the gathering action belongs not to the bridge's builder (who is after all trying to solve far more practical problems) but to the bridge itself as a *gebautes Ding*. Although the bridge is made by and for human beings, its efficacy as the constituter of the landscape belongs to its *thingness*, bound up in but also distinct from human being.[73] The effect of Heidegger's fourfold is to

70. Heidegger, "Building Dwelling Thinking," 152.

71. Ibid., 145. On neighbors see Žižek, Santner, and Reinhard, *The Neighbor*.

72. Heidegger, "Building Dwelling Thinking," 151.

73. Cf. "The Thing": "When and in what way do things appear as things? They do not appear *by means of* human making" (179).

cast humanity into a multidimensional environment: mortals are dependent on the earth, exposed to the sky, and apprehensively open to something other than themselves and the natural world.

In "Building Dwelling Thinking," Heidegger identifies human existence with dwelling: "Man *is* insofar as he *dwells*."[74] To identify man not primarily as a speaking or political animal, but as a being who dwells, drafts a humanism that places persons in a world composed of built and unbuilt things and the forms of cultivation that such things require. Dwelling belongs to humanism most definitely, but, as an insistent "staying with things" (149), its modes of sojourning habitation host an embedded humanism that invites ecocritical and object-oriented as well as theological trains of thought.[75] In this vein, Norberg-Schulz defines dwelling as "the establishment of a meaningful relationship between man and a given environment," and his phenomenological approach to architecture gave voice to a new place consciousness for architects and planners. Norberg-Schulz's attention to place has been given new urgency and purpose in sustainable design movements, which extend dwelling to include cohabitation with other forms of life.[76]

If in the main humanist tradition from Vitruvius onward, "man is the measure" of architecture, dwelling allows that measure to be conceived in vastly different ways: as a set of ideal proportions normatively established through a particular body type; or as embodied, ambulatory sentience; or as an instance of creaturely life coexisting with other creatures in a *wechselseitige Nachbarschaft*, a many-sided neighborhood composed of things as well as persons. This creaturely neighborhood is disclosed in Heidegger's division of *Bauen* between two forms of activity, cul-

74. Heidegger, "Building Dwelling Thinking," 145.

75. On Heidegger and ecocriticism, see Bate, *The Song of the Earth*, and McWhorter and Stenstad, *Heidegger and the Earth*.

76. Norberg-Schulz, *The Concept of Dwelling*, 13. On Norberg-Schulz's impact, see K. Smith, ed., *Introducing Architectural Theory: Debating a Discipline*, 361–52. For an "ecocultural" approach to dwelling, see Kemsley and Platt, *Dwelling with Architecture*. For a contemporary appreciation of dwelling and vernacular architecture, see Mansfield, *Dwelling in Possibility*.

tivation and construction, the latter having eclipsed the former in the history of architecture and engineering (145).[77] In identifying the builder with the *Bauer* (farmer), Heidegger asks the main tradition of architectural humanism, dedicated to acts of construction that memorialize and manifest human ingenuity, to make room for what we might call a *landscape-architectural humanism*, which situates dwelling-driven building projects in the metabolic field of their instigations and effects. Landscape architecture does not deny the primacy of human making in the arts of design, but rather relocates and rescales the human factor, whether by coupling human artifice and natural systems in new biotechnical partnerships; by redirecting light, air, and water flow between interior and exterior spaces; or by deriving more flexible building vocabularies from plant, animal, and mineral architectures.[78]

The emphasis across all design professions on the human user develops Heidegger's merging of building and dwelling by focusing on the routines of work, rest, and play housed by buildings and supported by the furnishings within them. The "universal" in universal design names not the normative body type of Vitruvian Man but rather the development of graspable tools and navigable pathways that facilitate the broadest possible use by the most actors. Putting the plurality of human users at the center of design research is also a landscape-architectural humanism, which attends to diverse bodily capacities and affective responses in a mode that emphasizes an environmental integration of persons and settings.

The sudden flourishing of landscape architecture and user-oriented design, broadly phenomenological in their commitment to supporting the embodied, ambulatory, and situated processes of dwelling, can also be read backward into the master texts of design writing. If Vitruvius's *De Architectura* is associated above

77. "This word *bauen* however *also* means at the same time to cherish and protect, to preserve and care for, specifically to till the soil, to cultivate the vine . . . Latin *colere, cultura*, and building as the raising up of edifices, *aedificare*—are comprised within genuine building, that is, dwelling" ("Building Dwelling Thinking," 145).

78. See Balmori, *A Landscape Manifesto*.

all with an architect's interest in symmetry and proportion and an engineer's commitment to function and efficiency, the Heideggerian frame brings out other aspects of this classical text. Vitruvius's comments in book 1 on "the site of a city" focus on the impact of winds and humidity on public health, and he suggests that the builder learn from "the common experience of many communities" about the debilitating effects of unregulated air flow on daily life. These considerations place Vitruvius in the tradition of what current architects, taking their cue from landscape design, call the "architecture of flows," which responds to and integrates human building projects with autopoetic processes in the surrounding environment.[79] Vitruvius goes on to recommend that planners test the location of a settlement by conducting a series of animal sacrifices, a ritual procedure that includes examination of the animals' entrails; if the priests consistently find abnormal organs, the planners should deduce that "the food and water supply found in such a place would be just as unhealthy for man."[80] Vitruvius's toxicity studies erect their own fourfold, combining sacrifice to the gods with empirical study of the earth.

Following Heidegger, Christian Norberg-Schulz writes that the task of architecture is to build on and support "existential space."[81] Theater, especially the minimalist theater of much Shakespearean dramaturgy, is ideally suited to contribute its own building forms to this phenomenology of architecture by establishing a basic typology of locations (plateau, balcony, canopy; sky, ground, gallery) for the exploration of human relationships in, to, and by means of space. Their interdependence is put on view in an exemplary way in theater, with its heightened spatial delimitation, its choreography of entrances and exits, its highly selective inventory of objects, and its initiatory "Let the show begin" stance toward human gesture and speech. Reading Heideggerian dwelling with Arendt emphasizes the action possibilities

79. Ballantyne and Smith, ed., *Architecture in the Space of Flows.*

80. Vitruvius, "Ten Books of Architecture," 314.

81. Norberg-Schulz, *Genius Loci*, 5.

that belong to drama while also bidding us to attend to the lived and built conditions of action in Arendt's discourse. This existential play with objects and places resonates with Arendt's image of action growing out of scenes of labor like weeds from stonework.

Gibson's "Neighborhood in Which We Live"

I make my own foray into the current *Wunderkammer* of clutter and clamor in Shakespeare studies through the theory of affordances, which, in Caroline Levine's formulation, "crosses back between materiality and design."[82] Affordances eminently belong to things in their tactile specificity yet address potential users in a double-facing posture that supports the setting-sensitive humanism I am developing here. The term "affordance" was first coined by ecological psychologist James J. Gibson to account for the way in which animals, including human ones, access their environments as scenes of action:

> The *affordances* of the environment are what it *offers* the animal, what it *provides* or *furnishes*, either for good or ill. The verb *to afford* is found in the dictionary, but the word *affordance* is not. I have made it up. I mean by it something that refers to both the environment and the animal in a way that no existing term does. It implies the complementarity of the animal and the environment.[83]

Affordances reside in the environment, and in this sense they are objective, but they only exist in relation to particular kinds of users (carpenters, carpenter ants, squirrels, bots), and in this sense they are relational. Affordances invite but do not cause actions in agents; affordances can be refashioned by cultural meanings. Affordances appear in tandem with the social routines that organize their employment, and they can be invented as well as discovered by users. For human creatures, any action that we take with things is also embedded within systems of meaning and commu-

82. Levine, *Forms*, 8–9.

83. Gibson, *The Ecological Approach to Visual Perception*, 127.

nication: a hammer can only afford pounding for an actor who lives in a world with nails and a tradition of building with them.

For Gibson, however, the social character of our interactions with objects does not mean that the affordance character of the physical world is rendered purely semiotic. Thus he develops the example of the mailbox:

> For Koffka, it was the *phenomenal* postbox that invited letter-mailing, not the physical postbox. But this duality is pernicious. I prefer to say that the real postbox (the *only* one) affords letter-mailing to a letter-writing human in a community with a postal system. . . . The main fact is that it is perceived as part of the environment—as an item of the neighborhood in which we live.[84]

Gibson nests perceptual levels: symbolic actions at the highest level still occur in physical environments managed through the skilled handling of tools that afford certain operations within communities that support their use.[85] Like Heidegger's *wechselseitige Nachbarschaft*, Gibson's "neighborhood in which we live" is a rich composite of creatures, things, places, routines, and meanings. This neighborhood constitutes the scene of actions that range from preparing food to building cities or waging war. Like Heidegger's landscape humanism, affordances are always relative to an actor (usually a human one), yet remain located within a world capable of putting humanity in its place.

Environmental anthropologist Tim Ingold would locate the postbox in what he calls the taskscape, the organization of locale by the skilled routines that support the needs of life. In *The Perception of the Environment: Essays on Livelihood, Dwelling and Skill*, Ingold brings together the phenomenological tradition of Heidegger and Merleau-Ponty with Gibson's ecological psychology in order to develop what he calls "the dwelling perspective," in which "the world continually comes into being around the inhabitant, and its manifold constituents take on significance

84. Ibid., 139.
85. On nested hierarchies in Gibson, see Heft, *Ecological Psychology in Context*, 68–73.

through their incorporation into a regular pattern of life activity."[86] Ingold's taskscape integrates ecological systems and social scripts through the actions and organisms they host. In the taskscape, he writes, "cultural knowledge, rather than being imported into the settings of practical activity, is constituted through these settings through the development of specific dispositions and sensibilities that lead people to orient themselves in relation to their environment and to attend to its features in the particular ways they do."[87] Gibson's postbox must be envisioned in a taskscape that includes streets, curbs, front doors, kitchen tables, and stamps as well as readers, writers, and collection agencies. Ingold develops the ecological and psychological orientation of Gibson within full-blown worlds of human sociality, but without sacrificing the object-rich framework that first hosted the concept.

If affordances were born in the environs of creaturely life, the concept has enjoyed the greatest impact in the world of design. A late note in Gibson's papers defines building as the organizing of affordances:

> The general purpose of "building" (both the altering of *old* surface-layouts and the making of *new* surface-layouts) is to change what the previous surface-layout *affords* (to modify what the "natural" layout of the environment *permits* a man—to *improve the affordances of the environment*).[88]

In Heideggerian terms, Gibson recomposes "building" around "dwelling," that is, around the uses and routines that building is meant to support and sustain. "Building" in this definition would include lean-tos erected against the hillside, holes dug into cliffs, gabardines unfolded in a storm, or arras hung up to enable hid-

86. Ingold, *Perception of the Environment*, 153. He compares Gibson and Heidegger: "Just as the point of departure, for Gibson, had been the perceiver-in-his/her-environment, so likewise [Heidegger and Merleau-Ponty] set out from the premise that every person is, before all else, a being-in-the-world" (168).

87. Ibid., 153. For more on the taskscape, see Ingold, "The Landscape of Temporality," a version of which appears in *Perception of the Environment*.

88. James J. Gibson papers, 14-23-1832, Box 5, Folder 24, Division of Rare and Manuscript Collections, Cornell University Library.

ing. Moreover, although Gibson's focus here is on human building, his definition easily accounts for animal architecture.[89] The note culminates in a miniature manifesto for design:

> We now aim for environmental design and environmental management, but with no theory to guide it. The theory of affordances would provide such guidance.

Here, Gibson considers the implications of this thinking: "environmental design" and "environmental management" are fundamentally concerned with the interface between building and dwelling, between the objects created by human hands and the settings that they forever reconfigure, yet these emerging disciplines lack a theory that would richly account for those connections. *Affordances*, Gibson suggests, *is that theory.*

Donald Norman, in contact with Gibson during the final years of his life, was the figure who made good on that bold statement, which Gibson had also shared publicly in a 1976 lecture to architects and engineers.[90] Like Gibson, Norman was an environmental psychologist. His work on design began as a response to his irritation with things that frustrate their users (recalcitrant door handles; inscrutable knobs). His landmark study *The Design of Everyday Things*, first published in 1988 under the tile *The Psychology of Everyday Things*, places affordances in the very specific context of handles, interfaces, and controls. Norman's influence is especially strong in human-computer interaction (HCI), which guides the design of buttons, touch screens, haptic feedback signals, and other features that facilitate life with computers.[91] Focusing on reaction times, attention spans, and intuitive responses to particular page layouts, HCI improves our sense of well-being and competence and helps prevent design-driven disasters such as Three Mile Island. Empirical design research is nominally hu-

89. See Ingold, *Perception of the Environment*, 172–88.

90. Gibson's talk, "The Theory of Affordances and the Design of the Environment" was delivered as a keynote address to the American Society of Esthetics in 1976 and published posthumously in *Reasons for Realism*.

91. Norman, *The Design of Everyday Things*.

manist in its orientation around the user. The calculated deployment of affordances also, however, increasingly guides our work and play experiences in ways that promote interests other than our own.[92] In response to new demands for sustainability and for more ethically integrated views of human action, designers are increasingly returning to the original environmental framework of Gibson's work in order to reconceive human use in larger scenes composed out of interdependent and precarious systems.

Writing from within the anthropocene, Gibson avers that man, in changing "what the environment affords him," has altered it "wastefully, thoughtlessly, and if we do not mend our ways, fatally."[93] There is a strong language of negative affordances in Gibson's work; fire affords burning, and cliffs afford falling off. Affordances, then, are not benign. Gibson's analysis of the costs of human-designed affordances is "ecological" in two senses: attuned to the complexity of systems, and concerned about the welfare of the environment. Gibson's *ecological psychology* becomes *political ecology* when we test the valences of affordances in the environments of contemporary capital. In the biopolitical clearings of today's cities, the design of a particular bench or park layout may benefit one demographic group (the middle-class mother, the well-heeled tourist, the neighborhood policeman) at the expense of another (the homeless person, the skateboarder, the migrant worker) in order to further specific civic and economic ends. In response to such concerns, architectural theorist David Leatherbarrow frames the following task for architecture:

> We [architects] have great trouble seeing design as something other than technique or planning, great difficulty seeing it as a mode of participation in an existing structure. Our methods are so effective, and our desire for a well-administered world so strong, that ordering has become the architect's chief service. If topography has a role to play in contemporary design practice, its job is to give "ordering"

92. Heft, "Affordances, Dynamic Experience, and the Challenge of Reification," 177; Gibson, *Ecological Approach*, 140. On the ideology of "the user" in design research, see Peter Lunenfeld, *User*.

93. Gibson, *Ecological Approach*, 130.

> techniques their orientation, to supply them with a frame of reference, a milieu, and a calendar. Were design practices to accept such a donation (the givenness described previously), our methods would not seek only the pleasure of their own productivity, but attempt to disclose the conditions of their genesis, out of topography and its structure.[94]

Topography here refers to the geological, vegetal, and climatic as well as vernacular features of the landscape, to which architecture is bid to respond in a more thoughtful and participatory way, harkening to Norberg-Schulz's *genius loci.*[95] Yet we can also think about topography more broadly, as engaging some of the other "scapes" of modern and early modern life—the sedimented grounds formed by the jostling of social classes, the swirl of emergent media forms, the monumental symbology of political institutions, and the various laboring efforts that shape urban terrains.

By folding forms of enskillment into the evolving features of the environment in which work takes place, affordances incubate a theory of distributed cognition that proves as relevant to early modern housekeeping as to modern landscape architecture. Take, for instance, the frontispiece to the work of another Hannah, Hannah Woolley's 1669 *The Queen-Like Closet*, which is divided into five sections, like compartments in a cabinet or cupboard where things might be stored. Although the word "closet" may seem largely architectural, denoting a private study, pantry or dressing room, it also announces a cognitive project, insofar as the closet designates a space for research into the secrets of nature, while its many shelving units suggest the distributed affordances of a memory theater. What the openings frame is not an inventory of objects so much as a set of scenes for engaged and skilled activity. The graphic resembles the elevation of a house, one in which every room is a kitchen. In each of these views, the

94. Leatherbarrow, "Topographical Premises," 73.

95. For an example of such topographic responsiveness, see Leatherbarrow, "Breathing Walls," an exquisite reading of a modernist chapel in Puerto Rico.

FIGURE 2. Hannah Woolley, *The Queen-Like Closet* (1681), frontispiece. Photograph: Reproduced by permission of the Huntington Library, San Marino, California.

kitchen appears as a taskscape, a layout defined by the purposeful movement of human and nonhuman actors through its layered terrain of affordances.

Woolley puns on *dwelling as living* and *dwelling as thinking* when she promises to "dwell most upon that which [housewives] cannot dwell without."[96] In cookbooks and husbandry manuals of the period, dwelling carries its primary meaning of residing, but often with a heightened sense of the expertise required for felicitous habitation. Gervase Markham's *Countrey Contentments* lays out the ways "to dwell upon, order, and maintaine a Farme, Meese, or Inheritance in the Fields": one *dwells upon* the land only by *ordering* and *maintaining* the complex operations that take place upon it.[97] These tracts cultivate comportments of care toward the places and things of the household; John Fitzherbert, in *The boke of husbandry* (1531), nominates "diligence," "attendance," and "discretion" as virtues that orient the householder toward the intricate exigencies of his property. Fitzherbert urges the proper construction of tools such as forks and rakes so that they "lye upright in they hand"; the goal is to make tools that are "handsome" and "easy to worke with," "handsome" commanding its original sense of "easy to handle or control."[98] Markham uses the phrase "outward virtue" to encompass the housewife's many responsibilities, including "Phisicke, Cookery, Banqueting Stuffe, Distillation, Perfumes, Wool, Hemp, Flaxe, Dairies, Brewing, Baking, and all other things belonging to an Household." Each of these "outward virtues" orchestrates skills in a setting that hosts humans, animals, plants, and microbes in a series of joint ventures. These arts are designed to profit the human managers most certainly, and thus belong to instrumental reason; insofar as they require the thoughtful ordering of a complex landscape, they become instrumental in a more musical sense, "playing" the environment for its autopoetic harmonies and capacities.

96. Woolley, *The Gentlewoman's Companion*, 6.

97. Markham, *Countrey Contentments*, 1.

98. John Fitzherbert, *The boke of husbandry*, addresses "How forkes and rakes shulde be made" (19).

Affordance theory invites us to consider the complexity of the worlds imagined by drama as well as the physical plant of performance spaces. Evelyn Tribble has developed both Gibson's affordances and Ingold's taskscape in her analysis of distributed cognition at the Globe.[99] Caroline Levine, in the most ambitious literary repurposing of affordances to date, argues that forms of all kinds, from rhyme and meter to the organization of time and space, open up "a generalizable understanding of political power."[100] W. B. Worthen has used affordances to shift the play text/performance relationship from a hermeneutic model (in which a particular production "reads" the text) to a relationship in which the play text invites new stagings solicited by shifting performance conditions. Worthen writes that "tools afford different acts in different technologies, which redefine the *affordance* of the tool," while "the utility of dramatic writing lies in the perception of what kinds of activity, performance, doing something, those properties might *afford* in the social technology of the theater."[101] Whereas Tribble is concerned with how actors do their work, Worthen uses affordances to understand how dramaturgy unfolds over time and across its constitutive components, thanks to the potentialities yielded by play texts under new dramaturgical conditions. Affordances can help explain how pieces of dramatic writing enable without determining future stagings: *The Winter's Tale*'s bear, *The Tempest*'s storm, *Pericles*'s sea, and *Macbeth*'s ambience have all instigated a range of scenographic responses by no means predicted by the Shakespearean texts, which know nothing of parachute silk, giant polar bear rugs, or postnuclear underground cities.

Gibson does not push the "invitation character" of affordances in an ethical or existential direction, but humanists and theologians have begun to take up that offer. Explicitly drawing on hospitality as a frame, theologian Douglas Knight has used

99. Tribble, *Cognition in the Globe*. For related work on affordances and the taskscape in modern dramaturgy, see Paavolainen, *Theatre/Ecology/Cognition*.

100. Levine, *Forms*, 7.

101. Worthen, *Drama between Poetry and Performance*, 21–22.

affordances in order to consider humanity's creaturely capture within a multidimensional world that hosts us.[102] In liturgical terms, the environment considered in terms of its offerings or affordances solicits the action of blessing or thanksgiving, insofar as the landscape consists of "givens" that are "gifts." Art and literature, including drama, may be especially suited to drawing out the existential affinity between hospitality and affordance theory, thanks to their attunements to places and things as reservoirs that harbor their own rhythms and efficiencies.[103] Both the artist and the hostess scan the landscape of creaturely constraints for surplus uses, soliciting them to think pragmatically but also in terms of occasion and gift. The affinity between hospitality and affordances allows us to discover the nimble architecture of nascent thought within the succor pledged by the pillow and the security assured by the saucer. Affordances can help us pose a theory of the spoon because the spoon is *already theoretical*, its slender stem and shallow bowl mumbling mutely of extension and transport, containment and flow, via the proprioceptive promises of hand love and mouthfeel.

Like Levine, I link the unfolding discussion of affordances in literary studies to both the original environmental setting of Gibson's work and the renewal of affordances within contemporary design research. Many of my readings center around what Kevin Lynch, writing in a mode that predicts many affordance issues, called "the environmental image."[104] By this he meant the

102. Douglas H. Knight, *The Eschatological Economy: Time and the Hospitality of God*. On affordances he writes: "J. J. Gibson argued that opportunities (affordances), not things, are our first objects of perception. Our behavior is best understood in terms of our alertness to opportunities for action. What we see are openings and advantages. . . . To touch any part of this tensed environment is to release a force that opens and closes various sets of options. These affordances are not casually related to the different behavioral capacities of different organisms but are another way of expressing these different capacities" (49–50). He goes on to suggest that "we are placed by, and contained within, the world of God's working" (51).

103. See, e.g., Edward T. Hall's turn to literature for data on proxemics: the literary attention ends up providing a quality of insight into human distances that social science and psychology cannot provide alone.

104. Lynch, *The Image of the City*.

mental navigational map built up by pedestrians in response to the wayfinding features of the urban landscape. I use the environmental image more broadly, to include images in dramatic poetry that probe the entangled engagement of human actors with location. (See my readings of Romeo's glove, Macbeth's martlets, Marina's leafy shelter, and Innogen's andirons for examples of the environmental image.) Poetry's intricate work with images describes and enacts the phenomenological flow among thought and its settings, a weaving, nesting, tunneling effort that opens spaces for reflection. This book remains a readerly project, though one that listens for the plays' alertness to theatrical and domestic urgencies and thus aspires to acknowledge the composite unity drawn by the phrase *dramatic poetry*.

Finally, I tap affordance theory's emphasis on movement, attention, and action to invite a dramatic view of how human creatures navigate "the neighborhood in which we live." If most dramatic action in Shakespeare unfolds in Arendtian fashion as transactions that occur between persons, those actions nonetheless take place in real settings shaped by work and labor. These moments often occur in scenes of hospitality, in which dwelling puts itself on display and opens itself to risk. When Perdita offers her disguised guests a bouquet garni of herbs, she chooses her flowers based on their kitchen virtues: rosemary and rue keep their properties (their "seeming and savour") through the winter months, and are thus resources for the Renaissance cook, who was also a doctor, a veterinarian, an accountant, and a conservator. Armed with her dibble, Perdita has one foot in Markham's husbandry manuals and the other in literary pastoral. Perdita's herbs help build her own queenlike closet that houses the practical with the aesthetic, the laborious with the ostensive, and the tactile with the semiotic. Temperamentally reserved like her mother Hermione, Perdita uses the gesture of handing flowers to her guests to tap her latent linguistic and expressive capacities, releasing Perdita into the perilous scene of human plurality hosted by hospitality. Here and elsewhere in Shakespeare, dwelling concerns the infolded routines through which we make our way in the worlds we build and inherit, transform and violate.

Over the course of five chapters, I build a model of dwelling designed to accommodate the poetic, phenomenological, and theatrical dimensions of Shakespearean drama. Shakespeare's plays build *spaces that afford dwelling*, and *dwellings that afford action*. I argue that a theater of affordances is an environmental and phenomenological theater, a space in which things, persons, settings, and forms of life are solicited to appear in the intricacy and volatility of their interdependence. I use affordance theory in concert with design, theology, and phenomenology in order to unfold the elasticities and resistances that hold together Shakespeare's fabricated worlds. These topics include proxemics and place-making in *Romeo and Juliet*; landscape, sleepscapes, and occasional architecture in *Macbeth*; artisanal taskscapes in *Pericles*; furniture design in *Cymbeline*; and dessert and holiday entertainment in *The Winter's Tale*.

Chapter 1, "Reading Dramaturgy in *Romeo and Juliet*," examines the poetics of things in space in Shakespeare's early tragedy. I show how joint-stools, torches, lanterns, curtains, marzipan, and crowbars are used to reset the space of the stage and the places of Verona for human encounter and subjective self-invention. This dramaturgy of dwelling takes shape around the scripts furnished by hospitality, which I read alongside Timothy Ingold's taskscapes and the architecture of flows. In this chapter, I also introduce the concept of proxemics, the study of distance and nearness in human relationships that stands at the center of much urban and environmental design as well as management and organization studies. The play's actions and images variously stretch and contract the real, symbolic, and psychic space among actors in order to create compelling opportunities for dramatic engagement.

My chapter on *Romeo and Juliet* introduces a pair of linked themes that return in my chapter on *Macbeth*: the ecology of sleep and the mobilization of soft architecture, or what I call the softscape. Contemporary shelter and dwelling magazines expend much attention on the sleeping spaces of the techno-gentry, including luxury bedding, smart mattresses, motorized window treatments, and lighting, heat, and sound systems. In *Macbeth*, this congeries of somatic and scenographic materials takes on a horrific cast. I read *Macbeth* as an oneiric assemblage of soft appliances, including bedtime prayers as well as sovereign sleeping quarters, that are subject to tragic violation and capable of redeployment for hostile action. I begin with scenes of investiture: the psycho-symbolic and political-theological appareling of persons and spaces with majestic fabric. I then turn to the revoking of prayer, examining bedtime blessings as part of a sleep ecology violated by the murder of Duncan. I end with Birnam Wood, in which a wall made of foliage moves across a militarized terrain in order to unfurl the hostility latent in hospitality. In the landscape architecture of Birnam Wood, scenography meets poetics, linking the affordances of setting to the language games of prophesy and curse. In *Macbeth*'s softscapes, the portable properties of impromptu building shape the ambience of a play characterized by both a terrible hardening of purpose and an apocalyptic rending of the fabric of reality itself.

The next three chapters are all devoted to Shakespeare's late plays. In *Pericles*, *Cymbeline*, and *The Winter's Tale*, Shakespeare visits messianic time and space by drawing on a fundamentally mixed set of religious and national traditions, including Roman, Hellenistic, and Hebrew antecedents as well as their humanist, Catholic, and Reform revisions. In *Pericles* the pluralist archaeology of Ephesus as well as the coupling of Jonah and Paul announce Shakespeare's messianism, a task taken up in *The Winter's Tale's* honoring of Whitsun (Shavuot-Pentecost) as the festival of a *ruach* or spirit of covenantal inclusion. In *Cymbeline*, set during the period of the Incarnation, Shakespeare travels to the messianic moment of an unwitnessed offstage nativity. As Thomas Betteridge compellingly argues, the romances reject the disciplinary and inquisitorial features of confessional Christianity in favor of a wider and more inclusive postconfessional faith.[105] The romances draw seasonal rhythms and geographical resources into their ethos of welcoming, as Randall Martin has convincingly demonstrated.[106] I argue that the ad hoc dwellings of the late plays contribute to the Pauline and messianic character of Shakespeare's romance landscapes.

"Grace and Place in *Pericles*" reads the first of the romances for its spatialization of chances for redemption. In the first movement of the play, I link Pericles's wandering to Jonah's journey in order to explore the hero's interactions with maritime taskscapes. In the middle movement, Marina founds a community of women dedicated to needlework, the performing arts, and the practice of eloquence and virtue, an establishment modeled on the house-churches of Priscilla and Aquila in the Epistles of Paul. The play ends in Ephesus, a city that enjoys a long and layered history of artisanal, liturgical, and curatorial collectivism associated with the Temple of Artemis. The viscous and resonant space-time of *Pericles*'s Asia Minor offers provisional sanctuary to messianism in its pluralist origins, mixed destinies, and imperfect completions.

Chapter 5, "Natality and Nativity in *Cymbeline*," revisits the play's setting during the time of the Incarnation in order to evaluate the play's inquiry into the virtues of fidelity and courage. I juxtapose the theological concept of nativity with the political concept of natality in order to distinguish religious and humanist conceptions of rebirth and to note their proximities in the liquid light of romance. In the first half of the chapter, reading Arendt with Auerbach, I focus on the exchanges between *figura* and *creatura*. In the second half of the chapter, I turn to the play's investigations of furniture. Beds, pillows, and lighting appliances as well as bedtime reading and evening prayers support the ecology of sleep explored in my chapters on *Romeo and Juliet* and *Macbeth*. *Cymbeline*, I argue, is a play that bids furniture to *furnish*

105. Betteridge, "Writing Faithfully in a Post-Confessional World."
106. Martin, *Shakespeare and Ecology*.

forth: to provide, to equip, to bring about, to apparel, to decorate, but also to arm and to occupy, in order to test the resilience of objects and persons.

The final chapter, "Room for Dessert in *The Winter's Tale*," looks to the dessert course for its capacity to open space for disclosure, encounter, and reflection, a dynamic between clearing and appearing that affiliates the rhythm of the meal with drama and dramaturgy. This chapter reads *The Winter's Tale* in the context of Whitsuntide observances. Whitsuntide marked the celebration of Pentecost, itself derived from the Jewish holiday of Shavuot. Set within the burgeoning world of creation while commemorating acts of revelation with the power to constitute and motivate human communities, the festival of Pentecost mediates between dwelling as creaturely routine and environmental engagement (Heidegger) and drama as scene of significant speech and covenantal action (Arendt).

In each of these chapters I attend to the environmental origins of Gibson's affordance explorations as they pass through the technological, theological, and philosophical complexities of modern and early modern life and are regathered existentially as the dwelling perspective by works of dramatic poetry. *Shakespeare Dwelling* aims to contribute to the phenomenology of theater, the ethics of habitation and hospitality, and the literary dimensions of design.

1

Reading Dramaturgy in *Romeo and Juliet*

In his comic exchange with the Capulet's illiterate serving man on the afternoon of the big party (1.2), Romeo caps his reading of the guest list with an evaluation and a query:

> *Romeo*: A fair assembly. Whither should they come?
> *Serving-Man*: Up.
> *Romeo*: Whither to supper?
> *Serving-Man*: To our house.
> *Romeo*: Whose house?
> *Serving-Man*: My master's.
> *Romeo*: Indeed, I should have asked thee that before.
> *Serving-Man*: Now I'll tell you without asking. My master is the great rich Capulet, and if you be not of the house of Montagues, I pray come and crush a cup of wine. Rest you merry. (1.2.74–84)[1]

The serving man's information-poor responses continue to draw laughs in the theater as Romeo drags out the key coordinates of the invitation from the ready but not able clown. In a rehearsal at my campus, the director and his cast discussed what to do with

1. All citations from *Romeo and Juliet* are from the Oxford edition, unless otherwise noted.

"Up." For a modern audience, the serving man might be referring to a part of the city, as in uptown, or the movement through it, as in the "jauncing up and down" on Juliet's errands that the Nurse complains of in act 2 (2.4.51); a time of day in the routines of eating (the "up" in "supper"); the "upper" class that he serves; the comic, upward movement of the play's first half; or features of the theater's architecture, such as the galleries where higher-paying patrons would be seated, the balcony where Juliet will later appear to Romeo as the rising sun, or the ladder he will use to join her.[2] The simple word "up," comic in both its semantic truncation and its buoyant arc, is one of many directional moments in *Romeo and Juliet* in which the play seems to surge and pop with its own burgeoning intentionality. Mapping civic space onto social space and merging both with the physical architecture of the theater, the serving man's "Up" contributes to *Romeo and Juliet*'s virtuoso conjuration of worlds.

In *New Dramaturgy: International Perspectives*, Katalin Trencsényi and Bernadette Cochrane define dramaturgy as "the totality of the performance-making process" and as "the inner flow of a dynamic system."[3] In the same volume, Joseph Danan writes that "dramaturgy cannot be separated from playwriting or mise-en-scène, because it is the process which crosses between the one and the other, and connects them both" (6). Drawing on dramaturgy as "*drama-ergon*," "the work of the actions," director Eugenio Barba defines dramaturgy as "the way the actor's actions enter into work," a technical as well as a literary procedure "inherent in the weaving and growth of a performance and its different components."[4] Dramaturgy, that is, treats the stage as a taskscape, a terrain of affordances that formats interaction. First coined by Tim Ingold as a phenomenological complement to James Gibson's ecological work on affordances, the taskscape speaks to what design theorists call an "architecture of flows,"

2. On horizontal and vertical patterns in the play that work both mythographically and dramaturgically, see Janice Valls-Russell, "Erotic Perspectives."

3. *New Dramaturgy*, ed. Trencsényi and Cochrane, 1.

4. Barba, *On Directing and Dramaturgy*, 8.

which approaches the built environment as an event rather than an object.[5] For architect and urbanist Keller Easterling, architecture "is not about the house but rather about housekeeping," beckoning us to reconsider spaces from a dramaturgical and dwelling perspective.[6]

In this chapter I argue that *Romeo and Juliet* stages architecture in the dynamic mode of dramaturgy, using the scripts of hospitality and urban space. Hospitality plots the gestures of entry, exit, offering, and encounter in the theatrical taskscapes of drama and life; in *Romeo and Juliet*, hospitality furnishes the drama with narratives of hosting and its risks, naturalizing classical myths into routines of dwelling internal to the story. At the same time, hospitality orchestrates the local affordances of objects (platters, torches, fabrics, floors, balconies, rope ladders) that help erect and maintain the environments of entertainment. *Romeo and Juliet* ensconces human life in an active environment built from the mixed media of torches and traffic, crowbars and dovecotes, household service and party planning. Because my focus remains phenomenological and literary-critical rather than theater-historical, I am interested in the role that poetic imagery plays in cuing action and inspiring future scenographic invention, as well as in dramatic poetry's life beyond performance, in readerly modes of engagement with dramaturgic possibilities that belong to no single stage. Such readings take place on imaginative planes that might infuse or inspire a particular production, but also bear their own literary power. These imaginative resonances might thematize the conditions of performance, but they are not bound by them. My aim is to remain true to the range of experimental clearings, both theatrical and poetic, managed by Shakespeare's lyric tragedy. *Romeo and Juliet*, with its absorption of neighboring entertainment forms into the language-rich and book-conscious medium of Elizabethan

5. See the essays collected in *Architecture in the Space of Flows*, ed. Ballantyne and Smith, particularly Yates, "Oceanic Spaces of Flow."

6. Easterling, *Organization Space*, 2.

drama, is continually integrating poetic and performative concerns in a manner that has proved endlessly productive for both scenography and literary criticism.[7]

Reading dramaturgy in *Romeo and Juliet*, then, encompasses a range of entries into the play, from concrete moments of staging and their immediate thematization in the text to the more diffuse scenographic and spatial sensibilities manifested by Romeo, Juliet, Capulet, and the Nurse as they move through their affordance-laden world. The first three sections address the dramaturgical dimensions of *Romeo and Juliet's* taskscapes, as defined by the scripts of child-rearing and domestic service, hospitality and entertainment, and urbanism and transport. In "Traffic Patterns," I look to the play for a phenomenology of transit in and between urban and domestic space. In "Consorting," I address the two lovers, but also Capulet, as scenographers avant la lettre who adjust the atmospheres of their worlds using the affordances of poetic language as well as available appliances. In "Dovehouse with Earthquake," I read the Nurse's memory of Juliet's weaning for forms of proximity and distance that organize both the scene recollected in the speech and its incorporation into the present action. The final two sections consider the taskscapes of dancing and housebreaking. In "Torchbearer" I argue that Romeo's decision not to dance mixes a festive urban choreography with lyric emblematics in order to design a space for close encounter with Juliet. Finally, in "Crowbar and Lantern," I evaluate the tonal consequences of Romeo's tools for opening the Capulet monument. A recurrent theme throughout these pages is the resources of light for poetic and theatrical expression; although modern lighting design lies centuries away from Shakespeare's original play text, *Romeo and Juliet* is a drama peculiarly alert to the emotional and spatial qualities of light and to the appliances available to dampen, amplify, and shape luminescent effects in early modern techniques of dwelling, from torches, candles, and

7. See Henderson, *Passion Made Public*. See also Slater, "Petrarchanism Come True in *Romeo and Juliet*."

lanterns to sparkling jewels and matte and shiny fabrics. Attention to affordances shapes these readings of dramaturgy, whether carried by tools, architectural features, and social arrangements, or communicated by poetic images that cue future scenographic invention in technical regimes to come.

Traffic Patterns

Romeo and Juliet famously launches its dramatic action and theatrical delivery under the sign of traffic. The story of the star-crossed lovers, the Chorus tells us,

> Is now the two hours' traffic of our stage;
> The which if you with patient ears attend,
> What here shall miss, our toil will strive to mend. (Prologue, 12–14)

A loan word from the French *traffique* and the Italian *traffic*, "traffic" suggests the coming and going of labor, business, trade, and transport in a cosmopolitan urban space. Encompassing not only the actions that transpire on stage but also the transactions between actors and audience, the final couplet spells out the responsibilities of both parties within the specialized architectural environment of the theater. The players are "toiling," engaged in a form of labor that involves the moving of furniture and the scaling of facades as well as the giving of speeches, and their labor is fraught with the risk that the performance will "miss" its mark. Such miscarriages can be mitigated by the audience's efforts to "attend," a word that implies an embodied and thoughtful listening that is also a kind of service, a sympathetic and solicitous *looking after* rather than a passive *looking at* the fiction unfolding before them. "Mend" rhymes with "attend," enlisting the efforts of both audience and actors in maintaining the "here" of the theater. "Here" may also refer to the book of *Romeo and Juliet* carried on stage by the Chorus, who might have been played by the bookkeeper or book-holder, forerunner of the modern stage manager.[8] If so, the reference simultaneously grants a certain presence to Shakespeare's text while also placing that text under the care of the theatrical house.

"Toiling," "mending," "attending," and "traffic" suggest the physical effort, emotional output, and attentive input that coproduce a theatrical experience, what theorists of work call "affective" or "emotional labor."[9] Affective labor is associated with service jobs that have no physical product and that engage the caring attention as well as the bodily expenditure of the worker; in the contemporary experience economy, affective labor ranges from the unwaged work of mothers to the highly paid performances of the celebrity chef. Affective labor characterized the artisanal and domestic arts of early modernity and, after losing prestige in the industrial period, has returned as a major component of communicative capitalism.[10] In *The Human Condition*, Arendt anticipates later discussions of affective labor when she draws comparisons between menial labor, including the skilled activities of cooking and housecleaning, and intellectual pursuits such as philosophy, medicine, music, and theater.[11] In Italian analyses of post-Fordism, this affinity comes to the fore as the key feature of the new service and experience economy: in the words of Paolo Virno, "The affinity between the piano player and the waiter that Marx glimpsed finds an unexpected confirmation in which all wage labor has something of the 'performing artist' about it."[12] For Arendt and Virno alike, the efforts of both the

8. See Oxford notes, 141–43, on the bookkeeper as deliverer of the Chorus. On the bookkeeper as stage manager, see Maccoy, *Essentials of Stage Management*, 11. For an analysis of "missing and mending" in the play that is attentive to questions of space, audition, and audibility, see Heyworth, "Missing and Mending."

9. On affective labor, see Hochschild, *The Managed Heart*; Hardt, "Affective Labor"; and Muehlebach, "On Affective Labor in Post-Fordist Italy."

10. Hardt, "Affective Labor," 90. For a critique of affect and communicative capitalism, see Dean, *Blog Theory*. For a discussion of Arendt and labor in the context of Shakespeare, see Halpern, "Theater and Democratic Thought."

11. Arendt, *Human Condition*, 90, 93, 207.

12. Virno, "Virtuosity and Revolution," 195.

laundress and the lutist disappear in the process of their performance, manifesting the affinity between the creaturely metabolisms of labor and the speech-based quality of action.

In the unfolding of affective labor from Aristotle and Smith through Arendt, Virno, and Hardt, theater is that form of art that develops performative affect as its primary medium and subject matter, while also drawing on domestic and manual forms of labor for its stage management, understood not only as the technical supervision of theatrical production, but as the deeper protocols that link the physical resources of the stage to the traffic of actors across it. *Romeo and Juliet*, with its many servants as well as its Nurse and Friar, seems keenly attuned to the role of emotional self-performance in both the routines of Renaissance dwelling and in theater's mixed status as action, work, and labor. Hospitality is a form of housekeeping and social work that enlists affective labor from all parties, ranging from the lord, lady, and young mistress of the house to their busy servants and their array of guests. *Romeo and Juliet* dramatizes the planning, effort, and social niceties that make such meetings possible, including inviting guests; clearing tables and moving furniture; adjusting light, heat, and sound; welcoming late arrivals; and saying good night. In *Romeo and Juliet*, hospitality's traffic ensconces the household within neighborhood, community, and cosmos.

The "traffic" announced in the prologue flows immediately into the first city scene, act 1, scene 1. Gregory and Samson, young serving men of the Capulet household, enter the stage looking for trouble:

> *Samson*: Gregory, on my word we'll not carry coals.
> *Gregory*: No, for then we should be colliers. (1.1.1–2)

No coals, of course, are actually being carried; the phrase refers to enduring insults. Yet labor rumbles in the background: colliers made charcoal out of wood, usually near the forests where the wood was hewn, and then hauled it into the city. The coal industry was a forest-city hybrid, as we know from Henslowe's diaries, which records the details not only of his theater business but also of his mining and coal operations.[13] Not to carry coals, then, is to belong more forcefully to the urban scene and its precious liveries of distinction. And to enter engaged in rapid wordplay that soon dissolves into the city ballet of the street fight is to link household service to the office of the *zani*, recently excavated from early modern *commedia* for post-Fordist analysis by Sianne Ngai. The *zani*, she writes, following Robert Henke, is "a temporary and itinerant worker in a household," like "the performers in the troupes who played him."[14] Samson and Gregory appear to enjoy a more permanent relationship to the house of Capulet, though the men playing them may have been hired on a temporary basis by Shakespeare's company. Samson and Gregory are zany in their office as servants and clowns who move between backstage and onstage labor in the houses they energetically serve. Contemporary zaniness, Ngai writes, concerns "performance, affective labor, and the post-Fordist workplace"; Renaissance zaniness, such as that on view in Shakespeare's Verona, concerns the traffic of affective labor in the pre-Fordist workplaces of early modernity.[15]

As zanies, laborers existing on the margins of the Capulet household, Samson and Gregory display a keen awareness of the urban topography of Verona as a space that affords particular kinds of appearance, encounter, and activity. Samson goes on to brag that he will "push Montague's men from the wall, and thrust his maids to the wall" (1.1.15–17). The wall defining the edge of the city street becomes the support against which young men perform their masculinity.[16] Unlike the boundary fortifications evoked by Romeo later in the play ("there is no world without Verona walls" [3.3.17]), the men's wall work conjures a cityscape of narrow alleys that encourage clandestine encounters and force indecorous crowding, backstage spaces that open onto a public square or suburban field that encourages roughhousing as well as commerce, festivity, and public judgment. The city's layout affords

13. *Henslowe's Diary*, xix–xxiv.
14. Ngai, *Our Aesthetic Categories*, 192.
15. Ibid., 3.
16. See Appelbaum, "'Standing to the Wall.'"

a range of behaviors that instantiate social and sexual tensions and hierarchies. The likely use of all three stage doors during the scene (the Capulets entering from one door and the Montagues from another, with the roused Prince and his entourage arriving through the august middle door) activates these spaces of contest and exchange, immediately rendering them as environments for action. Naomi Conn Liebler argues that *Romeo and Juliet*, unlike *The Merchant of Venice* or *Julius Caesar*, fails to generate "a legible map of an orderly city."[17] Yet we know where we are, not in a postcard way, but in a dramatic way: we are in *a scene of action*, swiftly brought into play by the rivalries of caste and class in a modestly modernizing urban economy, sparrings fanned by the openings and closings of city space.

Traffic of a more domestic and explicitly hospitable kind occurs in the brief exchange among household servants at the threshold between the young men's street scene and the beginning of the Capulet party. Romeo's gang and Capulet's serving men momentarily share the stage:

> *They march about the stage, and Serving-men come forth with napkins.*
> *[Chief] Serving-Man*: Where's Potpan, that he helps not to take away? He shift a trencher, he scrape a trencher?
> *First Serving-Man*: When good manners shall lie all in one or two men's hands, and they unwashed too, 'tis a foul thing.
> *[Chief] Serving-Man*: Away with the joint-stools, remove the court-cupboard, look to the plate. Good thou, save me a piece of marchpane, and as thou loves me, let the porter let in Susan Grindstone and Nell, Anthony and Potpan.
> *Second Serving-Man*: Ay boy, ready.
> *[Chief] Serving-Man*: You are looked for and called for, asked for and sought for, in the great chamber.
> *Third Serving-Man*: We cannot be here and there too. Cheerly boys, be brisk a while, and the longer liver take all. (1.4.113–28)

These lines rezone the stage from the streets of Verona to the interior of the Capulet house as the serving men prepare for the

17. See Liebler, "'There is no world without Verona's walls,'" 307.

party.[18] The servants, who are also stagehands, are engaged in the act of *making room*: clearing the domestic space of the Capulet house for dancing, while redistricting the space of the stage from city street to domestic interior. Hospitality provides the social script for these acts of making room: diegetically, the serving men are arranging for the party in which the visored Romeo will first encounter the feted Juliet, domestic preparations that momentarily merge with theater-making as a process that involves the traffic of persons and things in an architecture of flows.

The passage is laden with objects, including most immediately napkins, trenchers, joint-stools, a court cupboard, plate, and marchpane (marzipan), plus the objects that appear in the names of characters—Potpan, Susan Grindstone—indicating the affinity between the servant class and the world of utilitarian things. Unlike some other object scenes in Shakespeare, however—the dowry detailed by Gremio in *Taming of the Shrew* (2.1.346–56) or the scanning of Innogen's bedroom by Giacomo in *Cymbeline* (2.2 and 2.4)—this passage does not unfold as an inventory.[19] Instead, we see the serving men navigating a taskscape, "the entire ensemble of tasks, in their mutual interlocking," that compose an environment in active use, a scene that is "qualitative and heterogeneous" and "essentially social."[20] The tasks at hand involve clearing the table ("shift a trencher . . . scrape a trencher") and moving the furniture ("Away with the joint-stools, remove the court-cupboard, look to the plate"). The joint-stool, one of the household's most minimal and movable forms of seating, manifests the transitivity of furnishings on the stage and in Renaissance domestic spaces. Such stools would be moved constantly

18. This exchange does not appear in the First Quarto of 1597 and is often cut from modern performances. Brian Gibbons speculates that the First Quarto was streamlined to accommodate a smaller cast (introduction to Arden edition, 2n). In his new study of Shakespearean staging, David Bevington notes that the stage direction "bridges the two scenes with a continuous action; no scene break is to be found in the early printed texts of this play" (*The Wide and Universal Theater*, 131). See also Mariko Ichikawa, *Shakespearean Entrances*, 65–66.

19. *Taming of the Shrew*, in *The Riverside Shakespeare*.

20. Ingold, "The Temporality of the Landscape," 158.

throughout the day, used for eating, labor, or resting as well as becoming makeshift tables or stepladders. The court cupboard, on the other hand, standing at the end of the great hall to display and store the master's plate along with wines and fruits, would only be moved on major occasions like this one, to clear space for the dancing and perhaps protect the valuables within.[21] In this scene, insofar as objects appear on stage, they appear in movement, in the act of being taken away, in order to complete the act of clearing that makes hospitality possible.

What the scene affords the drama as a whole is the rezoning of the space of the stage from exterior to interior, from the streets of Verona to the great hall of Capulet. The young men *clear the stage* as a speaker might clear his throat: with an amplified phatic noisiness that signals a change. Although the scene is often broken here, the stage direction is continuous: "They [Romeo's crew] march about the Stage, and Servingmen come forth with Napkins." The connective fold in the Folio's single sentence bids us to imagine a moment in which the paths of the two groups, one carrying torches and the other bearing household goods, might cross then separate, in a choreography of bodies and things, as well as lights and sounds. Hospitality is at stake not only as the event for which the men are preparing the house, but more deeply, as the way in which things and persons interact in a scenario not fully governed by the opposition of active and passive or agent and object. In a moment like this, theater at its most mundane flashes its world-making magic.

The labor necessary to clear space for the banquet might have been elided altogether—as it often is in performance—to speed the drama forward to the scenes of revelry, infatuation, and feuding dominated by Verona's upper crust. The marchpane that establishes this moment in the party as a banquet of desserts is designed to delight the wealthy young people gathered to celebrate Juliet's coming birthday. Shaped, colored, sugared, and even gilded for maximum visual appeal, marzipan was the

21. See Gibbons's note, *Romeo and Juliet*, 114.

occasion for virtuoso confectionary in the highly theatricalized dessert course that composed either the final course or the main event in Renaissance banquets (see chapter 5).[22] Yet the serving men aim to commandeer some of this confection for their own party, planning an informal festival of leftovers to take place after hours. Thus the marzipan also points inward, to the backstage areas of house and stage that support the fanfare of entertainment. The scene's fleeting reference to leftover times and invisible service zones recalls the way in which the actors and stagehands will create their own scene when the theater closes, or an architect might insert a closet or a close stool in the space behind the stairs, or a rodent might establish his quarters beneath the stage. The environments of entertainment emerge here not as a single bounded space of pure representation, but as an open floor plan composed of variegated areas dedicated to different kinds of traffic. By opening service economies and representational economies to each other, the scene becomes an instance of the kind of dynamic rehearsed by Alice Rayner in her landmark essay, "Rude Mechanicals and the *Specters of Marx*." There she shows how "very concrete labor might participate in and reiterate the phantasm of the theatrical double, the visible and the invisible," an exercise she executes under the sign of Shakespeare.[23]

The serving men's rough music makes us suddenly privy to the labors that run behind the scenes of theater and hospitality as the self-erasing yet incessantly operating conditions of the main event to come. In her 1975 sociology of the theater, *The Living Monument*, M. C. Bradbrook tracks the emergence of drama proper—with its alternative world sustained by but also separate from the audience—from more immersive forms of pageant and holiday, and she takes the phrase "two hours traffic" as an entry into that process:

22. Sir Hugh Plat, in his cookbook *Delights for Ladies to adorn their Persons, Tables, Closets, and Distillatories: with Beauties, Banquets, Perfumes and Waters*, takes pleasure in the idea of molding fowl out of almond paste: "By this means a Banquet may be presented in the form of a Supper being a very rare and strange device" (B4).

23. Rayner, "Rude Mechanicals and the *Specters of Marx*."

> The variety of buildings that served as Elizabethan playhouses, the social constitution, size, and customary manners of the audience made up one part of the "two hours traffic of the stage," to which Shakespeare, more than anyone else, gave unity. The audience was part of the performance.[24]

Affective labor is at stake here insofar as theater creates an experience sustained by both actors and audience, a creation that involves forms of care and emotional expenditure as well as heavy lifting and technical expertise. "Sharing a task," writes Bradbrook, "is a sure way to stabilize personal relations—whether bringing up children or cooking a meal, whether customary or contractual."[25] In elucidating the new relationship between audience and spectacle in Shakespearean drama, balanced between the reciprocity of festive immersion and the distance of discrete fiction, Bradbrook turns to scenes of domestic care. But traffic also sends her to the city, which surrounds the theater while being pictured by it. From the traffic in coals that connects the city to the forest and the walled passageways that afford congress and conflict to the traffic in stools, trenchers, and marzipan that makes room for guests, *Romeo and Juliet* indexes its own composition out of work, labor, and action.

Romeo and Juliet, of course, is not "about" furniture, or leftovers, or even theater. Instead, Shakespeare lets the autopoiesis or self-organizing complexity of the taskscape appear and disappear before our eyes, rehearsing the continuity between stage management and household management. Each requires the zoning and rezoning of space. Each directs traffic among a variety of actants in an ensemble of undertakings. Each is sensitive to the sumptuary and seasonal shifts signaled by holiday, the "rites, feasts and ceremonies" that "are as integral to the taskscape as are boundary markers such as walls or fences to the landscape."[26] Each sports a deep relationship to hospitality, the suite of customs by which people manage their enmities and signify environmental depen-

24. Bradbrook, *The Living Monument*, 13.
25. Ibid., 13.
26. Ingold, "Temporality of Landscape," 159.

dencies. Moreover, this comparison rises above analogy insofar as the theater *is* a taskscape (an environment composed of affordances), and the taskscape *is* a theater (a setting for the performance of several kinds of action by multiple actors).

Consorting

We first meet Romeo obliquely, in the second half of act 1, scene 1. As the stage clears after the fight, Benvolio discusses Romeo's state of mind with the older Montagues. Benvolio reports,

> Madam, an hour before the worshipped sun
> Peered forth the golden window of the east,
> A troubled mind drive me to walk abroad,
> Where underneath the grove of sycamore
> That westward rooteth from this city side,
> So early walking did I see your son.
> Towards him I made, but he was ware of me,
> And stole into the covert of the wood.
> I, measuring his affections by my own,
> Which then most sought where most might not be found,
> Being one too many by my weary self,
> Pursued my humour, not pursuing his,
> And gladly shunned who gladly fled from me. (1.1.114–26)

Montague replies with a parallel picture:

> Many a morning hath he there been seen,
> With tears augmenting the fresh morning's dew,
> Adding to clouds more clouds with his deep sighs;
> But all so soon as the all-cheering sun
> Should in the furthest east begin to draw
> The shady curtains from Aurora's bed,
> Away from the light steals home my heavy son,
> And private in his chamber pens himself,
> Shuts up his windows, locks fair daylight out,
> And makes himself an artificial night.
> Black and portentous must this humour prove,
> Unless good counsel may the cause remove. (1.1.127–38)

In this matching pair of vignettes, Benvolio fills out the topography of the city by sketching the sycamore grove that "westward rooteth from this city side," like a libertine plant sprouting out from the walls themselves. The pastoral topography is lightly domesticated by the image of the morning sun "peering through the golden window of the east," a turn to architecture elaborated by Montague's description of Romeo's indoor habits; when the sun draws "the shady curtains from Aurora's bed," the lovesick, light-shy Romeo "shuts up his windows, locks fair daylight out, / And makes himself an artificial night." Romeo appears here as a scenographer who uses the affordances of shutters and curtains to adjust the bedchamber to his own dark mood.[27] Montague's description of Romeo "adding to clouds more clouds with his deep sighs" exhibits the pathetic fallacy familiar from lyric poetry; the passage as a whole, however, links such affective merging to specific techniques for shaping the sensory environment. The public theaters could not be artificially darkened, of course; what is at stake in Romeo's "artificial night" is a theatricality native to dwelling, presented as poetry and only later transposed to the theater proper.[28] Poetic description brings about a certain translation between *atmospheric effects* that could be achieved at home and *theatrical effects* that lay still very much on the horizon. Poetry does this translational work, moreover, precisely by heightening lyric literariness alongside and even in competition with the demands of the stage.

Romeo's teen sulking merges him with his environs, as when

27. Caroline Spurgeon identified the play's interest in light as part of its thematic texture and atmospheric effects in *Shakespeare's Imagery and What It Tells Us*, 310–16.

28. Robert B. Graves argues that in both indoor and outdoor theaters, "early English lighting emanated from around the actor, surrounding him with soft, indirect light. There was no impression of light focusing on the actor . . . nothing to suggest that the play created its own special light" (*Lighting the Shakespearean Stage*, 233). He believes that little or no attempt was made to darken theaters to increase the impression of night, and he credits Adolphe Appiah as the first scenographer to fully understand light "as an expressive element" (4). The plays themselves, however, are interested in verbally communicating light effects that would not be produced on stage for several centuries but that were manipulated in the more controlled spaces of dwelling.

in the orchard scene Benvolio notes that "he hath hid himself among these trees / To be consorted with the humorous night" (2.1.31–32). To consort is to associate or make music with someone or something, to dally with or espouse. Romeo withdraws into himself, retreating from the crowd to wallow in his complicated feelings and erotic fantasies. And yet, the division between Romeo's internal world and the external ambience of the evening dissolves in the figure of the youth "being consorted with the night," as Romeo is mixed up with the nocturnal landscape. In this moment, the humorous Romeo and the nightscape form what Drew Daniel calls a "melancholic assemblage," a figure "in which minds, bodies, and things melancholize each other."[29] Tybalt will later goad Mercutio for "consorting" with Romeo (3.1.44–48); read in a decidedly queer direction in Luhrmann's film, act 3's "consorting" exchange derives sexual, class, and cohort tension from Romeo's manner of orchestrating his social surround. Theater is a testing ground for such explorations, since it assembles objects and persons in an experimental zone fraught with the possibilities of directionality. Juliet asks Romeo, "By whose direction found'st thou out this place?" (2.1.122). This is a narrative question, but also a dramaturgical one, involving the taskscape of theater and the way in which its resources become organized through action.[30] Likewise, Benvolio's lines cue the actor to hide somewhere on stage, conforming his body to a set of available affordances—the lip of the balcony, the skinny silhouette of a post supporting it, the frame of a doorway at the stage's inner edge—in order to rezone the suite of architectural givens as "these trees." Consorting with the humorous night means embracing camouflage's environmental subterfuges as the actors duck in and out of multiple sight lines and hearing ranges in response to the dramatic situation's moment-by-moment re-

29. Daniel, *The Melancholy Assemblage*, 12.

30. Eugenio Barba emphasizes the organizational dimensions of dramaturgy in *On Directing and Dramaturgy*, 8–13. See also Easterling on "organizational space," *Organization Space*.

mapping of the stage.[31] In promiscuously "consorting" with his environment, Romeo, master of the melting mood, exercises an ambient theatricality, in which poetic posturing mixes with the built environment in an assemblage of words, limbs, and things.

Romeo is a scenographer of submergence, avoidance, and withdrawal, his erotic precocity also generating social hesitation. As the host of a major party, Capulet is a more other-oriented scenographer as he attends to the ambient factors of warmth, light, and sound in his managing of the space of hospitality: "Come, musicians, play. / A hall, a hall! Give room . . . More light, you knaves, and turn the tables up, / And quench the fire, the room is grown too hot" (1.4.138–40). Later he interrupts his argument with Tybalt by calling for more light (1.4.200), and his departing words to his guests also solicit illumination ("More torches here—come on—then let's to bed" [1.4.238]). These passages approximate the divided attention of the flustered host and the tools for tuning atmosphere at said host's disposal.[32]

Juliet is also a scenographer in training who gathers up much of the same imagery from the Benvolio/Montague diptych in her "Gallop apace" speech. She bids real, not artificial, night to come, but, like Romeo, she is well aware of the technical means available to imitate it. "Spread thy close curtain, love-performing night" (3.2.5), she says, unfurling an image of hanging bedclothes that she then reworks in the "sober-suited matron all in black," the night's "black mantle," and Juliet's own festival "new robes" (11–30). The strange image of Romeo's body "cut . . . out

31. I am indebted here to a fine essay by Christine Hoffman, "Much Ado about Planking." Vin Nardizzi notes this scene as a moment in which posts are bid to perform as trees (*Wooden O's*, 21).

32. The 2014 production at UC Irvine used Capulet's call for "more light, more light," delivered from above as he and Tybalt surveyed the dancers below, as the cue for a lightly simulated fireworks display that in turn stilled the assembled party during the sonnet sequence, which took place downstage. This lovely fusing of light and sound effects with intelligent blocking is an ensemble of choices afforded by Shakespeare's text yet dependent on the available technical and scenic-architectural capacities. The production was directed by Calvin Abbott MacLean with lighting design by Karyn Lawrence.

in little stars" implies some intimacy with appliqué, like Bess of Hardwick's magnificent gold-on-black hangings, designed for a bedchamber, or the knots and letters cut from marzipan, pastry, and sugar plate that show up in Renaissance cookbooks.[33] Unhae Lingis connects the image with the neo-Platonic idea of the astral body, "made of very fine, lucent stuff . . . corporeal but subtle."[34] Imagining her lover's glowing body as a sheer radiant material, Juliet plans a work of curatorial repair and scenographic commemoration in advance of their deaths. The image billows with future loss, launched into the heavens like a great canopy pushed aloft by ardor mixed with anguish.

Whereas Romeo's solitary softscape affords daytime sleep by shutting out stimuli, Juliet's softscape *á deux* uses light-blocking appliances to heighten rather than dim sensory perception: "Lovers can see to do their amorous rites / By their own beauties" (3.2.8–9). The darkness warmed by arousal amplifies the capacities of touch as a haptic component in the lovers' night vision. This ardent tactility, predicted earlier by the palmers' kiss, is communicated by Juliet's repeated references to fabric, whose affordances include its capacity to become a fluid, draping surface, a pliant second skin. Figuring Romeo as "new robes," she imagines him not so much entering as covering and embracing her, just as she pictures him lying "upon the wings of night," a reclining nude stretched out on a dark coverlet. Her cascade of images concerns the meeting of flesh and fabric, bed and bodies, in consort with the perceptual alterations wrought by nighttime.

So too, Romeo's desire to be a glove on Juliet's hand so that he can touch her cheek dissolves him into the proprioceptive interface of erotic self-touching, at once implying and eschewing the more legible topology of sexual intercourse. Both chaste and queer, Romeo's glove simultaneously reembodies Juliet after his cosmic flight, imagines physical congress with her, skirts her hy-

33. Levey, *The Embroideries at Hardwick Hall*, 134–79. Wall, *Recipes for Thought*, 112–66.

34. Lingis, "Love and Death: *Discordia Concors* in *Romeo and Juliet*," 6, citing Walker, "The Astral Body in Renaissance Medicine," 121–22.

men, and obliquely proposes the pleasures of nonreproductive satisfaction. Such imagery lends a whisper of weight—no heavier than Queen Mab's "lash of film" or "traces of the smallest spider-web" (1.4.61, 59)—to the floating abstractions of Romeo's balcony valediction: "Sleep dwell upon thine eyes, peace in thy breast. / Would I were sleep and peace, so sweet to rest" (2.1.232–33). He wants to become her coverlet, a light-adjusting, skin-touching, shelter-building aid to slumber, part of an ecology of sleep captured in the word "dwell." (I return to the ecology of sleep in my chapters on *Macbeth* and *Cymbeline*.)[35]

Fabric, too, shapes particular kinds of ambiences for household and theatrical productions. When in the balcony scene Romeo begins to swear upon the moon, what attracts him to this celestial body is its light-reflecting capacities: "Lady, by yonder blessèd moon I vow, / That tips with silver all these fruit-tree tops—" (2.1.150–51). Romeo scans his environment for luminous effects that prompt invention in later technical regimes. In the 2008 Salzburg Festival production of Gounod's *Roméo et Juliette*, for example, a huge silk sheet covered the entirety of the stage during the lovers' aubade. The minimalist metaphor (stage = bed) was subtly enhanced by the shimmering of the sheet under softly colored, digitally programmed lights, a scenography that enlisted the affordances of fabric in tandem with modern stagecraft and in response to poetic imagery. Lyric description becomes an experimental tool for exploring the "causal milieu" of affordances that bid objects, actors, and locale to consort with each other, across moments and media and between reading and performance.[36] The taskscapes that frame this ambient theatricality also concern the possibilities and dangers of erotic and spatial intimacy, the subject of the following section.

35. On ecologies of sleep, see Garrett Sullivan, *Sleep, Romance and Human Embodiment*.

36. "Causal milieu" is the expression of Teemu Paavolainen ("From Props to Affordances," 127). Worthen uses affordances to talk about the relationship of text to performance across time (*Drama between Poetry and Performance*, 22). See introduction for more discussion.

Dovehouse with Earthquake

Juliet enters the play for the first time in act 1, scene 3, at the behest of her mother and nurse in a scene that concerns the origins, limits, and spatial disposition of intimacy, or what sociologist Edward T. Hall in his 1966 book *The Hidden Dimension* called proxemics, the study of "social and personal space and man's perception of it."[37] Although Hall does not use the word "affordance," which postdates his book by some years, he cites Gibson's earlier work on the collaboration of sight and touch as modes of active exploration by animate beings (walruses and hounds as well as American office workers and French flaneurs); affordances everywhere resonate in Hall's claim that "what you can do in [a given space] determines how you experience it."[38] Proxemics has entered architecture, urbanism, and interior design around the question of what quantities and qualities of nearness and distance are solicited by different public spaces (subways in Japan, elevators in New York, offices in Silicon Valley) and social situations (meeting a stranger, buying a coffee, interviewing a job candidate).[39] In theater studies, Keir Elam links proxemics to both the physical architecture of the stage and "the ever-shifting relations of proximity and distance between individuals, thus applying, in the theatre, to actor-actor, actor-spectator, and spectator-spectator interplay."[40] While proxemics has many practical consequences for design, it also bears more existentially on questions of neighboring, intimacy, and estrangement as well as the aversions, inhibitions, and panics that accompany human development.

In his original exposition of proxemics, Hall turned to lit-

37. Hall, *The Hidden Dimension*, 1.

38. Ibid., 54. He cites Gibson (60) and analyzes American offices (52–53) and French boulevards (146) as well as Arab habits of congregating (154–64).

39. On proxemics and architecture, see Lawson, *The Language of Space*. On proxemics in anthropology, see *The Anthropology of Space and Place*, ed. Low and Lawrence-Zúñiga.

40. Elam, *The Semiotics of Theatre and Drama*, 51–53. Susan Bennett expands on Elam's use of Hall with special attention to audience spacing (*Theatre Audiences*, 131–35).

erature for phenomenological description of spatial sensibilities, since "great writers perceive and communicate the meaning and uses of distance as a significant cultural factor in interpersonal relations."[41] His first literary example is Edgar and Gloucester at Dover Cliff, but he could equally have turned to the scene with the Nurse, Juliet, and Lady Capulet, which plays the intimacy of the first two against the distance of the second two. The easy congress between the young girl and her caregiver can be enacted by having Juliet sitting on the Nurse's lap or pressed against her bosom, poses frequently featured in performance shots. If seated for all or part of the Nurse's reminiscence, the composite formed by their two persons requires additional support from a bed, bench, or stool. The Nurse and Juliet's interwoven postures, gestures, and affective responses draw the recollected scene into the present time and space of performance. Meanwhile, Lady Capulet strives for intimacy when she sends the Nurse away, but loses confidence and cedes the space of maternal care when she decides to recall the Nurse. During their conversation, Lady Capulet can exude alienation, impatience, or regret by circling around or turning away from the intimate couple. This is the same Lady Capulet who will later say to her daughter, "I have done with thee" (3.5.203). Whereas *Hamlet* splits the father into two figures, Hyperion and the satyr, *Romeo and Juliet* divides the maternal function between the prolix nurse and the inhibited mother. The full emotional range of the scene depends, that is, on a shifting organization and ongoing comparison of different proximities, from the warmth of bodies that touch to the palpable coolness of persons that drift.

The nurse's recollection is itself a long disquisition on relative proximities. She recalls,

> Come Lammas Eve at night shall she be fourteen.
> Susan and she—God rest all Christian souls—
> Were of an age. Well, Susan is with God;
> She was too good for me. But, as I said,

41. Hall, *Hidden Dimension*, 94–100.

On Lammas Eve at night shall she be fourteen.
That shall she, marry, I remember it well.
'Tis since the earthquake now eleven years,
And she was weaned,—I never shall forget it—
Of all the days of the year upon that day;
For I had then laid wormwood to my dug,
Sitting in the sun under the dovehouse wall.
My lord and you were then at Mantua—
Nay, I do bear a brain. But as I said,
When it did taste the wormwood on the nipple
Of my dug and felt it bitter, pretty fool,
To see it tetchy and fall out with the dug!
'Shake,' quoth the dove-house; 'twas no need, I trow,
To bid me trudge. (1.3.19–36)

Breast-feeding is one of the most proximate experiences available to mammals, belonging to what Hall calls "thermal space," in which creatures are close enough to feel changes in the other's bodily heat, and to "tactile space," composed by touching.[42] But the Nurse recollects the moment when that warmth required tempering: in order to wean Juliet, the Nurse had rubbed wormwood on her nipple, breaking up the fluid sweetness of early childhood with a sharp burst of gustatory betrayal. The separation between Nurse and charge coincided with the absence of the parents: "My lord and you were then at Mantua," the Nurse reports matter-of-factly, naming the same city to which Romeo will soon go into exile. Mantua becomes a psychogeography of proximity's denials, visualized by the uncanny spacing devices on the Apothecary's lonely shelves: "empty boxes, / Green earthen pots, bladders . . . thinly scattered to make up a show" (5.1.45–48).[43] Associated with estrangement, the word Mantua comes to resonate with what is lacking and wanting (*Manqua*, *Wantua*, *Verona manquée*). To such images of vacuity and sparseness the

42. Ibid., 54–63.

43. See Hugh Grady on the transformation of the play into "an empty panoply of objects, its immanent meaning lost" and the cluster of allegorical props, including crowbars, in the final scene. *Impure Aesthetics*, 215, 216.

emotional and ecological fullness of the Capulet orchard makes a compelling complement. The spatial notation of nurse and toddler "sitting in the sun under the dovehouse wall" mixes warmth and shade, open air and partial seclusion, the crafted solidity of architecture with the ambient presence of birds. The propping of child on breast is mirrored by the propping of the feminine couple in the sheltering vicinity of the retaining wall, an environmental composition in which ontic edges dissolve into tonal volumes.

Doves, famous for mating for life, are lyric emblems of proximity; "pronounce but 'love' and 'dove,'" chants Mercutio mockingly, in or near the same courtyard eleven years later (2.1.11). If the trite rhyme mimics the easy union promised by erotic verse, the dovehouse places the birds in a complex interspecies ecology; grown for eggs, meat, and dung, they nested in the dovecote, but procured most of their food off site. Doves could only thrive, however, where open land was plentiful, and in some parts of Europe dovecotes were restricted to the nobility; formal dovecotes are thus features of grander gardens. Usually stand-alone structures, their round or square volumes could also be incorporated into garden walls.[44] At once garrulous and thrifty, the Nurse's speech evokes a whole world defined by patterns of privilege and labor, work and rest, and human and animal cohabitation. What she evokes, in other words, is *an environment*. An environment is literally that which environs or surrounds (as the courtyard enveloped nurse and child that summer afternoon). An environment is also that which flows and interconnects, composed of a minimally coherent bundle of affinities at once strengthened by its web of exchanges and vulnerable to disturbance. The intensity of the bond between nurse and child is built on patterns of dependency in which the affective labor of the household staff supports the aristocratic citizenship of the Capulet family. The dovecote helps tune the courtyard in which nurse and child make their own nest, assembling a rhythmic composite of wall,

44. Hansell, *Dovecotes*.

ground, sky, breast, breath, and birds. Indeed, the space evoked by the Nurse dovetails for a moment with the open-air theater in which *Romeo and Juliet* was first performed; both the Capulet courtyard and the Bankside theater are spaces of congregation dedicated to human business while resting on material supports, open to the elements, and entertaining avian visitors.

Housing the conditions of its own diremption, this idyll exists to be interrupted. Weaning exacerbates the fault line between infant and caregiver; it separates forever a locus of connection (nipple and mouth) built on the rhythm of attachment and withdrawal. Such weaning, of course, also represents a first subjective birth, one that for Juliet will be repeated and intensified when her love for Romeo becomes the means by which she exercises her own capacities for speech and action, deeds that forever separate her from the bosom of the household, but also ultimately from Romeo as well. As Paul Kottman argues, if the lovers are "to claim their lives as their own, they must somehow actualize their separateness for themselves."[45] Juliet turns to the aviary kingdom to visualize the distance within proximity born by love as the fruit of mutual recognition:

> I would have thee gone;
> And yet no farther than a wanton's bird,
> That lets it hop a little from his hand,
> Like a poor prisoner in his twisted gyves,
> And with a silken thread plucks it back again,
> So loving-jealous of his liberty. (2.1.222–27)

The falconer's gyves visualize Hall's insight that "the boundaries of the self extend beyond the body" in the form of "an invisible bubble that surrounds the organism."[46] Juliet imagines Romeo as her hawk in training, attached to her by a string that determines the distance he can fly from her. An image of imprisonment and captivation, the "silken thread" also measures the space the lovers

45. Kottman, "Defying the Stars," 5–6.

46. Hall, *Hidden Dimension*, 11, 13. On falconry imagery, see Brown, "Juliet's Taming of Romeo"; and Heyworth, "Missing and Mending," 16–18.

require for their "liberty." So too, when Romeo dreams of being a glove upon Juliet's hand, he imagines entering the sphere of her thermal and tactile space while also inhabiting a margin of distance within the ecstasy of contact.[47]

These multiple fault lines, which both divide and connect child and breast, persons and environments, and servant and noble classes, are already part of the tremulous ecology of the courtyard. Moreover, in this passage, Shakespeare brilliantly associates the open architecture of built environments with the architecture of memory: both the instant melding of discrete spatial elements into memory-pictures by the refulgent flash of microtrauma, and the storage of memories via information technologies like liturgical and harvest calendars.[48] The exchange yields a range of gestures that draw the past into the present, making courtyard, closet, and stage reverberate in each other, for us. Distant places and distinct moments are infolded through the theater of memory, which erects its structures of recall in the *oikos* and the range of proximities it harbors. The function of the speech as a whole is to set the stage for Juliet's birth into action out of the recesses of dwelling. Her memory theater commandeers the affordances of architecture for the play's own dramatic, thematic, and atmospheric purposes while also allowing those affordances to manifest themselves, to "appear . . . within what is present."[49]

The scene explores the existential and dramaturgical calculus among proximity, precarity, and resilience. Proximity, the cherished zone of love and care, is subject to coercive policing, unexpected panic, and cooling drift. The mingling of persons, surfaces, organs, and orifices in breast-feeding and sexual congress rarely proceeds unchecked. Distance beckons, in the form of weaning,

47. Compare Valls-Russell on the function of the wall in the Pyramus and Thisbe subtext: "In Verona, resemblance compounded with proximity breeds intensity" ("Erotic Perspectives," 86).

48. On memory theater in *Romeo and Juliet*, see Wilder, *Shakespeare's Memory Theatre,* 59–60. On overlapping calendars in the play, see Berry, "Between Idolatry and Astrology."

49. Heidegger, "Building Dwelling Thinking," 157.

valediction, exile, or death, but also in the very operation of loving acknowledgment itself, which, in the words of Paul Kottman, "shows our separateness to be what is most immanently our own."[50] The wormwood on the nipple forces the toddler into a vertiginous freedom (the day before, she had fallen on her head), a plunge that is nonetheless buffered by the Nurse's buxom presence and the landscape architecture that openly encloses them. Both the proximity and the separation of the Nurse and Juliet are afforded by the resilience of physical supports: the edge of bench or bed on which they sit; the dovehouse wall against which they nursed; the ground that bears them, except when it shakes. As Bonnie Honig has argued in a brilliant integration of Arendt and Winnicott, the durability of the object world in tandem with the reassurances of loving routine compose a "holding environment" in which children build their own habits of resilience from the reliability of the things around them.[51] The right dose of distance creates more durable forms of proximity, in the form of ongoing relationships of trust, accommodation, and cooperation, intimacies that we see at work in the Nurse and Juliet's laughing recreation of trauma as jest.

But the scene also harbors a precarity that will overwhelm these limited protections.[52] The moment Juliet took the bitter nipple into her unsuspecting mouth, a small earthquake happened to occur; "Shake quoth the dovehouse," the Nurse says, attributing agency to the building in its capacity not only to shelter, but also to bury, like the temple in Gaza in the Samson story or the Christian church that implodes on the lovers in *Romeo and Juliet in Baghdad*.[53] (Perhaps what the Nurse heard was the sudden rush of doves leaving their abode.) The earthquake resonates with erotic tremors, but it also remains a contingent movement

50. Kottman, "Defying the Stars," 19.

51. Honig, "The Politics of Public Things," 59.

52. On precarity as an economic and affective condition of post-Fordism, see Lauren Berlant, *Cruel Optimism*.

53. On *Romeo and Juliet in Baghdad*, performed in London in 2012 as part of the World Shakespeare Festival and London Olympics, see Munro, "Performance History."

of the ground that rattles buildings and nerves, date-stamping the moment of separation from the breast as a birth into a subjectivity that is never simply autonomous, that relies on others and outsides for its identity and sustenance. If household duties knit the nurse into the *oikos* as a trusted member of the family, her indenturing to the Capulets renders the courtyard's nest of resilient routines unexpectedly perilous. The Nurse's own precarity—her dependence on the Capulets for her livelihood—becomes Juliet's precarity when the Nurse refuses to support the clandestine marriage she had helped broker. Her decision to side with the parents is of a piece with Emilia's delivery of Desdemona's handkerchief to her husband; in both cases, female solidarity is undercut by class interests. Dead Susan, moreover, both binds the Nurse to Juliet and indicates the factors of class and circumstance that forever divide them. Susan belongs to the Nurse's own private Mantua, the invisible city to which she withdraws when in act 4 she abandons Juliet to her secret plan.

This first scene with the Nurse combines novelistic reminiscence with cues for dramaturgy that imperfectly attach Juliet to the older women in her life and the world of dependencies they unevenly inhabit. Neither overweening nurse nor underwhelming mother is a resource for Juliet when she takes the sleeping potion; she considers calling them back "to comfort me," but then decides, "My dismal scene I needs must act alone" (4.3.17, 19). The Nurse's theater of memory builds what Lauren Berlant in her study of post-Fordist precarity calls the historical present, in which "memory and the past emerge in mediated zones of visceral presence distributed across scenes of epistemological and bodily activity."[54] Staged in the heart of dwelling, the scene seeds homely humor with tragic honesty in order to stress-test the oikonomic foundations that render Juliet's sheltered childhood into a scene of immeasurable danger, like some glorious Los Angeles landmark, all tiles and gargoyles, that was never retrofitted for seismic stress.

54. Berlant, *Cruel Optimism*, 52.

Torchbearer

The scene with the Nurse involves one kind of theatrical engagement with architecture and the scripts of dwelling, in which a recollected space comes to resonate in the space and time of performance. My final sets of reflections concern Romeo's wielding of objects on stage, first a torch and then a crowbar, in organizing the space he builds around himself and his movement through it. The torch belongs to a premodern lighting system that links urban choreography to theatrical semiosis. Whereas the torch helps create a lyric *Lichtung* for subjective encounter, the crowbar leverages a more violent set of associations and procedures that threatens the modal coherence of the play. Herbert Blau writes that "the primary architectural space of the theater is and always has been the body of the actor. . . . It is, of course, a transient architecture with a breathing skin, subject at any instant to the corrosions of time."[55] Torch and crowbar extend and supplement Romeo's bodily architecture with appliances drawn from the realm of dwelling, yielding case studies in theatrical affordances that help frame Romeo's actions in successive environments.

Urged by Benvolio to crash the party, Romeo agrees to join his friends, but only as a torchbearer: "Give me a torch, I am not for this ambling" (1.4.9). When Benvolio rehearses their plan, "Come, knock and enter, and no sooner in, / But every man betake him to his legs" (1.4.31–32), Romeo repeats his earlier declaration: "A torch for me . . . I'll be a candle-holder and look on" (33–36). Romeo's assumption of the role of torchbearer stands at the center of a complex of images, things, theatrical effects, and social scripts. In the tradition of masking, the torchbearer is he who serves rather than participates.[56] In Renaissance cities, torchbearers were youths or hired help who assisted gentlemen

55. Blau, *The Dubious Spectacle*, 213.

56. Early in the editorial tradition (1773), Steevens cited *Westward Ho!* ("He is just like a torch bearer to maskers: he wears good cloaths, and is ranked in good company, but he does nothing") and suggested that "a torch-bearer seems to have been a constant attendant on every person masked" (*The Plays of William Shakespeare*, 27n).

in their search for erotic pleasures. In the era before electrification, the streets were dark; gallants brought their light with them, moving with the roving pool of radiance cast by their linkboy.[57] The bearing capacities of the person and the illuminative virtues of the torch supplement each other, together casting the ambulatory illumination required by midnight maskers.[58] "Being but heavy," Romeo quips, "I will bear the light" (1.4.10): the word "heavy" describes Romeo's melancholic *gravitas*, but it also identifies him as the physical support of the torch; the composite figure, half-man, half-tool, makes room for the revelers as they edge through the darkened urban space.[59]

When Romeo first observes Juliet, he does so from the vantage point of attendant spectatorship announced by the torch he bears:

> *Romeo (to a Serving-man)*: What lady's that which doth enrich the
> hand
> Of yonder knight?
> *Serving-Man*: I know not, sir.
> *Romeo*: O, she doth teach the torches to burn bright!
> It seems she hangs upon the cheek of night
> As a rich jewel in an Ethiop's ear,
> Beauty too rich for use, for earth too dear. (1.4.154–60)

Romeo's comparison of Juliet to a jewel may seem of a piece with his earlier clichés for Rosalind. Yet it is the jewel's light-reflective affordances that Romeo's image catches here; like the shimmering fabrics that draped walls, tables, and chairs of state in the Renaissance softscape, jewels were worn not simply as

57. On torchbearers, linkboys, and early modern urbanism, see Tiffany, *Infidel Poetics*, 172–83.

58. Ann Pasternak Slater argues for the predominance of light effects in the party scene: "When Romeo meets Juliet, it is on a stage crowded with lights. '*Torchbearers*' (Q2 SD) accompany Romeo to the Capulets' ball, where Capulet constantly fusses about the lights. . . . Shakespeare's dialogue makes it clear that Romeo should himself be a torchbearer, and that their first hushed, intimate encounter should be illuminated by the torch whose light encloses them both" ("Petrarchanism Come True," 140).

59. Dessen and Thomson note that torch is sometimes used as a metonym for torchbearer, and confirm the supporting role played by torchbearers in masking (*Dictionary of Stage Directions*, 233–34).

ornaments or signs of status, but as tiny agents of reflective illumination. The reference to the Ethiop's ear evokes the pleasing contrast between glossy highlights and a dark matte background, an effect exploited to this day in the display of diamonds on velvet. The premodern lighting systems used in great halls and other spaces of entertainment included not only candles, tapers, torches, and their many holders, but also gold-threaded arras, metal candle plates, and mobile bling, whose reflective capacities amplified the precious effects of candlelight.[60] According to Gibson, it is reflected or ambient light, not the radiant light cast directly by the sun or other sources, that accounts for most animal perception: "Radiant light comes from atoms and returns to atoms; ambient light depends upon an environment of surfaces. Radiant light is energy; ambient light can be information."[61] The light-reflective capacities of surfaces, in other words, afford the visibility that helps communicate the more particular uses of objects to animate actors. And premodern lighting systems, more than electrified ones, worked that environment of surfaces in order to enhance the precious effects of ambient light. If the torchbearer Romeo handles one source of radiant light in the scene, the jewel-like Juliet is imagined to reflect back that light, becoming a second source of luminescence rendered more enchanting by virtue of *not producing* its own rays.

Romeo's torch, of course, is immediately caught up in a web of emblematic images; never simply a tool, it is always also an iconographic attribute of love and fidelity carried by angels, *putti*, watchmen, and Hymen in Renaissance poetry, prints, tapestries, plates, mantelpieces, and furniture, as well as bodied forth in the design of candlesticks both great and small.[62] Such objects visualize the composite form created by torch and bearer, often

60. Graves uses the term "lighting system" to describe the lighting arrangements of the Elizabethan stage (*Lighting the Shakespearean Stage*, 26–64).

61. Gibson, *Reasons for Realism*, 51.

62. On the interplay between print culture and the decorative arts in Renaissance England, see Wells-Cole, *Art and Decoration in Elizabethan and Jacobean England*. For caryatids on candlesticks, see examples reprinted by Thornton, *The Italian Renaissance Interior*, 280–81. Thornton also describes the lighting constraints of premodern rooms and the role of reflective surfaces in heightening the effects of ambient light (276).

couched in postures of supplication, service, and attendance at altarpiece or dinner table.

The vocation of torchbearer incorporates Romeo into an assemblage composed of print culture, home furnishings, festive custom, poetic conceits, old proverbs, and lighting techniques. We should resist placing the "real" torch and its material affordances at the center of a complex that becomes increasingly ideational. What the torch affords is phenomenal appearing: not only the emergence of visible figures out of the glooming dusk of indistinction, but also the reflective effects that link shine to *Schein* (semblance, appearance). Affordances, so tightly bound to use, actually exist in close proximity to aesthetics, insofar as each concerns forms of appearing and the "environment of surfaces" in which appearing can take place. In the public theaters, moreover, torches and tapers, whether or not they were actually lit, were properties that communicated "nighttime" in a space not conducive to artificial dimming.[63] Their affordances are semiotic as well as practical. It is ultimately words that must light the torch; Romeo's luminous comparison of Juliet to the jewel is a consummately poetic achievement that also makes theatrical and dramatic sense. In Shakespeare's poetic dramaturgy, images of things in their affordance-bearing capacities are drawn into the orbit of human thought and emotional life in order to build worlds that cue scenographies to come.

If the torch enters the play in part from love poetry's Petrarchan platitudes, Romeo manages to wake up these sleeping beauties from the coma of their commodification, using the torch to create a clearing—what Heidegger calls a *Lichtung*—in the field of conventional language. Romeo's decision to play the torchbearer is itself an act of partial exit from the society of spectacle in which he first glimpses Juliet, allowing him to become a kind of embodied, extended aside, to secrete and inhabit a *Lichtung* all his own. Like Juliet's silken thread, the torch calls atten-

63. Bevington writes, "The torch, as always, signals nighttime" (*This Wide and Universal Theater*, 133).

tion to the invisible envelope of personal space whose invasion can spark fistfights, road rage, and sexual panic. Candor is the virtue that belongs to that clearing: the shining ability to speak freely within a region defined by convention and spectatorship.[64] What Romeo shares with Hamlet is the desire *not* to subscribe completely to celebratory spectacle, thus reserving some element of purse and person. His resistance to decor, including the decorative resonances of his torchbearing posture, becomes the source of its own special illumination.

The circle of light cast by Romeo's ardent torch, then, not only contributes to the glamour of the happenings, but also signs his partial withdrawal from them, and thus makes a new kind of room for the two lovers. Ultimately, Romeo must draw Juliet aside—draw her, that is, into the clearing of *his aside*—in order to find an intimate space that is theirs and theirs alone, a space nested both within and beyond the environment of entertainment supervised by busy Capulet. In Baz Luhrmann's *Romeo + Juliet*, the lovers escape into a glass elevator, a dizzying embodiment of this translucent silo of proximate space. It is the work of the "little room" of the sonnet form itself to block such a locus out of language and gesture. When Romeo, addressing Juliet for the first time, speaks of "profaning" "this holy shrine" with his hands, he places Juliet in a metaphorical alcove; the conceit of the sonnet spins a kind of virtual shell around them. The word "profane" refers etymologically to that which lies before or outside the temple (*fanum*).[65] At once porch and alcove, the little room of roaming space that the two lovers build together draws on the affordances of the Catholic multimedia sensorium with its ritual choreography (pilgrimage, palmers' kiss) and its mood-inducing properties (candles, rich vestments, jewels). Yet their incipient idolatry is also iconoclastic: "profane is the term for something that was once sacred or religious and is returned to the use and

64. On the political virtue of candor, which belongs to the *candidatus* in Roman politics, see Green, *The Eyes of the People*, 134–36.

65. Wilcox and Todd, eds., *George Herbert*, vii.

property of men."[66] It is a moment of advent and annunciation, occurring, however, on a human plane whose summer heat holds the teenagers in the lambent *kairos* of the kiss. Their coy language of saints and pilgrimage fashions a setting for the birth of love, which is also, as Kottman argues, the birth of their own freedom as human actors out of inherited social scenarios.[67] At some point, Romeo must put down his torch. Bearing that torch, however, has helped light up the zone in which he and Juliet first kiss with the palms of their hands, the rhymes of their words, and finally with their lips.

Crowbar and Lantern

The torch guides Romeo's entry into his first encounter with Juliet. The crowbar guides his final movement into her region, though now manic forcefulness and a will to act at any cost replaces lyric reserve and receptivity. The crowbar links Romeo to mythic predecessors like Orpheus and Christ while also associating him with lower forms of labor and the backstage *oikos*. Designed to force open closed precincts (locked doors, sealed tombs), the crowbar leverages heterogeneous spaces and moods, tilting the play toward its tragic conclusion and final mortal setting, but also introducing a potential element of farce into the heaviness of the proceedings. Affordances bear here on the tool's real-world applications of forced entry and the transfer of those applications to more atmospheric and modal kinds of threshold action.

Paris has come to dress Juliet's grave with a dutiful bouquet of flowers. His obsequies are interrupted by the appearance of Romeo and his man Balthazar, "with a torch, a mattock, and a crow of iron." Romeo's first line upon entry is to demand the crowbar from Balthazar: "Give me that mattock and the wrenching-iron"

66. The jurist Trebatius, cited by Agamben, *Profanations*, 73.

67. On the cognitive affordances of religious objects, see Spolsky, *Word vs. Image*. On *Romeo and Juliet* as the tragedy of freedom, see Kottman, "Defying the Stars."

(5.3.22). The tools are rash Romeo's antibouquet. An instrument used in husbandry, carpentry, and sailing, the crowbar is associated in drama and fiction with breaking and entering. It shows up, for example, in an urban dictionary of the late seventeenth century,[68] but also in *The Comedy of Errors*, where Antipholus of Syracuse prepares to break into his own house with an "iron crow" (3.1.84).[69] In D'Avenant's *The Wits* of 1636, a character named Thwack enters a graveyard "with an Iron Crow and dark Lanthorn," preparing to rob an interred woman of her gold. Romeo "Thwack" Montague cuts himself from the same rough-and-ready cloth when he tells his servant that he is here to take "a precious ring" "from [Juliet's] dead finger" (5.3.30–31).

Echoing classical and biblical descents to the underworld, the moment borrows from Christ's Harrowing, in which Jesus is sometimes depicted as wielding the cross to pry open the mouth of hell much as Romeo invades the "detestable maw" and "rotten jaws" of the Capulet monument (5.3.45, 47). Although the mythic reference heightens Romeo's actions, the crowbar's homeliness simultaneously lowers it.[70] The crowbar is at once crude and precise, a simple tool whose bent and sometimes forked end (like the foot of a crow, hence the name) leverages the strength of its wielder. The opening of the grave with the crowbar resets the diegetic scene from graveyard to monument, efficiently moving us from outdoors to indoors. Whether executed from the gallery space into the stage below[71] or performed at the threshold of the discovery space in order to reveal Juliet's body within, the crowbar discloses entry as act in a scene that charts the emergence

68. B. E., *A New Dictionary of the Canting Crew*, 1699. See the entry for "*Mill-a-ken*, c. to Rob a House, Milling the Gig with a Betty, c. Breaking open the Door with an Iron-Crow. Milling the Glaze, c. Breaking open the Window· Mill them, c. Kill them."

69. *The Comedy of Errors*, in *The Riverside Shakespeare*.

70. For a stunning foray into the iconography and spatial disposition of Christ's Harrowing of Hell, see Cummings, *Mortal Thoughts*, 25–31. On this moment, he comments that "Romeo is crossing the door from event and consequence into a void in which time has no meaning" (183). Orpheus and Christ were linked in medieval exegesis and mythography; see Friedman, *Orpheus in the Middle Ages*.

71. As in Dominic Dromgoole's 2009 production at the London Globe.

of human action in relation to objects and architecture. Every entry onto the stage reframes and relaunches the actor into his assumed role out of the buzzing milieu of theatrical labor backstage. When the actor must force his way into a scene, the action character of entry is amplified; in this instance, the dependence of action on work and labor also makes an unscripted entry, as it does periodically throughout the play. And work and labor are bound up with hidden economies that threaten what little decorum this play manages to maintain. Describing himself as "savage-wild," this anti-Orpheus wields not a poet's lyre but a workman's tool, and Paris accuses Romeo of engaging in "unhallowed toil." He threatens to "tear [Balthazar] joint by joint / And strew this hungry churchyard with thy limbs" if the servant stays in the vicinity, a fantasy of dismemberment that seems to flow into *Romeo and Juliet* from *Titus Andronicus*, say, or *The Jew of Malta*.

The crowbar forces a gap between representational worlds. What or who exactly might spill out onto the stage when Romeo wields his wrenching iron? The semicomic friar most certainly, who enters the stage stumbling on tombstones and carrying—guess what—his very own crowbar. But what or who else might enter through the crack opened by the crowbar? How about the ghost of Tybalt imagined by Juliet, or Queen Mab, or Peter and his musicians, or the Apothecary, played by the company's comic "Thin Man" and surrounded by his Mantuan inventory of empty boxes and stuffed crocodiles? The gothic, but also the comic, lurk in the wings here, waiting for their cue—not the jolly banquet that warms act 1, but something colder, more macabre and grotesque. Meanwhile, Balthazar has fallen asleep beneath a nearby tree; awakened by the arrival of the Friar, he reports, "As I did sleep under this yew tree here, / I dreamt my master and another fought, / And that my master slew him" (5.3.137–39). This line doesn't get discussed much: after all, Balthazar's dream simply restates what occurred before us on stage. Yet the stage itself *has* been stalked by approaching phantasms, as a multitude of denizens representing netherworld and *Lebenswelt* crowd and mumble, seeking entry through the gap opened by Romeo's crowbar.

In other words, Romeo's crowbar dangerously pivots the play between tragedy and farce, or perhaps begins to lift the play beyond genre, into the more existential zone of *King Lear* and *Macbeth*.[72] Nonetheless Shakespeare brings in neither the ghosts nor the clowns. Instead, he lets in the light. As Romeo drags Paris's body into the monument, he glimpses Juliet:

> I'll bury thee in a triumphant grave.
> A grave—O no, a lantern, slaughtered youth;
> For here lies Juliet, and her beauty makes
> This vault a feasting presence full of light. (5.3.83–86)

In architecture, a lantern was the windowed structure erected above a dome in order to pour light into the room below. Liturgical spaces create an atmosphere in which divinity can "dwell": reside, suffuse, and become tangible in and as the atmosphere of a place. A lantern is also a portable lighting appliance, often carried on stage (as it is by the Friar in this scene) to indicate nighttime. Here, Romeo imagines the dark grave as a space miraculously flooded with the light of Juliet's presence. "Feasting presence" is short for "presence chamber," the great hall in which a monarch would receive guests and hold banquets.[73] The sovereign and ecclesiastical resonances are dominant, but the sense of an appliance and its real and semiotic affordances is not irrelevant, each borrowing light and structure from the other. Whereas earlier Romeo had imagined the tomb as a flesh-eating monster, here the same space recreates the party in which Romeo had first seen Juliet teaching the torches to burn bright. The lantern of

72. Ruth Nevo is one of the few critics to note the affinity between *Romeo and Juliet* and *Lear*: "*Lear* is the play in which Shakespeare presents the anguish of a mind fully facing the threat of chaos, a mind hovering above the void; in *Romeo and Juliet*, when he sets out to dramatize the vulnerability of young love, he places his young lovers not too great a distance from that terrifying terrain" ("Tragic Form in *Romeo and Juliet*," 242).

73. Levenson, Oxford edition, 343n.

the grave is the last theatrical space built out of and around the co-presence of the lovers. Its glowing bounds recall the imagined sonnet room that Romeo and Juliet designed out of language, imagery, and movement under the aegis of Romeo's torchbearing energy. Shakespeare begins to imagine here the pure volumes of light that would become building blocks of modernist stage design once electrification afforded them, as explored, for example, in Adolphe Appiah's landmark staging of Gluck's *Orpheus and Eurydice*, an opera that shares mythic materials with Romeo and Juliet: "In Appiah's hands, light had successfully created an environment that both amplified the human body in sculptural form and became itself 'a creation animated by an unencumbered vitality.'"[74] The image is Romeo's answer to Juliet's transcendent installation of lucent stars on velvet night. Her imaginary stagecraft issues from fabriculture and anticipates a scenography of scrims and projections. His comes out of political-theological experience design and anticipates a modernist scenography of poly-dimensional light forms. This feasting presence full of light is the play's final glass elevator, an intimate alcove lit up by the imaginative intensity of Romeo and Juliet's love.

After the risky bit with the crowbar, it's a great save. Yet the light here is not only the luminosity of Juliet's special brand of beauty (emergent erotic curiosity mixed with fidelity to a singular romantic attachment). Romeo associates her beauty as well as his own savage-wild energy with the "lightening" before death: what modern science now identifies as the rush of endorphins the body produces at the end of life. What lights up the grave is the lovers' own proximity within it; the illumination is the fruit of their actions. What also shines here is dramatic irony, the cool light of reason and the radiance of romance blending uneasily. After all, Juliet glows because she is *not* dead. Romeo's final blazon—"beauty's ensign yet / Is crimson in thy lips and in thy cheeks, / And death's pale flag is not advancèd there"—is horrible because it is true (5.3.94–96). If the passage reeks of res-

74. Salter, *Entangled*, 7, citing Richard Beacham, *Adolphe Appiah*, 78.

urrection, it's because Juliet lives. What is tragic about the play is not that they both die, but that they didn't have to, that manic Romeo ignores his own correct reading of Juliet's vital signs and precipitously joins her in death. Dramatic irony places us just outside the tomb, peering through the crack opened by Romeo's crowbar. If the image of the grave as feasting presence returns us to the dazzling hospitality of act 1, it also advances us into a zone marked by contingency, irony, and misprision. (To "dwell" originally meant "to lead into error," "to delude" [*OED*, 1].)

The golden statues that the fathers plan to erect in honor of the lovers manifests the bad faith of much public art and architecture, the self-aggrandizing permanence of their brazen reflectivities overwhelming the more performative and transient styles of lighting that characterize Romeo and Juliet's scenographies of love. The feasting presence, which mixes irony with epiphany, promises to be more real and true, something that we can *dwell in* and *dwell on* in its resonance and dimensionality. Temporary, site specific, dependent on embodiment, and revolving around ambience, Romeo's lantern image, a monument to the momentary, is closer to installation art than to statuary. Encapsulating different strains of the Renaissance lighting system within one glowing vault, the image assembles a reverberant space of appearing, a final consorting of Romeo with his environment.

In Baz Luhrmann's staging of this final scene, Romeo encounters Juliet surrounded by a host of votive candles. It is a case of dramaturgy responding to metaphoric cues in the play text; W. B. Worthen would speak here of the script affording its later performance. Whereas sacrifice involves offering up a human or animal victim who will die in the process of purifying or redeeming a community, votive offerings are tokens brought to a temple or church not for slaughter but for display and deposit or immediate use (see chapter 3). The votive character of those candles suggests curatorial economies of appearing that supplement the drama's beeline toward sacrifice while also drawing sustenance from the play's Catholic setting and sensorial imagery. The movement from crowbar to lantern, along with the other odes to dwelling that I've gathered together here, point us back to the environmental flows that sustain the theater. In *Romeo and Juliet*, I've argued, Shakespeare tests the scripts of habitation and hospitality for the risks and resiliencies they harbor, the leftover times and spaces they generate, and the chance for unexpected encounters that they court. Developed in environmental psychology, the concept of affordances has migrated to design, a discourse that draws together cognition, domesticity, and environmental complexity. In *Romeo and Juliet*, design delimits the revelatory passages between arts of place-making and processes of thought—between the techniques of spatial rezoning and the formations of affective and cognitive life. In reading dramaturgy in *Romeo and Juliet*, I have attempted to disclose the intricate topologies of consciousness, care, toil, and acknowledgment, of mending and attending, that the play harbors. My goal is not to bind the plays to a historical inventory of objects, but rather to understand the actions, atmospheres, and environments that torches, crowbars, and dovecotes solicit. At the end of act 1, scene 3, a servant tells Lady Capulet, "Madam, the guests are come, supper served up, you called, my young lady asked for, the Nurse cursed in the pantry, and everything in extremity" (1.3.102–4). *Romeo and Juliet* delivers to us the "everything in extremity" that characterizes hospitality as a taskscape: the dispersal and reorganization of things, persons, and spaces in the moment of the feast, and the dangers, distresses, and creative opportunities that hospitality as theater oversees with such bravado, and occasionally with real candor.

2

Macbeth against Dwelling

Now therefore, thou O most loving Father, which hast set me together: dissolve me in such wise as I may feele myself to be dissolved, and remember of whom I am overcome, and consider whither I must goe.
«RICHARD DAY, "A prayer to be sayd when we unclothe ourselves to bedward"[1]»

The real is a closely woven fabric.
«MAURICE MERLEAU-PONTY[2]»

In killing Duncan in his bed, Macbeth not only murders sleep, he also assaults the conditions of dwelling as such, rendering those conditions suddenly, nakedly, tangible. The murder of sleep (Duncan) leads to the disruption of commensality (Banquo) and to the assault on shelter (Lady Macduff and her dependents), actions that exile Macbeth from what Paul Kottman, following Hegel, calls "the friendliness of life."[3] By violating the routines of daily life, the Macbeths' actions take themselves, their worlds, and their audiences to the existential edges of those routines, where human being, both distinguished from and caught up in

1. Day, *A Booke of Christian Prayers*, 9.
2. Merleau-Ponty, *Phenomenology of Perception*, xi.
3. Kottman, "Introduction," in *Philosophers on Shakespeare*, 6.

the forms of life that buzz and hum around it, builds its house in the domain of a haunted creatureliness. As Benjamin Parris has argued, the play is *biopolitical* in its wresting of political ends (the crown) from pre- or protopolitical scenes of dormancy, and *political-theological* in its tendency to sacralize the slumbering life exposed to this violence.[4] The Scottish play is at once a *royal tragedy* of usurpation, which zones the castle as palace; a *domestic tragedy* of bad housekeeping and marital squabbling, which economizes the palace as household; and a *cosmic tragedy* that disposes the *oikos* within seasonal, liturgical, and media ecologies. Hospitality lays a very red carpet among the castle's political, domestic, and environmental offices, convening the social routines and mythic reserves that direct the fun-house flow among these convergent topographies. Bedtime prayers provide another repertory that configures somatic processes, affective attitudes, and poetic speech in the scenes of dwelling; constituting at once a liturgy, a dramaturgy, and a scenography, bedtime prayers help shape the play's murder of sleep and its seepage into the landscape of curses, a terrain composed by the concatenation of creaturely dependence, social trust, and cosmic accountability.

In murdering sleep, *Macbeth* gathers literary and theatrical atmosphere into the spaces cleared by dramatic action. In drama, atmosphere emulsifies mood and setting, an inmixing powered in this play by deeds against dwelling.[5] In architecture and ecological psychology, atmosphere mobilizes the affective affordances of sound and light as well as smell, smoke, temperature, and humidity. I do not address the performance history of *Macbeth* per se, whose successive productions have tapped the play's atmospheric invitations within evolving technological and hermeneutic frames. Instead, I seek out the play's commentary on the genesis of atmosphere as neither a technical addition to drama nor a merely semantic cushion of meaningfulness. Instead, atmosphere

4. Parris, "'The body is with the king.'"

5. On *Macbeth* and atmosphere, see Jonathan Gil Harris, "The Smell of Gunpowder," in *Untimely Matter in the Time of Shakespeare*.

in *Macbeth* emerges as a floating feature implied and produced by the actions of the characters, actions that occur as substantial speech (Arendt) and in locales cultivated by routines of habitation (Heidegger). The play's haunted house aesthetics, whether intuited through the reading process, teased out by theatrical production, or allowed to gather and lurk on the bare sunlit stage,[6] arise from the disturbances visited by the Macbeths on dwelling. In exploring *Macbeth*'s abuses of dwelling, I return to the idea of softscape, a term I borrow from landscape architecture, where the term encompasses the plantings added to the "hardscape" composed by paths, retaining walls, and landforms.[7] I use softscape to describe the use of fabrics and foliage to build temporary structures for purposes ranging from entertaining and repose to worship and protest. Soft architecture captures what is makeshift and transient in the spatial construction of human scenes of gathering. All architecture is in some sense soft (guaranteed of no permanence against the ravages of time, taste, or recession), but some forms of architecture curate their own moody alliances with atrophy more frankly than others. In the spaces cultivated by *Macbeth*, atmosphere is the ultimate softscape, its dusky sonority amplifying the moral consequences and residential origins of dramatic action.

Investitures

Having declared Malcolm his successor, Duncan rather abruptly announces that he will be traveling to Inverness. Macbeth's courteous response does not fail to exude a certain panic:

> The rest is labour, which is not used for you;
> I'll be myself the harbinger, and make joyful
> The hearing of my wife with your approach.
> So humbly take my leave. (1.4.45–48)[8]

6. On open air *Macbeth*, see Pamela Mason, "Sunshine in *Macbeth*," 335–37.

7. For an elaboration of softscapes in theatrical scenes, see Lupton, "Soft Res Publica."

8. All references to *Macbeth* are taken from the Oxford edition, ed. Nicholas Brooke.

Preparing to return to Inverness ahead of the king, Macbeth aptly elects himself the king's "harbinger." The term plunges him into the play's overleaping momentum, intemperately rushing ahead into a risky future, but it also lays out a relationship to place and place-making that concerns the protocols of royal dwelling. As Mary Hill Cole notes, the harbinger was the court official who preceded the monarch on his or her progresses in order to assure that "the bedrooms had chairs, beds, carpets, and hangings." These tasks were gathered under the rubric of "appareling," the same term used when great halls and banqueting houses were set up as theaters using timber frames and handsome textiles to assemble stages and seating.[9] Such appareling belongs to the hospitable softscape, the mobilization of fabrics, foliage, and furnishings for the shaping, lining, canopying, dividing, and outfitting of spaces for entertainment. Duncan had spoken of "investing" Malcolm as heir (1.4.41), one of many references to formal enrobement in the play that borrows from political theology's division between the symbolic accoutrements of office and the mortal body of he who wears them. What is at stake in the harbinger's charge is another kind of investiture, not of persons but of spaces, which will be decked with special fabrics whose affordances of enclosure and warmth also symbolize magnificence and support the tremulous sense of occasion.[10] Duncan will presumably meet his end in a properly outfitted state bed, a confection of elaborate tapestries hung on a wood frame that erected a chamber within the chamber, a holy of holies for royal guests.[11] The murder itself occurs offstage, a placement that pushes the bedchamber into the

9. Cole, *The Portable Queen*, 43. On "appareling" halls for theatrical performance, see Astington, *English Court Theater*, 29. The first meaning for "harbinger" in the *OED* is "One who provides lodging; an entertainer, a host" (1); the Knight Harbinger was an officer in the Royal Household until 1846 (2). The sense of a harbinger as a forerunner or announcer is metaphoric (3). "harbinger, n.," *OED Online*, March 2016.

10. On temporary stages and seating built on trestles and covered in fabric, see Astington, *English Court Theatre*, 93–94. On Renaissance England as a cloth culture, see Jones and Stallybrass, *Renaissance Clothing and the Materials of Memory*.

11. On state beds and their importance in Shakespeare, see Sasha Roberts, "'Let me the curtains draw.'"

recesses of the tiring house. We might even think of the murder as imaginatively rezoning the curtained discovery space as a canopied bed of state, its heavy drapery protecting the sleeping king from the prying eyes of the assembled audience.

This sovereign softscape affords, without prescribing, a variety of scenographic possibilities that resonate with contemporary scenes of displacement, encampment, and occupation, the appareled halls of Inverness flowing into present-day fabric architecture designed to host refugees and migrant workers. Picking up on the scriptural motif of dwelling as radical itineracy, Justin Kurzel's 2015 film depicts all of Inverness as a primitive collection of tents, save for a simple wooden chapel at the center of the wretched encampment. Like Holofernes at the hands of Judith, Duncan is killed in one of these tents, the makeshift fabric structure mirroring his physical vulnerability and the whole setup communicating the nomadic character of the Macbeths' life as a military family. Costume designer Jacqueline Durran eschewed "brocades and braids—anything you'd associate with medieval style" in favor of "bone, hemp, and nettle."[12] Durran's fabrications combine a deep historicism with a transcultural interest in design that responds to environmental exigency.

The readying of spaces for rest is not detailed in the text itself. Instead, we get several allusions to the kinds of soft implements that help support sleep by regulating light, sound, and temperature to create a sense of security. The most elaborate of these references to the investiture of space with equipment for sleeping is Banquo's description of the martlets' nests that deck the facade of Inverness with their avian artistry. Approaching the Macbeths' castle, Banquo remarks to Duncan,

> This guest of summer,
> The temple-haunting martlet, does approve,
> By his loved mansionry, that the Heaven's breath
> Smells wooingly here; no jutty, frieze,
> Buttress, nor coign of vantage, but this bird

12. Harris, "Michael Fassbender and the Robes of Royalty."

> Hath made his pendant bed and procreant cradle;
> Where they must breed and haunt, I have observed
> The air is delicate. (1.6.3–10)[13]

Banquo fills out the king's half line with an image of felicitous nesting, weaving a kind of virtual welcome mat that Banquo sees, or wants to see, decking the halls of Macbeth's castle with the promise of succor. The martlets' "pendant bed and procreant cradle" suggest temporary structures woven out of soft materials and subject to gentle movement, helping to fashion what Duncan calls the castle's "pleasant seat." The image visualizes the building as a contexture of affordances, in which the appurtenances and hollows that furrow the facade offer unexpected refuge for avian architects, creatures who remain perilously exposed to predators and weather shifts as well as random poeticizing. Editor Nicholas Brooke glosses the martlets as embodying "the benign spirit of the castle"; as embodiments of an architectural *genius loci* (Norberg-Schulz), the birds imply the adaptations and attunements that articulate landscape into taskscape, a repertoire captured in the evocative word "mansionry," which condenses the places (mansions) and arts (masonry) of building in a single substantive.[14]

According to J. P. Dyson, Banquo's meditation on martlets assembles the values of medieval hospitality, "caught in verse as light and delicate as the air it describes," that the play puts forward for tragic violation, like so many marzipan pigeons on a Renaissance banqueting tray.[15] To these ideals the Macbeths' hostile modes of dwelling will pose blistering antitypes: the act of murdering sleep replaces fertility with barrenness and openness with claustrophobia. Banquo himself may already be a bit unsettled by his own foreboding, with the martlet image as a defensive flip-

13. Hannibal Hamlin associates the passage with Psalm 84, rendered in the Sternhold and Hopkins psalter as "How pleasant is thy dwelling place . . . The sparrows find a roome to rest" (*The Bible in Shakespeare*, 292–94).

14. See Brooke, *Macbeth*, 114n.

15. Dyson, "The Structural Function of the Banquet Scene in *Macbeth*," 369–70.

ping of angst into optimism.[16] The martlets, in other words, are also harbingers of hospitality: their nesting prefigures the kinds of soft accommodation anticipated by the visitors within, while the picture of the birds' open architecture is riddled with the irony of its latticed voids. Duncan will very soon be murdered in his own "pendent bed" and "procreant cradle," reminders of sleep's perilous insecurity. Later, Lady Macduff will compare her own mansion to birds' nests as she anticipates the destruction of her household (4.2.6–11). As a map of leftover spaces carved out of permanent structures through skilled acts of scavenging, the image of nesting begins to visualize dwelling as an improvisatory orchestration of spatial and temporal remainders.

None of this appears before us as a prop or picture on stage; instead, the crenellated composite of birds, nests, and castle emerge and dissolve on the scrim of the imagination. In gazing at the loose tapestry formed by the martlets' nests and shaping it into a more formal image of human accommodation, Duncan and Banquo are imagining their own rooms at the inn. And as we gaze with these visitors at these conjured nests, we gain a passing phenomenological access to our own coigns of vantage, pendant beds and pleasant seats in theater, inn, great hall, nursery, and dormitory. The passage engages "apprehension" in the two senses employed in Theseus's famous speech on the imagination: first, as the broad intuiting of a fluid landscape that is both environmental and affective ("apprehend[ing] / More than cool reason ever comprehends") and, second, as the "apprehensive," objectless anxiety solicited by vertiginous heights and unprotected spaces, a state of nervous excitation in which bushes might appear to be bears. Banquo engages in an act of ekphrasis that merges several

16. Carolyn Spurgeon writes about this passage, "From my experience of Shakespeare's methods, I was convinced that the vivid picture of the masses of swallows' nests on the outer walls of Macbeth's castle was not purely imagination on his part, but that he had somewhere *seen* such nests on a castle's walls" (*Shakespeare's Imagery*, 374, 189). Bruce Smith associates Spurgeon's image analysis with the phenomenological project in *Phenomenal Shakespeare*, 32.

subjects (Duncan, the audience, himself) as they approach diverse objects and affects: the open weave created by martlets, twigs and bits of building; the memories of work and rest caught up in this fair assemblage; and the floating disquiet and lurking insomnia that attend its exposed structure.[17] This act of poetic apprehension, moreover, occurs as the sojourning speakers move toward their destination across the stage; if the image *reflects on* hospitality as theme, it is also *produced by* hospitality as a spatial routine.[18]

Banquo captures the martlets' mix of inventiveness and vulnerability in an explicit evocation of atmosphere: "Where they must breed and haunt, I have observed / The air is delicate" (1.6.9–10). "Haunt" carries its original meaning of a familiar action or habit, but already begins to invite its secondary sense of visitation by ghosts.[19] "Air," especially coupled with "delicate," implies an affective redoubling of the setting, gathering an aural sense (air as melody) into its penumbra of associations. "Delicate" suggests the charm of the setting as well as the receptiveness of the visitors to the world they encounter. Although this "delicate air" will be swiftly displaced by the cold front of crime, even the play's later, darker atmospherics, thanks to Macbeth's own canine keenness, participate in a kind of delicacy, in the sense of being "responsive to very slight influences; finely sensitive."[20] All atmospheres, in other words, are "delicate," animated by the vibrant relay between objective and subjective factors. The delicate atmosphere of welcome on display in Banquo's ekphrastic ode to the martlets also gestures toward the fragility of hospitable environs; as Harry Berger notes, "'The air is delicate' trembles between its summery and precarious senses,"[21] an ambivalence that seeps into the soft wrappings of the play's object world.

17. On ekphrasis and phenomenology, see Rapaport, "The Phenomenology of Spenserian Ekphrasis."

18. On the theater as a workplace, understood in cognitive and organizational terms, see Tribble, *Cognition in the Globe*, 27–28.

19. For the latter sense, see "haunt," verb, *OED*, 5b, with citations beginning in 1597 and including Shakespeare. "haunt, n.," *OED Online*, March 2016.

20. "Delicate" (III.10.b), "delicate, adj. and n.," *OED Online*, March 2016.

21. Harry Berger Jr., *Making Trifles of Terrors*, 96.

The end of Lady Macbeth's "Unsex me here" speech, thickened by figures of hardness, also alludes to the soft implements that support sleep:

> Come, thick night,
> And pall thee in the dunnest smoke of Hell,
> That my keen knife see not the wound it makes,
> Nor Heaven peep through the blanket of the dark
> To cry, "Hold, hold." (1.5.49–53)

A "pall" is a rich cloth or vestment, often ceremonial, including the black, purple, or white drapery that covered hearses and corpses; it could also refer to a light-obscuring cloud, an atmospheric sense picked up in Lady Macbeth's reference to smoke.[22] By handling the noun as a verb, the speaker invokes the cloaking and clouding properties of the pall along with its liturgical and funereal associations. The pall shares affordances with the blanket introduced in the next fold of imagery, an item drawn from a homelier inventory of objects. Samuel Johnson used this passage to measure the impropriety of low words in heightened situations: "This sentiment is weakened by the name of an instrument used by butchers and cooks in the meanest employments; we do not immediately conceive that any crime of importance is to be committed with a *knife*. . . . Who, without some relaxation of his gravity, can hear of the avengers of guilt *peeping through a blanket*?"[23] Johnson's response to the improper mixing of the tools of dwelling with the themes of tragedy helps orient us in the play's atmospheric architecture. Lady Macbeth compares the night to a blanket, from *blanquette*, referring to white or undyed woolens; indeed the submerged contrasts between pall/dunn and blanket/dark begin to insinuate a checked pattern into the speech's Scotch softscape. Lady Macbeth, however, emphasizes not the color but the thickness of the blanket ("Come,

22. "Pall, n. 1" (I.1, I.4, and III.9.a), *OED Online*, March 2016.

23. Johnson, "Number 168," in *The Rambler*, 254. Blankets show up in the extensive textile inventories at Hardwick House, as recorded in *Of Household Stuff*, 24. On these and other household words in *Macbeth*, see Hopkins, "Household Words."

thick night"): in the domestic economy, this attribute affords the sleeper warmth and a sense of provisional protection, a "security blanket" reinforced in Duncan's case by the ring of guards outside his door. These things of darkness join a sequence of phrases that suspend image and idea in mood and milieu (e.g., "Light thickens" [3.2.53], "thick-coming fancies" [5.3.37]).

Lady Macbeth wants the murder of Duncan to be invisible to "Heaven," a figure for forms of conscience, witnessing, and acknowledgment potentially shared by the murderers, their victims, and onlookers, whether human or divine. The specter of a divine force unable to peep through its blanket (un)covers the figure of the king himself bundled in his bed. Lady Macbeth wants the blanketing darkness to hide the act from her "keen knife," the instrument of her sharp intention; compare the obfuscating functions of the arras in *Hamlet*, in which the hanging tapestry allows the prince to pierce Polonius with his weapon by releasing the agent from the burden of witnessing his own bloody work. Her "keen knife" figures the prick of conscience, which literally means "thinking with": in *Macbeth*, conscience merges with atmosphere and arms the accoutrements of dwelling with a new sting, inviting us to "think with" the play about the way in which intention ricochets into remorse by retooling the appliances of dwelling.

The "Sleep no more" passage twists the beneficent strands of idealized repose into a curse hurled against sleep itself. In his inventory of the blessings conferred by rest, Macbeth associates sleep with a suite of technologies and routines:

> Methought I heard a voice cry "Sleep no more;
> Macbeth does murder sleep, the innocent sleep,
> Sleep that knits up the ravelled sleeve of care,
> The death of each day's life, sore labour's bath,
> Balm of hurt minds, great nature's second course,
> Chief nourisher in life's feast." (2.2.34–39)

Sleep is "sore labour's bath," a moment of rest and cleansing that renews us for labor's inevitable resumption, part of a fundamental rhythm of attachment and withdrawal. Waking hours comprise the first course in the feast of life, a hospitable gathering that is at once subjective, sumptuary, and sociable. In this image, sleep allows us to digest the day by resting but also by dreaming. Far from merely vegetative, sleep so conceived honors the elements of autopoiesis resident within bodily processes that are always also social and ecological events; in the feast of life, sleep is a dynamic dormancy, an incubational restfulness. The most obscure and compelling image in the cluster, however, is the description of sleep "knit[ting] up the raveled sleeve of care." Sleep mends the frayed sleeve of the day or its untwisted "sleave" or thread; in these images of repair sleep winds a tunnel of comforting darkness around the self-abandoning consciousness of the sleeper. If care names what the sleeper releases, care is also exercised by the makers of beds and the singers of lullabies in the social work of slumber.[24] Sleep emerges in this set of images and localizations as part of a household economy involving the rhythms of work, labor, and rest, a vulnerable state imperfectly sheltered by a panoply of soft technologies that included pillows (e.g., 2.3.106), blankets, and bed curtains, as well as security teams and bedtime drinks.[25] As Kevin Curran argues, in *Macbeth* "knowledge and thought [form] part of a larger sensual experience that extends beyond the mental or spiritual into a real, material world of things and actions."[26] Both sleeping and thinking are distributed among a number of supporting players, as part of what Garrett Sullivan calls an "affective landscape" and Benjamin Parris describes as

24. For a sensitive reading of these different valences of care in the Renaissance scenography of sleep, see Parris, "'Watching to banish Care.'"

25. Holinshed describes a ruse by which the Scots delivered ale and bread laced with "mekilwoort berries" (nightshade) to their enemies the Danes: "the operation of the berries spread in such sort through all the parts of their bodies, that they were in the end brought into a fast dead sleep, that in manner it was impossible to wake them up. Then forthwith Duncan sent unto Macbeth, commanding him with all diligence to come and set upon the enemies." At Duncan's command, Macbeth slaughters the Danes in their sleep, *Macbeth: Texts and Contexts*, 140. Buchanan describes the "Night-Shade" at great length, and describes its "virtue" as "soporiferous," although it will also "make men mad" (129).

26. Curran, "Feeling Criminal in *Macbeth*."

"the humoral environs of sleep."[27] Guiding our attention to this distribution, however, does not decrease our sense of the characters' moral agency, but rather heightens our awareness of the forms of trust required to maintain a world in which we depend on other persons and things for our dwelling as well as for the forms of acknowledgment that make dwelling worth pursuing.

Revoking Prayer

The props that sustain sleep are linguistic as well as physical. Macbeth's ode to sleep occurs in a sequence that begins with the prayer exchanged by two men roused from their rest:

Macbeth: There's one did laugh in's sleep,
And one cried "Murder," that they did wake each other.
I stood, and heard them. But they did say their prayers,
And addressed them again to sleep.
Lady Macbeth: There are two lodged together.
Macbeth: One cried "God bless us," and "Amen" the other,
As they had seen me with these hangman's hands;
List'ning their fear, I could not say "Amen"
When they did say "God bless us."
Lady Macbeth: Consider it not so deeply.
Macbeth: But wherefore could not I pronounce "Amen"?
I had most need of blessing, and "Amen"
Stuck in my throat.
Lady Macbeth: These deeds must not be thought
After these ways: so, it will make us mad.
Macbeth: Methought I heard a voice cry "Sleep no more. . . ."
(2.2.20–34)

Responding to sounds in the night, the sleepers wake up briefly and exchange a blessing, a truncated version of the more elaborated prayers that prefaced sleep in the early modern period. Richard Day's *A Booke of Christian Prayers*, first published in

27. Sullivan, *Sleep, Romance and Human Embodiment*, 20; Parris, "'The body is with the king,'" 127.

1569 and popularly called "Queen Elizabeth's Prayer Book," offers a total of nine prayers associated with the night, including "A Prayer to be sayd at the setting of the Sunne," "A prayer to be sayd at the lighting up of candles," two prayers "to be sayd in the Evening," "A prayer to be sayd when we unclothe ourselves to bedward," and another two prayers offered at bedtime itself. The prayers express gratitude, air anxieties, and request shelter and protection, and they proceed by comparing the human gestures of dwelling (kindling, undressing, sleeping) to cosmic processes and principles (the light of God's knowledge and love; taking on and off the body; death and rebirth). Phrases like "bedward" manifest prayer as an act of orientation in relation to the room and its affordances as well as to the time of the day and its atmospheric shifts. In *Cymbeline*, Innogen gives a brief bedtime prayer, one that turns out to be woefully ineffective: "To your protection I commend me, gods. / From fairies and tempters of the night / Guard me beseech ye." (2.2.8–10).[28] We know from Giacomo's inventories that Innogen's slumber is further insulated by arras, perhaps hanging like curtains around her bed as in *Lucrece* as well as draping the walls, and that, like Lady Macbeth, she sleeps with the lights on ("The flame o'th' taper / Bows toward her" [2.2.19–20]). Innogen's bedtime routine includes (rather less piously) reading a few pages from Ovid. Delivering microdramas of sin, betrayal, and accident, bedtime prayers integrate ritualized speech with physical gestures in order to build enough trust to risk falling asleep. Such prayers contribute to a larger ecology of sleep that includes home furnishings, circadian shifts, and metabolic deceleration, detaching consciousness from the world by melting the sleeping subject into her soft surrounds.

Duncan may have intoned such a sequence of prayers before climbing into his bed at Inverness.[29] Banquo delivers his own

28. Citations from *Cymbeline* are from the Oxford edition, ed. Roger Warren.

29. See Muir on the account of Donwald's murder of King Duff: "Holinshed tells us that the day before his purposed departure the King was at his prayers till late into the night" (*Shakespeare's Sources*, 209). See Holinshed: "It chaunced, that the king vpon the

brief anticipatory rendition of a bedtime prayer when he enters with Fleance and a torch in act 2, scene 1:

> There's husbandry in Heaven,
> Their candles are all out.—Take thee that too.–
> A heavy summons lies like lead upon me,
> And yet I would not sleep; merciful powers,
> Restrain in me the cursèd thoughts that nature
> Gives way to in repose. (2.1.5–10)

Bedtime prayers commonly include a request to be shielded from wicked or desirous thoughts. Banquo's reference to husbandry evokes the range of dwelling technologies that will be drawn into the vortex of the Macbeths' crime, from the candles whose lighting warranted their own prayer in Day's book to the challenge of sleeping when "cursèd thoughts" displace thankful blessing. When Banquo in his horror at the crime says, "when we have our naked frailties hid, / That suffer in exposure, let us meet" (2.3.128–29), he captures the sense of creaturely vulnerability that the specter of violated sleep arouses in the party at large. The entire company has been stripped of their blankets; bereft of the comforts evoked in prayers said upon undressing for bed, they are caught instead in the valley of nakedness through which those prayers are designed to guide the supplicant.[30] Moreover, it is not only Macbeth whose access to the affinity circle of blessing is broken; Donalbain and Malcolm decide "not [to] be dainty of leave-taking, / But shift away" (2.3.147–48), a pragmatic eschewal repeated later by Macduff, who abandons his wife and child in "rawness . . . Without leave-taking" (4.3.26–28). These aborted valedictions attest to a more general unraveling of trust and care in the wake of Macbeth's murder of sleep.

Most of Richard Day's meditations end with the recitation of the Lord's Prayer or with a tonic "Amen." Hebrew for "So be

---

day before he purposed to departe forth of the Castell, was long in his oratoric at his prayers, and there continued till it was late in the night" (*Chronicles*, 208).

30. In the 1978 video directed by Trevor Nunn, Malcolm and Donalbain are shirtless when Banquo addresses these lines to them, underlining their nakedness.

it," "Amen" is an expression of assent; whether appended to one's own prayer or provided as the conclusion to the public prayer of another, "Amen" asserts the dialogic and communal character of prayer, even when said in private.[31] Macbeth's failure to say "Amen" marks, in the words of Daniel Swift, his "exile from the community of shared experience."[32] Arriving shortly after this revocation of prayer, the "Sleep no more" curse comes to Macbeth as still another voice, vocalized from somewhere in the castle but clearly linked to his own guilty conscience—the acoustic equivalent of the phantom dagger.[33] Macbeth's swallowed "Amen" is regurgitated as a hallucinated execration; these broken and twisted prayers, moreover, are narrated by Macbeth to his wife, whose own impatient pragmatism ("Consider it not so deeply") constitutes a second failure to say "Amen," to acknowledge the validity of her husband's dawning compunction. Macbeth's agonizing reconstruction of the brief journey back from Duncan's chamber is counterpointed with Lady Macbeth's eagerness not only to complete their evidentiary scenography by decking the sleeping grooms with bloody daggers, but in doing so, to avoid her husband's stricken gaze. Daniel Albright sees in Lady Macbeth's frantic activities an aspiration "toward a condition of perfect detachment, as if by such aesthetic operations as framing and composing she could desensitize herself to gore," a dramaturge who "approaches assassination in the spirit of an interior decorator."[34] Bedtime prayers provide the liturgical and domestic score for the play's murder of sleep.

The cascade of gentle sleep metaphors that bubble up from the horrific phrase "Sleep no more" shares imagery with nighttime prayers: compare, for example, Macbeth's ode to "sore labour's bath" and Richard Day's request that Jesus "refresh the pores of

31. On the collective and ratifying function of the Amen, see Targoff, *Common Prayer*, 40.

32. Swift, *Shakespeare's Common Prayers*, 173.

33. Parris calls it "the disembodied voice of judgment." "'The king is with the body,'" 123.

34. Albright, *Musicking Shakespeare*, 137.

[the] silly bodies" of the faithful. More striking, however, are the semantic undertows connecting Macbeth's image of sleep knitting up the raveled sleeve of care and Day's remarkably existential "Prayer to be sayd when we unclothe our selves to bedward":

> Now therefore, thou O most loving Father, which hast set me together: dissolve me in such wise as I may feele myself to be dissolved, and remember of whom I am overcome, and consider whither I must goe.[35]

Acknowledging that his creaturely estate has been "set together" by God, the speaker accepts the coming slumber as a temporary dissolving of consciousness that anticipates the final dissolution effected by death.[36] He asks not to avoid death tout court, but rather to be *dissolved in such a way that he feels himself to be dissolved*: he wants the courage as well as the opportunity to experience his death, to witness the onset of that final sleep as it undoes, strand by strand, the sleeve of cares that constitute the effortful entanglements of living. That Day frames these anxieties in the process of *undressing for bed* subliminally associates fabric with consciousness, each capable of raveling and unraveling.[37] Clothes afford donning and stripping, protection but also exposure; moreover, in the act of dressing and undressing, the fabric that becomes largely continuous with our skin as we move about our daily tasks separates and becomes tangible as an occasion for proprioception, of feeling oneself feel. More precisely, Day wants to "feel himself dissolve": he wants to experience a transitional phenomenon that itself frays the edges of the agent undergoing

35. Day, *Booke of Christian Prayers*, 9.

36. On the semantics and theology of dissolution in the period, see Cummings, *Mortal Thoughts*, 196–98.

37. In "A Prayer at the putting on of our Clothes," Day evokes the clothing and the act of dressing in them, transforming dressing into metaphor (for being clothed in the flesh, for being clothed in God's protective love), without losing a sense of the physical act and its choreography of objects: "Be thou our clothing and apparel, to keep us warme from the cold of this world. For if thou be away, all things become noume [numb], weake, and stark dead . . . And therefor like as I wrap my body in these clothes, so clothe thou me all over, but specially my soule, with thine own selfe, Amen" (4–5).

both the dissolution and its apprehension. A kind of immanent and affective Cartesianism draws the melting into air undergone each time we fall asleep into a knot of something permanent (thought, mind, soul). Prayer as form of "thinking with" concerns the threshold between existential finitude and the immortality of the subject as the thinking thing. Duncan neither gets to feel himself dissolve, nor to "remember of whom [he is] overcome." To murder sleep is not simply to strip the victim of his life (all killing does this), but to deny the forms of recognition that confirm the personhood of the creature even as both personhood and creatureliness melt, thaw, and resolve into a dew. Day's attention to overlapping dissolutions provides a template for *Macbeth*'s phenomenological interest in border phenomena conducted in the innards of dwelling and at the edges of ensoulment.

In his essay on Shakespeare's sleeping sovereigns, Benjamin Parris writes,

> Holy and accursed, sanctified and bare, the sovereign body in sleep not only betrays the antitheses of doubled life that it encrypts—it also opens the sleeping body to the volatile humoral flows and cosmological forces animating living substance at large.[38]

Like Parris I am interested in the transitivity between the "holy and accursed" suspended in the condition of sleep, as well as the sleeping being's environmental bleed into her spongy surrounds. Following Björn Quiring's dramatic and linguistic analysis of Shakespearean curses and blessings, I would like to call attention to the routinized and scripted character of bedtime prayers and their part in the larger ecology of sleep, in which bedclothes merge with nightgowns and bushes become bears. Sleep in the play is cursed as well as murdered, subjected to liturgical disruption in a networked scene of sensations floating in a darkness thick with thought and sound. In their organization of mood and mindfulness, evening prayers are atmosphere responders, mood regulators, and soul stewards that tune the speaker to her im-

38. Parris, "'The king is with the body,'" 135.

mediate setting and to the cosmic rhythms in which she counts her days.

In murdering sleep, Macbeth unmoors himself from his embeddedness in the routines and material scaffolding of dwelling, entering a landscape of curses that is simultaneously premodern and postsecular. Macbeth tells his half-dressed company, shocked into knowledge of their nakedness by the murder of Duncan, "Had I but died an hour before this chance, / I had lived a blessèd time" (2.3.93–94). "Blessèd" means being gifted with the chance to exercise one's virtues in the intersecting circles of public life and domestic dwelling. In Macbeth's words, after the murder his "way of life" has "fall'n into the sere, the yellow leaf, / And that which should accompany old age"—the blessings of honor, obedience, and friendship—has been replaced by "Curses, not loud but deep, mouth-honour, breath / Which the poor heart would fain deny, and dare not" (5.3.22–28). The low rumble of curses sounds his exclusion from familiar forms of social communion, the phrase "way of life" indicating that dwelling itself as a repertory of integrative routines is at stake.[39] These curses are not the deceptive prophesies of disenfranchised cunning women, or the singular antiprayers of a hero bent on blunting his own moral capacities, but something closer to communal curses, like the annual recitation of the curses of Leviticus (26:14–43) and Deuteronomy (27:28:15–68), chanted by Jewish congregations in a low voice in respect for their power. The biblical curses evoke a fragile world of provisional shelters and incessant agricultural effort threatened by bad weather, disease, and enemy incursion, a taskscape that depends on kinship, cooperation, and border patrol in order to bring forth and sustain its precious outcomes. Curses can feel archaic and primitive, implying a wrathful God who visits his rage on those who break faith with him. Yet the curse can also arrive more indirectly, as what happens when commu-

39. Engle writes of this passage, "Macbeth invokes the community of watchers as here offering a meaningful response to his choices: they curse him subvocally while fearing him" ("Pragmatism," 661).

nities breach contracts, forge weights, or scorn their neighbors. The landscape of blessings and curses is *a consequential landscape*, a setting that lends its bounty within a scene of intricated exigencies that require ritual as well as practical management. Thus theologian Douglas Knight locates biblical oaths in a "participative ontology," "a complex, social fabric of attachment, connectedness, and contract."[40] The reverberation of the curse defines a space of risk that threatens the speaker as well as receiver with dangers to dwelling.

In *Macbeth*, the people's muttered curses are described as "not loud but deep," contributing to the atmosphere of thickening distrust while also weaving a kind of secondary trust among those who are turning against Macbeth. Blessings and curses call attention to the inherently contingent, erratic, and causally comingled character of a world in which neither nature nor God establishes a consistent horizon for ethical action. Curses actualize prayer's uncertainties and conceptualize the limits to thankfulness, because blessings often remain fruitless, social justice cannot be chanted into existence, and trust depends on fictions that are too often revealed as lies.[41] Blessings and curses are antimodern (in ascribing to primitive forms of magical thinking), but they are also protomodern, since they harbor within their micronarratives of abundance, dearth, disease, and incursion a range of conceptualizations of what it means to inhabit bodies and live in worlds we never fully possess or control. In *Macbeth*, the hero's revocation of prayer neither lands him in secular modernity nor traps him in a hidebound hell, but instead makes visible forms of thinking-with that belong to prayer as life practice, as equipment for dwelling. I agree with Paul Kottman that "Shakespeare forces us to regard any perspective on human actions as deeply provisional, historically bounded, and contextually determined."[42] Unlike Kottman, and like Hannibal Hamlin and Daniel Swift, however, I see the

40. Knight, *Eschatological Economy*, 56.

41. On the phenomenology of the unheard prayer in Shakespeare, see Sterrett, *The Unheard Prayer*.

42. Kottman, "What Is Shakespearean Tragedy?"

religious allusions and speech patterns of the play not simply as residual, abandoned, or accessory, but as resources for continuing to work with and through the forms of provisionality tested by Shakespearean drama.[43] Macbeth's approach to prayer is thus best understood as postsecular, involving the creative reencounter with religious appliances in a world in which those technologies are no longer under warranty, but haven't been donated yet to the Goodwill.

Gathering Atmosphere

Macbeth's repertory of curses blends the poetic, the environmental, and the theological.[44] In the medieval metaphysics of the play, the heavens may indeed have peeped through the blanket of the dark and nature itself may convulse into tempest, eclipse, and earthquake in horror at the deed. Upon entering the castle in search of Duncan, Lennox reports that

> The night has been unruly: where we lay
> Our chimneys were blown down, and, as they say,
> Lamentings heard i'th' air, strange screams of death,
> And prophesying with accents terrible
> Of dire combustion and confused events
> New-hatched to th' woeful time. The obscure bird
> Clamoured the livelong night. Some say the earth
> Was feverous and did shake. (2.3.54–62)

Lennox describes a state of affairs that combines meteorological, geological, and biological disruptions in an ominous mélange of strange sounds. "Lamentings" are "heard i'th'air," an atmospheric amalgam that dissolves verbal expressivity into "confused" sono-

43. Hamlin writes, "There are many voices in the Bible, however, and at least some of them raise serious questions about whether God is really in control, or cares, whether good will triumph over evil, and whether time will have an end. Some of these voices are ventriloquized in *Macbeth*" (*The Bible in Shakespeare,* 304). See also Swift, who argues that baptismal rites provide the play with "its greatest metaphor for the perils of attachment" (*Shakespeare's Common Prayers,* 243).

44. See Kristin Poole on Macbeth's theology of environment, *Supernatural Environments in Shakespeare's England.*

rous effects that mix and hang in the darkness. A. C. Bradley uses the word "atmosphere" to describe the distinctive tone of *Macbeth*, which "gives the impression of a black night broken by flashes of light and colour."[45] By atmosphere Bradley seems to mean the emotional associations that attach to the setting's changeable aspects, what Jayne Lewis describes as "the evocative and enveloping spaces that can seem to thicken between lexical lines."[46] In architectural theory, atmosphere is associated with the mood or *Stimmung* that knits a building to a place, climate, and way of life; drawing on dwelling as the relay between architectural form and environmental opportunity, atmosphere keeps open the Heideggerian fourfold of air, earth, mortals, and divinities.[47] Atmosphere belongs to air, but it mixes with earth (see the witches as the earth's bubbles [1.3.79]) while implying divine supervision and binding itself to the activity of human dwelling. In drama, atmosphere concerns what the setting affords the actor, and how the actions taken by the actor reverberate spatially. At stake in theatrical atmosphere is not stage design (originally affiliated with painting and often illustrative) but rather scenography, the art of shaping the spatial and acoustic experience of theater in the time of performance. Scenography encompasses not only the outfitting, layout, and lighting of the stage, but also the actualization of that space by the actors, in collaboration with the audience's attention and imagination. Scenography is atmospheric in the sense that it concerns the collectively produced and sustained multimedia sensorium of the theatrical event.[48]

45. Bradley, *Shakespearean Tragedy*, 267. Wells also links the play's atmosphere to its environment, which he sees as fundamentally theatrical, exacerbating the paradoxes of mimesis: "The play's iterations of Macbeth as a paradox of being and non-being not only form an important part of the play's environment, they are themselves environmental" ("'To be thus is nothing,'" 225).

46. Lewis, *Air's Appearance*, 3.

47. See Christian Norberg-Schulz: "The constituent elements of a domain [are] distinguished by a *Stimmung* or atmosphere . . . a general object of identification" that "completes man's being in the world" (*The Concept of Dwelling*, 25).

48. On scenography and atmosphere, see McKinney and Butterworth, *The Cambridge Introduction to Scenography* on Adolph Appiah, a major figure in both the theory and practice of modern scenography, who "proposed that the domination of painted flats be relegated" in favor of the curation of "the scene's atmosphere" (11).

One way into understanding *Macbeth*'s experiments with atmosphere is through blessings and curses, the revocation of the former leading to the terror of the latter and each knitting modulations in mood to the consequentiality of action. Blessings and curses have a special role to play in *Macbeth*'s constitution of worlds because of their alertness to a layered and causally complex reality in which agency, social accountability, and the "thinking with" of conscience unfold within seasonal localizations of cosmic ordering. The witches' occult actions against the sailor are curse-like in their visitation of bodily and mental distress on their victim ("I'll drain him dry as hay; / Sleep shall neither night nor day / Hang upon his penthouse lid" [1.3.18–20]") as well as the imputation of communal exclusion ("He shall live a man forbid" [1.3.21]).[49] Macbeth curses no one, if by curse one means a ritualized speech-act aimed at the well-being of an addressee; instead, he becomes cursed by virtue of deeds that violate routines of dwelling shaped by acts of prayer. In need of blessing but no longer able to participate in prayer's collective forms of assent, Macbeth, another sleepless "man forbid," finds himself in his own version of Lear's heath. Unlike Lear, he is not subjected to nakedness or bad weather, but like Lear, he confronts his own creaturely existence within an agitated and erratic environment. The dwelling perspective calculates these disturbances in the landscape neither as expressions of divine judgment nor as merely subjective projections of a guilty mind, but rather as the assertion of the intractable existence of the world, an ontological upsurge suddenly palpable in the new forms of sensitivity that accompany the Macbeths' concerted inversion of care.[50]

By persuading themselves that "the sleeping, and the dead, / Are but as pictures" (2.2.52–53), the Macbeths have managed to

49. On witches, curses, and occult action, read within an environmental perspective of networked causalities, see Floyd-Wilson, *Occult Knowledge*.

50. I admire Michael Bristol's characterization: "Macbeth was careless of his own beauty, profligate in the expenditure of those virtues central to his identity as a person." As a result, "Macbeth realizes that he has destroyed his capacity for self-repair and self-maintenance." "Macbeth the Philosopher," 658.

scarf up the eyes of their own consciences long enough to complete their deed, but the radical world-denial that makes murder possible is belied in the appearance of an enhanced and overactive reality. Putting aside self-defense and crimes of passion, the only way a human being can commit murder is by denying the reality of the world; he must experience the lives of others as a play, dream, or video game, as the malleable extension of his will and imagination, or as the fantasy of an evil god, state, or computer programmer. Ex post facto, the reality of the world flashes in an explosive, regurgitated burst of noise and color: "Whence is that knocking? . . . Will all great Neptune's ocean wash this blood / Clean from my hand?" (2.2.56–60).[51] Likewise, Lady Macbeth's studied assault on her own cognitive capacities ultimately leads to her heightened sensitivity to setting ("she has light by her / Continually" [5.1.21]), an unbearable hyperawareness that will eventually drive her to suicide.

In the AMC television series *Breaking Bad*, Walter White's decision to allow his partner Jesse's girlfriend to choke in her bed while overdosing from heroin (another "murder of sleep") leads through a series of incidents and accidents to a plane crash that scatters its mortal jetsam across Walter's neighborhood. In Lars von Trier's film *Melancholia*, neurasthenic horses, precocious locusts, and electromagnetic spikes respond to the approaching planet whose impact will destroy all life in the cosmos. In both works, disturbances in the environment unfold in concert with, but not simply as projections of, human moods and moral choices. When the smart, underachieving Walter White "breaks bad," he is not struck dead by lightning or covered with boils; his actions, however, breed effects he cannot control, filling him with horror while stoning his heart. He is, in Macbeth's phrase, unable to "trammel up the consequence and catch / With his surcease, success" (1.7.3–4), a failure powerfully visualized in the image of sub-

51. Swift associates knocking with the action of prayer; he cites the baptismal liturgy, whose effects he sees at work in *Macbeth*'s concern with water's cleansing powers: "'Ask and you shall have; seek and you shall find; knock and it shall be opened unto you'" (*Shakespeare's Common Prayers,* 207).

urban streets and swimming pools littered with limbs, toys, and fuselage. Macbeth also "breaks bad," a decent enough man whose moral cracking destroys lives and communities in such a way that the environment itself begins to look and sound different, rendering him both sensitized to his surroundings and increasingly mechanical in his decision making. The Macbeth of acts 4 and 5 is not smart like a moral agent but rather smart like a bomb, homing in on the weaknesses of others while increasingly blind to his own.

In *Melancholia*, no human decision making has led to the end of the world; instead, a quasi-allegorical mirroring affiliates the depression of the heroine Justine (Kirsten Dunst) and the planet Melancholia, a relationship that more closely approximates the pathetic fallacy than does *Breaking Bad*'s plane crash. In the pathetic fallacy, however, the outer world reflects the inner state of the lyric subject; in *Melancholia*, real changes in the physical world afford new occasions for agency in Justine, since her depression not only allows her to apprehend the upcoming dissolution with a certain clear-eyed joy, but also to symbolize it for others in ways that make the end bearable.[52] In the final scene of the film, Justine, her sister Claire, and Claire's young son Leo huddle together in an open tepee built out of branches harvested from the nearby forest. Justine has erected this hut in response to Leo's repeated plea to build him "a magic tunnel." As the end of the world approaches, they work together to build this open structure, a pure fenestration of space and sky; beneath this minimalist sukkah they will greet the end of the world together. Justine's makeshift scenography channels the humoral and somatic into the symbolic and architectural without negating her structure's fundamental relationship to site and occasion.

The aptly named Justine finds herself suddenly capable of both adjustment and judgment; against all odds and without altering the outcomes, she is able to rescript apocalypse into a scene of repair and acknowledgment. Edgar's Dover Cliffs is a similar

52. See Bonnie Honig's fine reading of the film in the spirit of Winnicott and Arendt, *Public Things* 73–80; and "'Out Like a Lion': *Melancholia* with Euripides and Winnicott."

FIGURE 3. "Magic Cave" from Lars Von Trier, *Melancholia* (2011). Drawing by Jennifer Tobias. Reproduced by permission of the artist.

kind of magic tunnel that works through without reversing catastrophe from the edges of abjection. The accelerated causality of *Breaking Bad* matches the untrammeled and unraveling tempo of *Macbeth*. The sympathetic landscape of *Melancholia*, with its skittish horses and wayward weather, borders on the Scottish play, but reaches toward the world of the romances, where the damaged charisma of Marina, Innogen, and Pericles renders them newly receptive to the affordances of their surroundings.

In tragic dwelling, the antihero, the exploiter of negative affordances, reencounters the consequences of his deeds as environmental disturbances that trumpet the reality of the forms of personhood and the varieties of creatureliness disavowed by his murderous actions. Atmosphere is one form taken by the landscape of curses. Macbeth, planning Banquo's slaughter as he makes his way back toward dinner, describes to Lady Macbeth the time of night in which the act will occur:

> ere the bat hath flown
> His cloistered flight, ere to black Hecate's summons
> The shard-born beetle with his drowsy hums
> Hath rung night's yawning peal,

a nocturne that continues with his evocation of the light that thickens as "the crow makes wing to th' rooky wood" where "good things of day begin to droop and drowse" (3.2.43–55).[53] In the Trevor Nunn video of 1978, McKellen's Macbeth whispers these last lines into the ear of Dench's Lady Macbeth, delivering a desperate lullaby that calms only by chilling her. Macbeth's ode to dusk folds its rooky wings around a formal antiprayer that repeats Lady Macbeth's earlier imprecations:

> Come, seeling night,
> Scarf up the tender eye of pitiful day,
> And with thy bloody and invisible hand
> Cancel and tear to pieces that great bond
> Which keeps me pale. (3.2.49–53)

Jewish congregations witness the liturgy of blessings and curses at the conclusion of the recitation of the law.[54] Macbeth's curse aims not to support the law but rather to tear it to pieces, smashing anew the tablet that contains the precept "Thou shalt not kill."[55] To do so means making war against what is "tender" and "pitiful," in the surrounding world but also in himself. Around this tear in the contexture of values composed by the warp of justice and the woof of mercy, the rooky wood collects its dusky gloom. The atmosphere evoked here is both eerie and beautiful, the air alive with flying creatures and their flight patterns, channeling bits of *Midsummer* and Queen Mab into the biosemantic soup of the witching hour. Although bat, beetle, and crow have displaced the martlets of Inverness, *the air remains delicate*: teeming with traces of creaturely life whose amplitude becomes both ominous and oneiric. It is not only Macbeth, but the world itself that is always, somewhere, awake—a nocturne that does not pathetically manifest Macbeth's guilty conscience as an interior fact, but instead asserts the coexistence of other things and thus manifests conscience as a "thinking with" the world.

53. For an ecocritical reading of this passage, see Kerridge, "An Ecocritic's *Macbeth*," 199–201.

54. On this point, see Quiring, *Shakespeare's Curse*, 2.

55. Bevington is one of several critics to associate *Macbeth* with the commandment against killing ("Tragedy in Shakespeare's Career," 65).

Does the shard-born beetle inhabit the landscape of blessings or the landscape of curses? The beetle's flight reveals them as the same landscape. To dwell is to cultivate a mindfulness that builds resilience by anticipating precarity, to encourage independence by practicing gratitude, and to exercise ingenuity by responding to affordances as invitations to see feelingly. Blessings are a form of dramatic poetry that scan the environment for its offerings, not in order to maximize them as resources or standing reserve but to receive them as gifts that come with strings attached: the bonds of trust and accountability oiled by the virtues of respect, pity, and covenant love. Curses respond to the same landscape of exposure and risk cultivated by blessing, but founder on the negative edge of those dangers, transmuting pity into fear and respect into horror. In Macbeth's atmospheric ode to the shard-born beetle, the echoes of blessing continue to color the dusk of descending curses because they belong to the same humming, yawning, summoning world. Although we might infer divine intervention in the earthquakes of *Macbeth*, whose cosmos often feels retrograde, the preternatural and supernatural in the play can also be taken as alibis for the real effects of moral actions that engage forms of living (such as sleep) that are themselves not directly political yet do their work by knitting together social and biological processes in a bundled sleeve of care. If curses and blessings participate in a theological economy that posits God as just distributor, they remain fundamentally human efforts that invoke divinity in order to sustain social relationships that arise out of the management of life processes and ripple outward into myriad causal conduits. Macbeth's act against sleep throws the hero into the landscape of curses, a teeming biosphere whose uncanny manifestation of agency everywhere reveals the incalculable consequentiality of the antihero's deeds.

Merleau-Ponty speaks of the "unmotivated upsurge of the real" as what the phenomenological perspective allows us to encounter.[56] *Macbeth* is indeed phenomenological in soliciting such *Umwelt*-ing, but with the crucial difference that the upsurge is

56. Merleau-Ponty, *Phenomenology of Perception*, xv.

not "unmotivated": the sudden overabundance of world occurs as an involuntary testament to the real effects of the motivated actions of human agents. Soon, airplanes will fall from the sky, or horses will eat each other: although these are different kinds of consequential landscapes, the one more secular and the other more enchanted, in both instances the curse, like the blessing, delivers the real in its environmental complexity, wrapping the agent in the creaturely folds of a thick "causal milieu"[57] that strips him of his idealist disavowals and autochthonous fantasies.

Leafy Screens

Visualizing Macbeth's murderous intention, the dagger is a piece of signage indexically pointing the way into the landscape of curses.[58] The approach of Birnam Wood actually landscapes *with curses*, by taking the witches' riddling prophesy as a scenographic invitation to design a softscape that treats words as things and things as words. Like the festival architecture of the Renaissance or the pop-up stores and food trucks of today's instant urbanisms, Birnam Wood uses the sound, color, and aroma of leafy branches in concert with their affordances of cutting, bearing, and screening in order to expose *theatrum* and *theatrum mundi* to their constitutive engagement with the world of things.

Anticipated over the course of several scenes, the branches of Birnam finally march onto stage at the beginning of act 5, scene 6:

> *Drum and colours.*
> *Enter Malcolm, Seyward, Macduff, and their army, with boughs*
> *Malcolm*: Now near enough: your leafy screens throw down,
> And show like those you are. (5.6.1–2)

This is a moment of multiple manifestations. The "leafy screen" metonymizes the forest while composing its own moving wall,

57. The phrase is Paavolainen's, based on Gibson. See Paavolainen, "Agents and Objects: A Primer to Concepts and Approaches," in *Theatre/Ecology/Cognition*.

58. A version of the commentary in this section appears in Lupton, "Shakespearean Softscapes."

materializing architecture out of environment in order to mobilize architecture as event. Cast down, the soldiers "show" themselves, revealed as the movers behind the illusion, but also bid to assume their proper personae in the theater of war. The soldiers bearing boughs are accompanied by "Drum and colours," the stage direction slurring together stage properties, the effects they make, and the men who bear them into what Simon Palfrey calls a "formaction," a theatrical device that is also a dramatic event.[59] The free float of "Drum and colours" signals the scene-marking surge of effects onto a stage that is bare in one sense, but full in another, animated by a soft congeries of sound, fabric, foliage, and bodies in motion. The boughs themselves, of course, play a more immediately semiotic role, framed as emblems of both nature's insistence and culture's uprootedness by their role in the prophetic irony of the action. At the same time, their verdant sway and smell are swept into the scene's haptic climatology, a cloud of sound, sign, stuff, and color.[60] Words like "screen," "show," and "shadow" (5.6.1, 5.6.2, 5.5.24) delimit the forms of appearing shared by theater and hospitality, whose overlapping softscapes are composed of music, cut foliage, and textile coverings.[61] Birnam's leafy screens resemble the woven verdure tapestries that Bruce Smith recovers in *The Key of Green*; these or other fine fabrics would have decked the hall at Hampton Court Palace, where the play may have been performed for James in August, 1606.[62] In modern productions, fabric can substitute for

59. On "drum and colours," see Dessen and Thomson, *A Dictionary of Stage Directions*, 53. See also Palfrey, "Formaction."

60. Cf. Bruce Smith, who announces his turn "from the body to the ambient world," and does so under the umbrella of "green" as an ensemble of color, sound, smell, and touch (*The Key of Green*, 6).

61. On the decorative use of foliage, see, e.g., Thomas Tusser, who recommends that housewives use spring gardens "to trim up their house, and to furnish their pot" (*Five Hundred Points of Good Husbandry*, 129). He also provides a list of "herbs, branches, and flowers, for windows and pots" as well as herbs for strewing on the floor for their aromatic and medicinal properties (121–22).

62. Bruce Smith, *Key of Green*, 44–46. On *Macbeth* at Hampton Court Palace, see Kernan, *Shakespeare, the King's Playwright*, 71–89. On the royal tapestry collections at Hampton Court Palace, see Thomas Campbell, *Henry VIII and the Art of Majesty*.

foliage in order to create an undulating wall to hide the soldiers and partition the stage space.[63] Macbeth's office as harbinger resounds anew in the couplet and encrypted stage direction that close the Birnam Wood scene: "Make all our trumpets speak, give them all breath, / Those clamorous harbingers of blood, and death" (5.6.9–10). A harbinger is an omen or messenger, but also one who prepares spaces for enjoyment and thus a kind of scenographer. These space-time functions of the harbinger grant the softscape its plasticity, its sense of both moment and movement.

The Birnam Wood episode has been largely read in terms of nature's revenge on Macbeth's alienating, deracinating, and destructive actions, whether nature is conceived ritualistically (Goddard) or ecocritically (Kerridge).[64] In Kurzel's 2015 film, the approaching army sets the forest on fire, turning its groves into an angry cloud of smoke and ash: Birnam Wood dissolves into atmosphere, the softest scape of all. Harold Goddard's seasonal reading associates these leafy props with Maying rituals in which branches of greenery would be brought back from the forest in order to beat out the winter king.[65] If this ritual action reconciles humanity and nature, *cut* branches already bear a deracinated relationship to the forest from which they are culled. In being cut, however, the boughs by no means belong fully to a culture conceived as distinct from the nature that it colonizes and expro-

63. In a 1979 production of *Macbeth* at the National School of Drama in Delhi, "Birnam Wood was the central symbol of the play, 'which was performed before a great spreading tree up-stage, a full moon shining through its branches. The tree became, for Karanth, the labyrinthine jungle of ambition, which snares and destroys. The half-curtains, behind which the witches were first concealed, had emblematic designs suggesting the three branches of the tree. Similar drapes, as the symbol shifted its meaning, concealed Malcolm's troops, when they advanced in a sliding two-step rhythm, bringing new life to the wasteland Macbeth had created" (Trivedi and Bartholomeusz, *India's Shakespeare*, 206).

64. Goddard, *The Meaning of Shakespeare*, vol. 2, links the Birnam Wood episode to Maying rituals. For a green reading of *Macbeth*, see Richard Kerridge, "An Ecocritic's *Macbeth*," in *Ecocritical Shakespeare*, 193–210.

65. Goddard, *Meaning of Shakespeare*, 134.

priates. As every flower arranger and sous chef knows, the cells of cut vegetation continue to live long after they are severed from their root systems, while foliage releases its odors when it is broken or bruised. Although Macbeth is appropriately incredulous, forests *do* in fact move: in the slow time of natural history, woods encroach on commons, twist sidewalks, and block views; in the fast time of tempest, mudslide, and tsunami, they crush roofs, down power lines, and crucify cars. What the dwelling perspective allows us to apprehend is the extent to which environments of entertainment, including their battlefield inversions, immerse human action in a network of dependencies.

The arbors of the softscape shelter mixed polities, from hired men employed as actors and stagehands to the "Drum and colours" of haptic fanfare and the climate conditions that form and dissolve between poetic language, the scenes of playing, and audience responsiveness. At the end of the play, Macbeth has himself become a broken branch, his head first imagined "painted upon a pole" "as our rarer monsters are" (5.7.55–56), and then stuck before us like an apple shaken from the tree (5.7.85; 4.3.237–38). Macbeth becomes a tree, but also a flag: the first standards consisted not of fabric panels, but of three-dimensional figures (bird, beetle, boat, head, hand) impaled on the tip of a spear or staff in order to be carried aloft or tied to a wheeled vehicle.[66] Macbeth has indeed died into the forest, but only insofar as the forest has itself become a crenellated city of messages, part of a dense mediascape whose communicative resources include emblems, objects, surfaces, and signposts. Whether composed out of branches, silk, or smoke, Birnam Wood theatricalizes architecture in response to verbal prompting. As such, Birnam Wood is a design problem: a node of multiple affordances in which the entanglement of words and things in the daily work of place-making becomes the occasion for dramatic action and scenographic ingenuity. Like Justine's tepee in *Melancholia*, Birnam Wood is a mixed bouquet

66. MacGeorge, *Flags*, 12–17.

set into motion by actors in concert with an environment that harbors its own seeds of causality.

In *Macbeth*, atmosphere is not simply a subjective projection of internal states onto the external world, but rather the reencounter in features of the setting of the consequences of crimes that themselves bear a locative dimension. In *Macbeth*'s softscapes, the sheltering properties of fabric feed poetic imagery, which in turn can inspire scenographic invention. Prayers join with pillows, blankets, and sleepy drinks in building routines aimed at securing a good night's sleep; in their management of circadian rhythms, such prayers provide a template for the nighttime action and imagery of *Macbeth*. To "murder sleep" is to cut through the layers of protection and repair promised by the soft affordances of both pillows and pillow talk and to hold up those layers for phenomenological analysis and scenographic exploration.

Macbeth, unlike *Othello*, and perhaps less than *Lear*, is not in any technical sense a domestic tragedy, since the play dramatizes the actions of monarchs in a kingdom that weeps and bleeds, yet it is most certainly a drama in which the *oikos* is key to the action, atmosphere, and image banks of the play. The play's environmental vistas, dipping into hospitality, housekeeping, and husbandry discourses, reassert the forms of dependency that Macbeth and Lady Macbeth strive to cut off. The many references to homely needs couched in diurnal rhythms ("lodge," "supper time," "wine and wassail," "husbandry in heaven," "curtain'd sleep," "droop and drowse," "comfort") reassert the connections violated by the murder of sleep. Throughout the play, creatureliness and personhood undergo a series of reductions, expansions, and convergences that are horrific for the characters involved, yet summon an unexpected assonance and amplitude for an audience newly trained by Shakespeare's dramatic poetry to listen to the place-making.

3

Grace and Place in *Pericles*

The waters compassed me about, even to the soul: the depth closed me round about, the weeds were wrapped about my head. I went down to the bottoms of the mountains; the earth with her bars was about me forever: yet hast thou brought up my life from corruption, O LORD my God.
«JONAH 2:4–6»

What seas what shores what granite islands towards my timbers
And woodthrush calling through the fog
My daughter.
«T. S. ELIOT, "MARINA"»

T. S. Eliot's lyric monologue "Marina" begins with an epigram from Seneca's *Hercules Furens*: "Quis hic locus, quae regio, quae mundi plaga? [What place is this? What region, what quarter of the world?]."[1] In the poem that follows, Eliot transposes the moment of lucidity at the delirious end of life onto the process of coming ashore in a small boat, perhaps to a summer house on a lake where one's grown daughter calls through the fog from

1. Seneca, "Hercules Furens," 1137. Returning to consciousness out of the rage in which he had killed his wife and children, the hero's first mental work is to re-locate himself in place and time.

the embankment. Boat, lake, fog, and woodthrush, ambient carriers of the daughter's presence, allow the speaker to find some easement from the rank scandal of death, manifesting what Eliot calls "this grace dissolved in place." To dissolve grace in place is to discover an immanent messianism, a redemptive or reparative potentiality that resides in human relationships and the promises of locale.[2]

Pericles offers a fitting place to test the possible shapes such a dissolved messianism might take; as Sarah Beckwith has argued, the play's conversion of chance into providence occurs "through the touching of human voices."[3] In Eliot's poem, however, grace belongs to the ebb and flow of the father's consciousness, but does not address either the world-building and soul-healing capacities exercised by Marina, or the setting itself as a set of *données* that help direct human action. Eliot's poem tells us *what* to read for: the phenomenology of spatial experience as the means by which transcendence becomes world in the late plays. He does not quite tell us *how* to read the play, however, if we seek a fuller account of the ways in which dramatic action coalesces in response to places that harbor their own durations, histories, and capacities. In *Pericles*, I argue, Wilkens and Shakespeare bid place to appear by staging collaborative and self-organizing actions; in this play, the layered significances, environmental affordances, and economic and ecological dependencies that converge in a location link human action and community to setting. *Pericles* dramatizes dwelling as the assemblage of architectural, ecological, and theological features brought together by the lived routines and symbolic investments of human habitation in its sojourning character. After establishing the parameters of messianism through a brief reading of *Pericles* and the Book of Jonah, I look at the messianic dissolution of grace in place in three distinct

2. On the poem's phenomenology, see the excellent reading by Stephen Thomson, "The Adjective, My Daughter: Staging T. S. Eliot's 'Marina.'" For a theological reading of grace and place from a Christian and environmentalist perspective, see Willis Jenkins, *Ecologies of Grace*.

3. Beckwith, *Shakespeare and the Grammar of Forgiveness*, 102.

moments of the play. "Net Work" takes us to the shores of Pentapolis, where the hapless prince of Tyre finds himself shipwrecked among fishermen. "Edifications" leads us into the brothel in Mytilene and the academy founded by Marina at the city's edge. Finally, "Votive Offerings" tours the Temple of Diana at Ephesus at the end of the play in order to query romance's relationship to both human community and worldly things. In each case I am interested in the dramatic action of the play, especially the role of speech and recognition in subjective rebirths, following Sarah Beckwith and Paul Kottman. But I also show how action comes out of and reflects back on setting, locale, and environmental embeddedness, an orientation that draws me closer to the work of Steven Mentz. Finally, insofar as my reading concerns messianism, I build on work by Bradin Cormack on sovereignty as well as Randall Martin on Paul and *Pericles*.[4] My larger goal is to understand the intrication of messianism, in both its religious and its profane valences, in the styles of action and forms of dwelling tested by the romances, a theme that continues in the subsequent chapters on *Cymbeline* and *The Winter's Tale*.

Placing Messianism from Jonah to Pericles

The Book of Jonah has long been associated with *Pericles*.[5] The tossing of Thaisa's body overboard at the behest of sailors concerned for the welfare of their ship (scene 11) echoes Jonah's passage into the sea, while Pericles's elegiac musing on "the belching whale" (11.61) recalls Jonah's psalm of thanksgiving (2.3–10).[6] Jonah's international itinerary, including his flight to Tarshish,

4. In addition to Cormack's *Pericles* chapter, see "Shakespeare's Other Sovereignty" and "Decision, Possession: The Time of Law." Relevant work by Randall Martin includes "Rediscovering Artemis in *The Comedy of Errors*" and "Shakespearean Biography, Biblical Allusion and Early Modern Practices of Reading Scripture."

5. E.g., Hannibal Hamlin, *The Bible in Shakespeare*, 122. Hamlin emphasizes the typological connections between Jonah and Christ rather than Jonah's status as a prophet.

6. I cite the Oxford edition edited by Roger Warren (Oxford: Oxford University Press, 2003), unless otherwise noted. Following Warren's procedure, scene and line number but no act numbers will be cited.

associated with Tyre and Tarsus in some commentaries, links him to both Paul and Pericles.[7] Jonah's depressive retreat into the bottom of the ship while the tempest rages ("But Jonah was gone down into the innermost part of the ship; and he lay, and was fast asleep" [1:4]) resembles Pericles's catatonic state in act 4. Jonah's flight from his calling to preach to the Ninevites colors the fugitive character of Pericles's behavior in the first half of the play, and Marina's leafy shelter by the sea (21.50) recalls Jonah's sukkah or booth east of Nineveh (4:5–8) at the end of each text.

Messianism, stretched between ancient and modern as well as exegetical and philosophical instances, captures the way in which the Jonah material helps shape the sense of place as well as the narrative arc and temporal infoldings of *Pericles*. Messianism names the Jewish hope for the redemption of the world, a vision that conceives Israel's future in universal as well as national terms: *national*, because the temple will be rebuilt, Israel restored, and exile reversed; *universal*, because the nations will speak one language and praise one God: "He will prepare the whole world to serve the Lord together. As it is said, 'For then I will change the speech of the people to a pure speech, so that all of them shall call on the name of the Lord and serve him with one accord' (Zeph. 3:9)."[8] Messianism involves a state of expectancy that cultivates attitudes of incompleteness in relation to future scenarios of peace and right rule that require the participation, but not the hegemony, of human action in their

7. I use the Soncino edition of *The Twelve Prophets*, which includes the Geneva Bible translation and facing Hebrew text plus Jewish commentary. The editor suggests that Tarshish "maintained a mineral trade with Tyre" (138n). George Abbot's lengthy 1600 commentary, *An Exposition upon the prophet Ionah*, published by Shakespeare's townsman Richard Field, identifies Tarshish with Tarsus, the birthplace of Paul. For a reception history of the Book of Jonah, see Barbara Green, *Jonah's Journeys*. For another modern Jewish commentary see *The JPS Bible Commentary: The Book of Jonah*.

8. Maimonides, *Ethical Writings*, 182. In Svante Lundgren's summary, "Messianism is a synthesis of national and human elements. In the messianic age first Israel and then the city of mankind will be built up as the fulfilled kingdom of God. The messianic humanity will not be Jewish, but will be elevated over all presently existing categories, and Judaism, having fulfilled its mission, will abdicate from its separateness. Until then, however, Judaism must remain separate and not mix with other cultures"; *Particularism and Universalism in Modern Jewish Thought*, 78.

realization. In the words of Martin Kavka, Jewish messianism "moves from a philosophy of nonbeing to the passionate faith in a redeemer still to come . . . whom I represent" (ellipses his).[9] Of Paul's three theological virtues, hope, love, and faith (1 Cor. 13:13), hope is the most properly messianic; although messianic hope is realized and then deferred a second time in Christianity, it continues as an independent line of Jewish thought and life, including the failed messianic movement of Sabbati Svi in the seventeenth century and the secular messianism of the Zionist project in modernity.[10] Jewish messianism has been read existentially and philosophically rather than confessionally by modern thinkers including Gershom Scholem, Walter Benjamin, Martin Buber, Jacques Derrida, and Giorgio Agamben.[11] Sometimes called "weak messianism" or "messianism without messianism," this postsecular rendering of the messianic emphasizes "a logic turned toward the future no less than the past, in a heterogeneous and disjointed time," an attitude that emphasizes human incompleteness, vulnerability, and accountability in and to the world at large.[12]

Jewish messianism is divided between visions of catastrophe leading to the radical suspension of both ritual law (*halakhah*) and the laws of nature on the one hand, and an insistence on a worldly messianism announced by more modest and mundane transformations in human institutions, forms of knowledge, and social outlook. Maimonides, whose rabbinic Aristotelianism continues to guide much normative Judaism, downplayed millenarian scenarios: "Let no one think that the custom of the world will in any way cease to exist during the days of the Messiah or that something new will occur in the Work of Creation."[13] Maimonides was responding to Jewish mysticism and folkways

9. Kavka, *Jewish Messianism and the History of Philosophy*, 2.

10. See Scholem, *The Messianic Idea in Judaism*.

11. On messianism in contemporary critical theory, see Eleanor Kaufman, "The Saturday of Messianic Time."

12. Jacques Derrida, *Specters of Marx*, 181. Cited by Owen Ware, "Dialectic of the Past/Disjuncture of the Future," 99.

13. Maimonides, *Ethical Writings*, 182.

that emphasize the wholesale disruption of life as we know it; in Scholem's summary of this tradition, "In the Prophets this stage is called 'the Day of the Lord,' which is wholly unlike other days; it can only arrive after the old structures have been razed."[14] Benjamin cites the tradition, more Maimonidean than mystical, that the Messiah will not "change the world by force, but would only make a slight adjustment in it" (compare Maimonides: "The days of the messiah are in this world").[15] Paul's declaration that Christ is the "end" (*telos*) of the law (Rom. 10:4), which can be read as either heralding the law's destruction or celebrating its consummation, participates ambiguously in both strands of messianism.[16] Countering the long tradition of reading Paul as simply anti-Jewish, New Testament scholars after World War II reinterpreted Paul's relationship to messianic and prophetic thinking in more expansive and continuous ways. W. D. Davies, for example, characterized Paul as "a Pharisee who believed the Messiah had come," a prophet who derived his pneumatism—his understanding of the creativity of the Holy Spirit active in human community—from Judaism's harboring of Wisdom as the ground plan of Creation and the Shekhinah (feminine divine presence) as Wisdom's divine aspect.[17]

What does it mean to read Shakespeare and messianism together?[18] After all, for Shakespeare, the Messiah could only be Jesus the Christ (*christus* translates *moshiach*, "the anointed"). Shakespeare is unlikely to have been aware of messianism as an

14. Scholem, *Messianic Idea*, 38.

15. Benjamin, *Illuminations*, 14; Maimonides, *Ethical Writings*, 179.

16. On Paul and Jewish messianism, see, e.g., Matthew V. Novenson, *Christ among the Messiahs*. Novenson reads Paul's letters as evidence of the "diverse strands of messianism in ancient Judaism," including Hellenizing-philosophical and Davidic-historical accounts. Novenson draws on and responds to an important body of work on Paul and Judaism; see my chapter "Paul Shakespeare" in *Thinking with Shakespeare* for a review of this literature in relation to Shakespeare (219–46).

17. Davies, *Paul and Rabbinic Judaism*, 216, 176–226.

18. A number of scholars have read Shakespeare for messianism, usually working through Paul and his rereading by Giorgio Agamben. See, e.g., Donovan Sherman, "'What More Remains?,'" and James A. Knapp, *Image Ethics in Shakespeare and Spenser*.

ongoing feature of Jewish thought, and although he was deeply attracted to Old Testament texts, he tended to read them typologically. I'd like to suggest, however, that prophetic and wisdom literature, such as the Books of Jonah and Job as well as Ecclesiastes resonated for Shakespeare as expressions of existential yearning in a mode that combines Jewish, humanist, and creaturely strains. Written in Hebrew, works of wisdom and prophesy translate Jewish history and theology into affective postures (complaint, litigiousness, anger, sorrow, self-deprecation, resentment, wit) and portable styles of dwelling, which include patriarchal householding, prophetic nomadism, and cities of sanctuary, that retain their Jewish stamp. These works are humanist when they dramatize moments of individual and collective agency, explore cosmopolitan contact, and aspire to a universal accountability. Finally, this literature is creaturely when it enlists vast landscapes, unexpected animals, and psychosomatic metabolisms in an effort to probe what is more than human in the human condition.[19] Following Eric Santner, I understand creatureliness not as sheer exile in vitality but as our constitutive prematurity and incompleteness as persons and hence our inventive reliance on linguistic, social, and biotechnical forms of nurture, shelter, and sexuation. The Judeo-creaturely humanism that I am identifying with messianism accords with Christianity without being identical with it, and thus becomes a means of sounding Christianity for its ecumenical, pre- and postconfessional possibilities.[20] Shakespeare's late plays are messianic in the sense that they explore the attitude of hope and the forms of open address practiced by the Jewish prophets and the Pauline epistles. By freely mixing Jewish and Pauline motifs in a fluid Hellenistic

19. Eric Santner has emphasized the creaturely character of messianic thinking: "Benjamin's messianism, which was a constant through his career, must in turn be understood in direct relation to this figure of the creaturely, of life captured at the (ever shifting and mutating) threshold of the juridicopolitical order." *On Creaturely Life*, 109.

20. On confessionalization and its alternatives in English literature, see Betteridge, *Literature and Politics in the English Reformation* and "Writing Faithfully in a Post-Confessional World."

geography, the late plays disclose messianism as a call to action, congregation, and fellowship within a horizon of emergent universality, a scene on its way to Christianity but not Christian yet.[21] The theo-political actions of atonement, patience, forgiveness, and benediction brought forward so definitively by Sarah Beckwith are staged by Shakespeare in allusive terrains built up from the deposits left by multiple religious traditions, which the romance outlook tends to read syncretically rather than schismatically.[22]

Although all of the late plays are awash in Pauline references, *Pericles*'s Pauline travelogue, including stops at Antioch, Tarsus, and Ephesus, has been especially striking to editors and critics of the play. In *Pericles*, Paul is shadowed by Jonah, who, like Paul, was a Jew who became a reluctant prophet to non-Jews. Liturgically, the Book of Jonah is part of the Yom Kippur service and thus conscripted into the kind of public penance that the Ninevites undertake in the biblical story. The rabbis associate Jonah's great fish with the Leviathan that will be eaten at the messianic banquet beneath a sukkah canopy made from its skin, drawing an eschatological link between the whale that God "prepares" (*yaman*) for Jonah and the vine that he later also "prepares" (*yaman*) to grow above the prophet's head.[23] In his psalm of thanksgiving, Jonah describes a visionary voyage down "to the bottoms of the mountain," where "the deep was round about me" and "weeds were wrapped about my head" (2:7; 2:6). The mystics believed that a "Tzohar-like pearl" was suspended in the belly of the whale,

21. Davies, *Paul and Rabbinic Judaism*; E. P. Sanders, *Paul, the Law, and the Jewish People*. I make this argument in more detail in the chapter entitled "Paul Shakespeare" in *Thinking with Shakespeare*. For a Protestant reading of Paul in *Pericles*, see Richard Finkelstein, "*Pericles*, Paul, and Protestantism."

22. Beckwith, *Shakespeare and the Grammar of Forgiveness*.

23. *Yaman* is from *manah*, to count, reckon, number, assign, appoint, prepare (Strong's 04487). On the role of the Leviathan in the menu and decor of the messianic banquet, see Schwartz, *Tree of Souls*, 145–48. Schwartz notes that the tradition of eating fish on the Jewish Sabbath (Friday night) is "that eating fish anticipates the feast of Leviathan." The origin of this messianic motif is Job 40:30, a line relevant to both Jonah and *Pericles*: "Will bands of fishermen make a banquet of him?"

illuminating the underwater world for Jonah to see and wonder at.[24] The whale's cavernous interior is both an anticipation of hell and a sacred space prepared by God for the salvation and edification of his prophet. Thus the medieval rendering of the Book of Jonah in the poem "Patience," ascribed to the so-called Pearl Poet, depicts the whale's jaw as a "munster dor [cathedral door]" and his belly as a "bour [bower]," the same word later used in the poem to describe Jonah's suburban booth.[25] From great fish to makeshift bower, the Jonah story explores creaturely encampments as scenes of exposure, forms of shelter, and models of an open *ecclesia*.

Pericles, too, is a Pearl Poet. When he prepares to cast Thaisa into the sea, he laments that "the belching whale and humming water" must stand in for "a monument upon thy bones / And aye-remaining lamps" (11.60–63). If he aims to present the whale and its submarine echolocations as a sorry tomb for a royal princess, his language manifests awe at the places hidden beneath the water. In Pericles's liquid lyricism, the unbuilt environments and muffled music of the sea eerily translate while also estranging the works of human artifice. Like Jonah's psalm of thanksgiving, Pericles's "priestly farewell" to his wife (11.68) conjures a drowned world that is both terrifying and beautiful, the horrific siphoning of human meaning making room for a sudden rush of creatural significance.

The Book of Jonah broaches the messianic tension between Judaism's universalist and particularist strands. The Ordinary Gloss associates Jonah with Paul, acknowledging that both men spoke as Jews to broader communities of listeners. Glossing the line, "And Jonah was tormented" by his mission to Nineveh (4:1), the Ordinary Gloss writes, "The apostles also preach first to Israel. Paul also wishes to be cursed for the sake of his brethren (Rom. 9:3)."[26] The ecumenical theologian Rosemary Reuther

24. Schwartz, *Jewish Mythology*, 87.

25. Pearl Poet, "Patience," lines 268, 276, 437. My thanks to Elizabeth Allen for pointing out these resonances.

26. McDermott, "The Ordinary Gloss on Jonah," 436.

notes that the Book of Jonah was written after the return of Jewish leaders from the Babylonian exile and "was meant to promote tolerance and coexistence of Jews with other communities within the Persian empire."[27] Jonah is a reluctant cosmopolitan who first flees his mission and is then distressed by his success: commentators debate whether he prefers justice to mercy, Jews to gentiles, or a true prophesy of doom to a sentence overturned by human repentance and divine forgiveness.[28] The Book of Jonah places its Hebrew hero in dialogue with two different groups of gentile interlocutors; in addition to the Ninevites are the sailors, a mixed multitude who "cried every man onto his god" (1:5) when the tempest rages and become God-fearers when the storm ceases (2:16). This scene of interfaith participation in a shared religious truth inspired Jean Bodin's 1588 ecumenical dialogue, *Colloquium of the Secrets of the Sublime*, which includes the tale of "a most hazardous sea voyage" in which each passenger prays in his own language.[29] Although *Pericles* does not explicitly thematize a diversity of faiths and languages, the play's cosmopolitan itinerary and its fierce and vigilant tendering of Catholic narrative forms evokes the political program of Jacobean irenicism. In Tom Betteridge's formulation, the play yearns for "a pre-confessional world in which liturgical words, the language of faith, united rather than divided Christians."[30] *Pericles* draws on the messianism of the Book of Jonah when it reaches out of schism toward painfully secured shared meanings within a sublime soundscape that crests and surges at the limits of meaning.

Jonah and Paul form a typological sequence, in which the Hebrew prophet anticipates aspects of the Christian saint as well as Christ himself. Jonah and Paul can also, however, be read as

27. Reuther and Reuther, The *Wrath of Jonah*, xx.

28. For these lines of interpretation and their basis in early midrashim, see the introduction to the text by Simon, viii–xx.

29. Jean Bodin, *Colloquium of the Seven about the Secrets of the Sublime*, 6–8. Cited by my student Sheiba Kian Kaufman in her dissertation, "The Hospitable Globe," 80.

30. Betteridge, "Writing Faithfully," 225. On *Pericles* and Catholic narrative and dramatic forms, see Womack, "Shakespeare and the Sea of Stories."

responding to a prophetic vocation that remains distinct from typology, drawing on Hebrew resources that are messianic without simply being Christian. The depressive character of Jonah, his flight from vocation, his willingness to argue with God, and the opacity of his thoughts and motives contribute to prophesy as not only a lurch toward but also a swerve away from typology's vertical integration of the Jewish and Christian testaments.

Pericles surfs both the lurch and the swerve. One of the play's most striking differences from Gower's poem is the relative lack of scriptural influence in the former as compared to the thickly biblical design of the latter. The story of Apollonius of Tyre in the *Confessio Amantis* is preceded by a long disquisition on incest in the Bible, but the romance narrative itself is remarkably Homeric in its recitation of maritime wandering, island hospitality, and delayed intergenerational recognitions.[31] Gower is to Wilkens and Shakespeare as Odysseus's scar is to the binding of Isaac in the opening chapter of Auerbach's *Mimesis*: Gower's Apollonius, like Auerbach's Odysseus, enjoys a certain translucency of motive and aspiration, while Wilkens and Shakespeare's Pericles, like Auerbach's Abraham, is "explained not only by what is happening to him at the moment, nor yet only by his character . . . but by his previous history . . . his soul is torn between desperate rebellion and hopeful expectation; his silent obedience is multilayered, has background."[32] While Gower places the Bible outside his romance, Wilkens and Shakespeare suck scripture inside *Pericles*'s dramatic world, from the opening tableau linking Antiochus and his daughter to Adam and Eve to the play's finale in Ephesus, city of the Acts and the Epistles. The play's meandering structure is organized by the successive reinscriptions and partial corrections of the initial incestuous couple, so that Antiochus and his daughter are replaced by Thaisa and her father and finally by Pericles and Marina; the typological associations of the two women with Mary effect the classic typological reversal of "Eva"

31. Gower, *Confessio Amantis*, 8:1–201.
32. Auerbach, *Mimesis*, 12.

by "Ave."[33] If these Marian restructurings channel the messianic in a Christian-typological direction, the Jonah material not only supports typology, as Hannibal Hamlin has argued, but also measures the mood that persists when Christian fulfillment remains unknown, uncertain, incomplete, or otherwise inadequate to its Hebrew instigations. Michelangelo captures this mood in his Sistine portraits of the prophets; burdened with a dark wisdom, they know without knowing what they know; more profoundly, however, they also refuse to relinquish the open address of their truth to a determinate confessional knowledge. Michelangelo's Jonah is a muscular, masculine version of Botticelli's Chloris/Flora in the *Primavera*, his head tilted toward an unseen god while his body twists away in revolt and resistance. Meanwhile, the great fish appears to munch his exposed and widespread thigh, a reminder that the calling of human creatures into subjectivity passes by way of sexual trauma and the riddle of language, a theme shared with *Pericles*.

The elements of flight, resistance to vocation, and depression that dog Jonah are part of Pericles's prophetic inheritance. Daniel Keegan describes the "prophetic dramaturgy" of early modern drama as "stimulating and engaging with different facets of theatrical life"; on Shakespeare's prophetic stage, Keegan writes, "multiplex prophetic constitutions set in motion a sort of inductive process that cues our thinking to more general, more complex topologies of theatrical constitution and theatrical life that abide beyond—perhaps not even in contact with—the representation and the performance."[34] *Pericles* spirits Gower into the schismatic present and prismatic future through the liturgical power of performance and affirms the vitality of Catholic narrative and dramatic forms within a deeply Hellenistic and strikingly creatural scene. In doing so, *Pericles* anoints Keegan's

33. Thaisa gives birth on the road and dedicates herself to the Temple of Diana; Marina's name as well as her exemplary chastity evokes the lives of several Marys.

34. Daniel Keegan, "The Prophetic Stage: Constituting Performance in and after Shakespeare," 3.

prophetic dramaturgy as a messianic dramaturgy that boldly exposes historical worlds, theological epochs, and kinds of environment to each other.

Net Work

The first half of the play concerns the young Pericles, a prince of Tyre who early seeks adventure only to find himself derailed by his own melancholic responses. The play begins at Antioch, where the king Antiochus is living in incest with his daughter. Any suitor who can solve the riddle of the king's relationship can marry the daughter; those who fail are condemned to death. Pericles easily solves the riddle; instead of exposing the king's secret, however, he decides Jonah-like to flee, retreating from the rage of the bloat king but also from his own knowledge of human error. This pattern of flight continues. Back home at Tyre, Pericles sinks into a deep melancholy. Leaving Tyre again, he eventually finds himself the sole survivor of a shipwreck, leading to the play's first great scene, likely written by Shakespeare's collaborator George Wilkens.[35]

Cast cold, wet, and naked upon the shore, Pericles observes a group of fishermen, who enter the scene preparing to fix nets damaged by the storm:

> *Master* [*calling*]: What ho, Pilch!
> *Second Fisherman* [*calling*]: Ha, come and bring away the nets.
> *Master* [*calling*]: What, Patchbreech, I say.
> [*Enter a Third Fisherman with nets to dry and repair.*][36]

The fishermen are caught up in what Tim Ingold calls a taskscape: the organizational space composed by the total "pattern of dwelling activities," "the entire ensemble of tasks, in their mu-

35. I follow what appears to be the current consensus, that the play was coauthored by George Wilkins and Shakespeare, with the first ten scenes (or first two acts) largely written by Wilkins and the remainder by Shakespeare.

36. Warren supplies the stage direction from Wilkins's *Painful Adventures*.

tual interlocking," that engage groups of people occupied by a shared set of undertakings.[37] In Wilkens's piscatory pastoral, the fishermen respond to the aftermath of tempest in a topography of affordances cultivated by their craft and profession. Relating the men to their environment, the shoreline workplace also associates the laborers with each other: the Master calls to the other fishermen, one of whom, Patchbreech, may be younger than the others; this apprentice to the older men would also likely be an apprentice in the theatrical company.[38] Here as so often in Shakespearean drama, the mise-en-scène of a dramatically imagined locale for labor (ship, shore, great hall, kitchen, graveyard, sheepcote) overlays and brings into visibility the taskscape of the theater as a collaborative enterprise involving its own patterns of command and enskillment in a specialized setting.

Ingold conceives of an environment "in terms of *function*, of what it affords to creatures—whether human or nonhuman—with certain capabilities and projects of action."[39] Action here is intended in a tactile, corporeal, and immediately instrumental direction, like the men's work with their nets or, later in the play, Cerimon's manipulation of heat, linens, and sound in order to revive Thaisa. Such motions would not count as action in Hannah Arendt's fuller sense of substantial and risky intersubjective speech, but rather would remain submerged in the more routinized zones of labor and work. Yet the fishermen's minimal language of call and response flowers into political discourse as they shift from repair of the nets to repair of the social body:

> *Third Fisherman:* Master, I marvel how the fishes live in the sea.
> *Master:* Why, as men do a-land: the great ones eat up the little ones. (5.67–70)

37. Ingold, "The Temporality of the Landscape," 153, 158. I borrow the term "organizational space" from Easterling, *Organization Space*.

38. Warren speculates that the Third Fisherman may have been played by the same boy who will later personate Marina and who may also have been one of the reporters of the defective Q text (78–79). On apprenticeship in the theater, see Kathman, "Grocers, Goldsmiths, and Drapers."

39. Ingold, "Temporality of the Landscape," 156.

Picturing class inequality using the metaphors at hand, the fishermen are what Antonio Gramsci calls "organic intellectuals," skilled workers who incubate political vocabularies out of their artisanal expertise and self-organizing activities. Through their allegorical speech, the fishermen's work with the nets becomes affective labor in the sense suggested by Michael Hardt, writing in the autonomist tradition initiated by Gramsci. Labor becomes affective labor when, in Hardt's terms, it produces "social networks, forms of community, biopower," visible here in the forms of satiric camaraderie that knit the fishermen together in their employment by the sea.[40] Here action begins to approach Arendt's intersubjective benchmark, though connected to economic activity in a manner that Arendt does not usually choose to spotlight.[41]

The fishing nets are pliant and portable instruments of capture, entanglement, and hauling that connect men, shore, sea, and city. In Hans Blumenberg's famous analysis of the philosopher's "shipwreck with spectator" motif, the shore forms the fold dividing immersion in existence from the possibility of reflection.[42] In the shore as taskscape, however, the shore remains the site of ebb and flow, with the men working its margin ever pulled back into the sea. They ride its energy in order to reap its resources, actions that sweep them back into the city in a double apprehension by ecological and economic cycles. The cooperative rhythms of labor and affect (what management experts call "workflow") spawn more fully formed social actions, including the political speech of the fishermen and their charity toward Pericles. In this extraordinary scene, the taskscape spawns an array of actions, from highly focused deployments of effort and skill to world-building and self-disclosing acts of speech, gift, invention, and acknowledgment. Although it is perhaps unavoidable to think of these ac-

40. Hardt, "Affective Labour," 96.

41. For a generous reconstruction of work, labor, and action in Arendt, conducted under the canopy of architecture and with an eye to autopoesis, see Markell, "Arendt's Work."

42. Blumenberg, *Shipwreck with Spectator*.

tions along a spectrum that extends from the manual, embodied, and object-oriented endeavor of fishing to the more capacious and contingent speech of strangers on the shore, the Wilkens-Shakespeare taskscape stages the proximity, co-intrication, and environmental situatedness of these actions. In *Pericles*, the shore is defined by patterns of use that are both environmentally responsive and critically cognizant of their own capture in the great net of emergent capital.

The work of the scene as a whole is to clothe the naked prince. Responding to Pericles's plea for assistance, the head fisherman gives the naked prince one of his own sea gowns. This outfitting enters a new stage when the fishermen draw up a net containing the rusty armor bequeathed to Pericles by his father.[43] Handing Pericles the beachcombed booty, the Master reminds him of his debt: "Ay, but hark you, my friend, 'twas we that made up this garment through the rough seams of the water. There are certain condolements, certain vails. I hope sir, if you thrive, you'll remember from whence you had this" (186–88). The fisherman presents the garment as the collaborative creation of the sea and its skilled workers. Wielding a key term for all of the late plays, the actors on the shore use the word "provide" to characterize this impromptu act of costume design. To provide is to equip, furnish, or outfit; it also means to look to the future (*pro-videre*), which shadows the providential with the provisional. Although the recovery of the armor from the sea partially rebuilds Pericles's princely identity, the armor itself is rusty and its seams are rough.

By the end of the encounter, however, this angler's apprentice has begun to appropriate a style of action that moves ably between material affordances and linguistic capacity. In the next scene, Pericles marches off to the nearby court of Pentapolis in order to try his luck in a tournament in honor of the birthday of Princess Thaisa. When Pericles appears at court, Thaisa remarks:

43. For a theatrical reading of Pericles's armor, see S. Harlan, "'Certain condolements, certain vails.'"

> He seems to be a stranger, but his present is
> A withered branch that's only green at top.
> The motto, *In hac spe vivo.* (6.46–48)

One of the lords comments,

> He well may be a stranger, for he comes
> Into an honoured triumph strangely furnished. (55–56)

Whereas the other knights are properly outfitted with painted shields, Pericles has used his lessons in beachcombing to fashion a makeshift emblem from materials under foot.[44] The lord describes Pericles as "strangely furnished": "furnish" means to equip, provision, or make ready. "Furniture" can refer to equipment for horses, hunters, ships, armies, and banqueting tables as well as houses and churches, that is, to any ensemble of supplies that allows workers to organize and manage a specialized taskscape. The withered branch and the rusty armor comprise Pericles's chivalric furniture, appareling him for the sumptuary ordeal of pageantry while signifying his situation in a thingly and environmental manner that distinguishes his habit from the handsome painted shields of the other knights.

The withered branch at once recalls and radically prunes Pericles's earlier image of sovereignty as "the tops of trees / Which fence the roots they grow by" (2.30–31). The figuration of the state as a sylvan political ecology composed of multiple roots, stems, and branches does not yield an image of personal sovereignty as readily as other political-theological metaphors such as the body politic or the ship of state. Combining Macbeth's sere leaf with the upstart verdancy of Birnam Wood, the margin of green atop Pericles's blasted branch draws an inch of inventiveness from his melancholia's dark roots. Hope, one of Paul's three theological virtues (1 Cor. 13:13), germinates in the play's complex

44. I would like to thank my student Chris Dearner for connecting the fishermen's beachcombing to Pericles's emblem in the following scene. On beachcombing and other maritime labors in Shakespeare, see Steven Mentz, *At the Bottom of Shakespeare's Ocean.*

exchanges among objects and worlds. Proffered like the frankincense and myrrh of an epiphany king, Pericles's bit of tufted driftwood symbolizes his rebirth out of the storm, manifests his education in affordances, and initiates a new action, insofar as the gift constitutes a first joist or brace around which a set of human relationships might begin to be built. As Randall Martin has noted, it is this humble offering, and not the tournament itself, that the authors of the play choose to depict. Presenting the bough to Thaisa with "graceful courtesy" (6.45) elevates the branch into the support of a new beginning.[45]

Pericles's capacity for action remains perilously imperfect. In the airless scenes at Pentapolis, Pericles is remarkably unassertive as a lover, while in the next tempest and its aftermath he too willingly relinquishes Thaisa's body to the sea and delivers their baby to foster care. Both Pericles and Leontes cause the assumed deaths and extended seclusions of their wives and daughters. What one hero undergoes as suffered disaster is replayed by the second as self-authored delusion; in both cases, the father signals his culpability by sinking into a penitential paralysis that can only be lifted by the healing action of another. At once bad bouquet, walking stick, and wilted priapus, the withered branch becomes a figure of assisted reproduction and indeed assisted living, flagging Pericles's venture into relationships of partnership and dependency. Always a prince of potentiality and never a king of sovereign self-possession, Pericles cannot enter into action on his own; for this he will need Marina. Yet the point of the play is not to prop up the phallus in order to revive its damaged potency but rather to explore forms of weak sovereignty and soft power that might organize action and agency differently. In Evelyn Tribble's account of work and labor at the Globe, the theatrical taskscape distributes cognition among multiple actors and memory architectures in order to bring off the miracle of live performance. In *Pericles*, the birth of subjectivity out of affordances and into action is parceled out among several generations, genders, classes,

45. Randall Martin, personal communication.

spatial dispositions, and social scenes, and the play is unusually attuned to a range of workplaces that include Cerimon's clinic, Marina's school, and the brothel in Mytilene. The enterprise of the play, and of the romances in general, is to acknowledge the collaborative, creaturely, and networked character of all forms of action and authorship, including their always only partial release from capture in structures of alienation and exploitation.

Edifications: Marina in Mytilene

As Randall Martin has demonstrated, Marina's experiments with space begin inside the brothel itself, where she makes the bawdy house into an edifice for edification, in the tradition of Saint Paul.[46] In *The Pauline Renaissance*, John S. Coolidge points out that to edify (from *oikodomeo*, to build a house) is to build up, to use the power of the word to construct the church as community.[47] In the house-churches of Pauline Christianity, domestic settings afforded table fellowship and acts of worship that in turn rezoned the *oikos* as semipublic places of congregation and witnessing. Marina will eventually found her own house-church by the sea, but she already begins that work here in the brothel through her edifying practices. The governor of the city, Lysimachus, comes to the brothel seeking to deflower a virgin, not because maidens are more lovely but because they are less likely to infect him with syphilis. Such a man hardly seems ripe for dissuasion. In the extraordinary exchange between Lysimachus

46. On Paul, women, and ministry, see Gritz, *Paul, Women Teachers, and the Mother Goddess at Ephesus*.

47. John Coolidge, *The Pauline Renaissance*, 23–54. For a literary application of Coolidge's account of Pauline edification, see Gregory Kneidel, *Rethinking the Turn to Religion in Early Modern English Literature*. Rebeca Helfer explores the link between edifices and edifications in *Spenser's Ruins and the Art of Recollection*. See also Karsten Harries: "Originally 'edify'—from the Latin *aedificare* (*aedes*, 'dwelling' + *fiacre*, 'to make')—meant simply to build, to construct. Long ago this meaning fell into disuse, but the word found a new home especially in religious discourse: 'to edify' came to mean to build up the house or the soul, to provide something like spiritual shelter"; *The Ethical Function of Architecture*, 11.

and Marina, the governor insists that the space Marina inhabits determines her vocation: "Why, the house you dwell in proclaims you are a creature of sale" (19.82–83). She responds by recalling him to the carnal knowledge manifested by the very fact of his entry into this space: "Do you know this house to be a place of such resort and will come into it?" (19.84–86). "Dwelling" shifts here from mere occupancy and social determinism ("the house you *dwell in* proclaims you") to a form of dramatic and cognitive engagement in which every entrance and exit reveals something real and risky about its denizens.[48]

Increasingly agitated by her frank and open handling of language as an instrument of truth, Lysimachus dissolves into authoritarian bluster: "Come, bring me to some private place. Come, come" (19.102). Although his command identifies the room they occupy as a parlor or antechamber, a deeper renovation of space is at work here: Marina's speech, qualifying as action in the Arendtian sense, has rendered the *oikos* into a provisional polis insofar as their exchange prompts each actor to risk self-disclosure. Through her use of words, Marina has instituted a scene in the sense developed by Paul Kottman: whereas *skena*, he argues, began as an architectural term, it has come to designate both the location of an action and the action itself, "moving from a valence dominated by technical fabrication to a valence that privileges the unpredictable here-and-now interactions of human beings."[49] In this scene of scenes, Lysimachus may be aroused by Marina's comportment, but he is also, far more profoundly, revolted by the person he has revealed himself to be in her presence: tyrannous, preemptory, and equivocal; empty, needy, sordid, sorry, and sad. *Come, bring me to some private place*: that is, *lead me away from the terrible visibility hatched by your speech; grant me refuge from the self you have led me to publish.*

48. I am drawing here on ongoing research by Christopher Wild and Juliana Vögel at the University of Constance on entries and exits in drama. See also Rayner, "Rude Mechanicals and the *Specters of Marx*," 535.

49. Paul Kottman, *A Politics of the Scene*, 10. See also Sarah Beckwith's stunning reading of Marina's use of language in this scene, in *Shakespeare and the Grammar of Forgiveness*, 99.

The marriage of Lysimachus and Marina at the end of the play, a scandal to eighteenth-century readers, still has the capacity to shock. (*That guy* with *this girl*?) If we find Lysimachus an unlikely lover in this scene, he exercises Arendtian courage when he actively courts the very woman who has made him reveal his own frailty: courage, writes Arendt in a passage I read at greater length in my chapter on *Cymbeline*, begins with the act of "leaving one's private place and showing who one is, disclosing and exposing one's self."[50] A public man seeking private pleasures, Lysimachus has discovered in Marina the possibility of new forms of publicity that issue from the rezoning of space through the action of eloquence.[51] He is brave enough to want more. The leafy shelter that Marina builds with his funds partially translates and provisionally institutionalizes that minimal clearing for courage into a place infused with grace.

Thus Pericles's withered branch returns at the end of the play in the form of the ad hoc housing that Marina has constructed for herself and her community of followers at the edge of the sea:

> She in all happy,
> As the fairest of them all, among her fellow maids
> Dwells now i'th'leafy shelter that abuts
> Against the island's side. (21.38–41)

"Leafy shelter" suggests a form of minimal architecture, like Viola's willow cabin, Lear's hovel, or Justine's tepee at the end of Lars von Trier's *Melancholia* (figure 3).[52] Essayist Lisa Robertson writes of the shack that it is "a thickening, a concentration, an opacity, in the lucid landscape"; Marina's leafy shelter is a shack

50. Arendt, *Human Condition*, 186.

51. Bradin Cormack identifies Marina with privacy: "No one in the play inhabits space (although not place) more fiercely and privately than Marina"; *A Power to Do Justice*, 289. I would argue a little differently that through her wielding of speech Marina is able to design new forms of publicity, and to institutionalize those new forms of publicity in the architecture of the leafy shelter.

52. Jonah 4:6: The Hebrew *sukkah* is rendered as "booth" in the Geneva and King James Bibles. In his lengthy commentary on Jonah from 1604, George Abbot describes it as a "booth, or sommer-house of boughs" (561) and "a silly house, a cottage, or a cabben" (570).

in this sense.[53] Letting in the salt air along with the wind and the rain, Marina's leafy shelter participates in what contemporary designers call "an architecture of flows," which approaches buildings as improvisational elements perched in larger economic and ecological systems.[54] True to her name, Marina has chosen to build her house of flows as close to the sea as possible—and as far as she can from the urban brothel from which she has used her active eloquence to escape. Yet her establishment remains connected to the city insofar as "her gain / She gives the cursèd Bawd" (21.10–11), since she remains indentured to her original investor and continues to pay off her purchase price.[55] Like the fishermen, Marina remains caught up in, but also cognizant of, the economies of exploitation from which her actions give her provisional independence. Rob Watson writes that ecocriticism too quickly prefers "reverence for nature" to "tolerance of complexity."[56] Open to both the city and the sea, Marina's pastoral pavilion renders the simple complex, in the scientific sense of complexity as an intricate system of dependencies and feedback loops. Her name becomes an emblem of that complexity: she is "Called Marina, / For [she] was borne at sea" (21.145–46).

Pericles's stunted branch, single and almost bare, has now been multiplied and assembled into a church of craft and an edifice for edification. Marina's leafy shelter transplants the prince's original image of sylvan sovereignty into a form of architecture that builds itself out of the available forms and resources of its site. Here and elsewhere, Shakespeare participates in a topos of architectural theory that derives primitive buildings from the spatial disposition and growth habits of trees. In this line of thought,

53. Robertson, *Occasional Work and Seven Walks from the Office for Soft Architecture*, 176. She also writes: "When the shack dweller lays in supplies, she is composing a politics" (180).

54. Ballantyne and Smith, *Architecture in the Space of Flows*.

55. For a related reading of sex trafficking, precarity, and education in *Pericles*, see Joseph Campana, "The Traffic in Children."

56. Work in progress/personal communication. On Shakespeare and complexity theory, see Henry Turner, *Shakespeare's Double Helix*, and Robert Watson, "The Ecology of Self in *Midsummer Night's Dream*."

all architecture begins as landscape architecture and only later hardens into something more decisively artifactual.[57] The word "academy" originally designated "the grove of Akademos," and it is surely an academy that Marina has founded in her frondescent pavilion. Randall Martin associates Marina's school with the house-churches of Priscilla and Aquila at Ephesus and Corinth. (This missionary couple were, like Paul, Jewish Christians and tent-makers by trade, and hence architects of the ad hoc.)[58] Feminist theologian Elisabeth Schüssler Fiorenza writes that house-churches "provided equal opportunity for women" because the house was already associated with women's work and capacity for leadership; such house-churches, moreover, were structured less like "a patriarchal family" and more like a "religious association"—based on free affiliation rather than kinship, and hence becoming exercises in citizenship and self-governance.[59]

Mytilene is on the island of Lesbos, home to another academy, the school of Sappho.[60] The island itself is associated with the

57. Landscape architect Diana Balmori and Joel Sanders cite the frontispiece of Marc-Antoine Laugier's *Essai sur l'Architecture* of 1753, which depicts "columns emerging from the trunks of trees to form a primitive dwelling; *Groundwork,* 37.

58. Fiorenza, *In Memory of Her*, 178.

59. Ibid., 176, 179. See also Fiorenza, *But She Said*: "Both Prisca and Aquila were well-known leaders in the early Christian movement, of which their house-*ekklēsia* in Corinth, Rome, and Ephesus was a center. Their example shows that the house-*ekklēsia* was fashioned after the organizational form of private associations rather than patterned after patriarchal household structures. Not only Paul but the entire gentile church had reason to give thanks to them" (169).

60. In the *Tristia*, Ovid represents Sappho as a teacher: "What did Lesbian Sappho teach girls, if not to love?" (2.364–65). In the poem to Phaon in the *Heroides*, Sappho speaks to her community in strikingly marine terms: "Lesbian women of the water, offspring wed and about to be wed, / Lesbian women, names spoken to the Aeolian lyre, / Lesbian women, you who having been loved made me disgraced, / Stop coming as a throng to my musical performances." In *Bisexuality in the Ancient World*, Eva Cantarella describes the *thiasoi* as "communities of women, the existence of which is documented not only in Lesbos where, as well as Sappho's *thiasos* there were also the *thiasoi* of her rivals Gorgo and Andromeda, but also in other parts of Greece, especially in Sparta. . . . They were groups with their own divinities and ceremonies, where girls, before marriage, went through a global experience of life. . . . And the girls received an education within this community of life. With reference to Lesbos, in particular, the *Suda* names three *mathētriai,* meaning three 'pupils' of Sappho, who was called '*didaskalos,*' or 'schoolmistress'"

curative powers of music; thus Agrippa von Nettesheim writes that "Therpander, and Arion of Lesbos cured the Lesbians, and Ionians by Musick."[61] In Ephesus, Cerimon had used "rough music" to revive Thaisa, and Marina will be brought to Pericles's ship to use "her sweet harmony / And other choice attractions" to cure him of his melancholy. Arion, the mythic poet who was captured by pirates but saved by dolphins when he sang a poem to Apollo, is sometimes associated with Jonah.[62] In Acts, Paul stops briefly at Mytilene on his way to Ephesus (Acts 20:14). As a place, then, Mytilene is associated with the curative powers of music, the poetic and associational inventiveness of women, the travels of Paul and Jonah, and the mysterious agency of the sea and its creatures. Marina's Lesbian mission can be placed in the line of what Susan Fraiman has called "shelter writing." In contemporary periodicals, shelter writing refers to mainstream home-and-garden journalism; Fraiman boldly retools the phrase in order to capture the more militant and beleaguered writings of "those whose smallest domestic endeavors have become urgent and precious in the wake of dislocation, whether as the result of migration, divorce, poverty, or a stigmatized sexuality."[63] In her negotiations with the bawd Bolt (his very name an architectural innuendo), Marina has asked to be placed "among honest women" (19.240). Although most of her students are probably paying full tuition, there is no reason not to think that at least some of Marina's "fellow maids" resemble their leader: refugees

(79). Subjects included "music, singing and dancing" as well as grace (*charis*). Thomas Heywood refers to the poet as "Sapho Mitelaena," "a singer and a strumpet." *Gynaikeion* (1624), 544. He writes further that Horace "cals her Mascula Sapho," on account of "preposterous and forbidden luxuries" (550).

61. Cornelius Agrippa, *Three Books of Occult Philosophy*, 256. Peter Heylyn's *Mikrokosmos: A Little Description of the Great World* (1625) cites "Mitilene" as one of the chief cities on Lesbos, whose famous residents included Sappho, Theophrastus, Arion, and Alcaeus (426–27). The association of Arion and Lesbos is a commonplace: e.g., *The Famous History of Herodotus* (1584).

62. George Abbot, *An Exposition upon the Prophet Ionah*, 323–24. On the association of Arion and Lesbos, see, e.g., Giacomo Affinati, *The dumb diuine speaker*, 68.

63. Fraiman, "Shelter Writing," 37.

from parental abandonment, abusive foster care, and sex trafficking who seek new forms of autonomy through the skills taught in Marina's messianic house of hope. Marina's leafy shelter is an academy, a trade school, and a cottage industry; her halfway house is also a refuge for the survivors of sexual shipwreck and an architectural testament (not unlike Timon's seaside earthwork)[64] to the tempestuous and exposed character of creaturely life in the age of primitive accumulation.

Still another precedent for Marina's leafy shelter is the sukkah, the booth or bower that Jonah briefly inhabits outside Nineveh. When God spares Nineveh, Jonah "went out of the city, and sat on the East side of the city, and there made him a booth [sukkah], and sat under it in the shadow, till he might see what would become of the city."[65] God supplements Jonah's temporary shelter with the gift of a fast-growing vine: "And the Lord God prepared a gourd, and made it to come up over Jonah, that it might be a shadow over his head, and deliver him from his grief" (4:6). The next day, however, God sends a worm that destroys the vine, and Jonah is angry again. In the final lines of the Book of Jonah, God explains his action: "Thou hast had pity on the gourd, for which thou hast not labored, neither madest it grow, which came up in a night, and perished in a night, and should not I have pity on Nineveh, that great city, wherein there are more than sixscore thousand persons that cannot discern between their right hand and their left hand, and also much cattle?" (4:10–11). God has created a living allegory for Jonah, a parable *about creaturely life* that engages the growth patterns and actants *of creaturely life* in an act of divine poiesis that participates in the autopoiesis, the self-organizing capacities, of the teeming world.

Both Mytilene and Nineveh are cities of sinners who are nonetheless capable of conversion; not only Lysimachus and the other johns but also Bolt are transformed by Marina's speech and

64. Hugh Grady calls Timon's tomb "a work of environmental art;" "*Timon of Athens*: The Dialectic of Usury, Nihilism, and Art," 449.

65. Jonah 4:5 (Geneva Bible; Soncino Bible, *Twelve Prophets*, ed. A. Cohen, for Hebrew *sukkah*).

action. And in both texts, these opportunities for redemption are conceived in environmental as well as human terms: the very last word of the Book of Jonah is *behamah rabah*, "much cattle." Commentator George Abbot (1600) refers to the gourd as a "creature" and reads the scene as instructing us "to take benefite of all things, which God doth offer to us, or wherewithal honestly and justly our labour and our wit may furnish us."[66] Commentators speculate as to whether Jonah builds his sukkah out of gathered branches that are then adumbrated by the vine, or sets up his shelter out of the plants "prepared" by God;[67] in either case, his architecture is an exercise in affordances, of "taking benefit" from what is "offered" in a manner that weds human invention to the gifts of place. Like her father's beachcombing, Marina builds her shelter from leavings of the natural and scriptural worlds. The Ordinary Gloss reads Jonah's sukkah typologically: "Israel is compared to this ivy or gourd. Israel once protected Jonah under its own shade—that is, Christ—awaiting the conversion of the nations. The vine provided no small joy, making for him a bower, which has the appearance of a house but is not one, because it does not have foundations."[68] Considered typologically, the bower is a limited type of the universal church to come. Read more prophetically, as an open-ended message, the sukkah shelters a range of affects (fear, hope, anger, dismay, regret) and possible comportments (patience, resilience, hospitality, care) that continue to proffer designs for the theater of life.

In her modes of dwelling, Marina is the un-Miranda. The contrast between these two romance heroines is visible in their differing orientations within the "shipwreck with spectator" motif, Hans Blumenberg's blueprint for the origins of conceptuality. Miranda, as her name declares, is the archetypal spectator, watching disaster unfold off shore and then going home to a rocky cave recessed into the earth as a natural fortification. Marina's name,

66. Abbot, *Exposition*, 373, 374.

67. Ibid., 561.

68. McDermott, ed., "Ordinary Gloss on Jonah," 437.

on the other hand, announces her as what Bradin Cormack calls "a creature of the limit itself";[69] unlike Miranda's cave, the soft and airy structure of Marina's coastal tree house places her in the closest possible proximity to the ocean and its insurgencies. Marina dedicates her architecture of flows to the condition of permanent sojourning that Blumenberg associates with the sea.[70] If she lives, however, as a resident alien in the fluctuating now of existence, she also cultivates in that same site forms of enskillment, place-making, communication, and community that scaffold a future for those who gather with her.

Gower describes Marina's embroidery as making the cambric "more sound / By hurting it" (15, 24–25). Just as Cerimon's restorative music is unexpectedly "rough and woeful" (12.84), Marina's soft stitchery requires a surgical sharpness. These same handicrafts also afford opportunities for fellowship, conversation, and self-sufficiency, fragile assemblages whose mending can also inflict harm. The image of needlework as a form of wounding links Marina's handicraft to the nets of the fishermen, to the airy architecture of the leafy shelter, and to the gaps and gashes that at once perforate and hold together the loose weave of this meandering play. (Think also of Juliet's appliqué project, which imagines a celestial darning of Romeo before any damage has been done to him [3.2.21–25].) In the environs of Marina, messianic means seeking a livable future from within an immanence characterized by forms of repair that are not themselves without violence.

G. Wilson Knight writes of *Pericles* that "we have poetry, as it were, writing itself and are to see what new thing unfolds."[71] In Knight's analysis, the play as a whole is an autopoietic experiment generated out of the associative movement of imagistic rumination, as Shakespeare and Wilkens take up the metaphor of the sea of existence and allow that symbol to course in multiple

69. Cormack, *A Power to Do Justice*, 289.

70. "We are always already embarked and on the high seas," Blumenberg, *Shipwreck*, 19.

71. Knight, "The Writing of *Pericles*," 80.

directions: roiling as the ocean of fortune, contingency, and disaster; cresting with the promise of birth and renewal; and always subsisting as an environment supporting travel, trade, communication, and industry. If autopoiesis describes the compositional movement of the play as a piece of writing, autopoiesis also describes the modes in which its two central characters become actors by responding to the affordances of their situations. Pericles inhabits the most passive edge of autopoiesis, insofar as he literally "goes with the flow," allowing the currents of the sea to take him from port to port. Marina, on the other hand, meets occasion with a more active sense of virtue, building her leafy shelter out of materials at hand and allowing the intrication of those preexisting conditions to resonate within the form and disposition of her building. Knight goes on to identify Marina as "art incarnate," administering a total program of aesthetic education that includes "arts both of melody and of design."[72] Merging Knight's remarks on autopoiesis with his comments on Marina as designer allows us to envision Shakespeare's heroine as a social and environmental artist whose sweetness is always sharp. Marina practices what Hugh Grady calls an "impure aesthetics," which, through its living link with labor, entails "a transformation of the given . . . using forms and techniques developed in a complex historical process of collective social interaction."[73] A new Jonah as well as a new Sappho, a second Cerimon as well as another "herb woman" (19.90), Marina's *hortus inconclusus* dramatizes her cosmopolitan origins, her environmental connectedness, and her prophetic ministration to the social body.

Votive Offerings: Thaisa at Ephesus

The play ends in Ephesus, the setting of Shakespeare's much earlier drama *The Comedy of Errors*. Mythically associated with the Amazons, Ephesus is another city historically hospitable to

72. Ibid., 102.
73. Hugh Grady, *Impure Aesthetics*, 57.

female fellowship. As documented in Saint Paul's Letter to the Ephesians, it is also the place where early Christians, drawn from diverse backgrounds, confronted and rethought the challenges of marriage as a model of corporate community.[74] In both *Errors* and *Pericles*, shipwrecked mothers separated from their children devote themselves to religious service in Ephesus. In both plays, the sanctuaries where they have found refuge and meaningful work set the scene for the plays' final reunions. In late antiquity, Ephesus housed Asiatic, Hellenistic, Roman, Jewish, and early Christian cults and cultures; today, as in Shakespeare's time, it is a Muslim city, host to its own traditions of universalism. The philosopher Apollonius of Tyana (ca. 15–100 CE) wrote to the Ephesians about the Temple of Diana: "Your temple is thrown open to all who would sacrifice, or offer prayers, or sing hymns, to suppliants, to Hellenes, barbarians, free men, to slaves."[75] Written in the same century as Paul's own letter to the Ephesians, this Neopythagorean speaks in universalist and cosmopolitan terms that resemble Paul's open address.

In *Errors*, Emilia joins an abbey, marking the city as Catholic. In *Pericles*, the same space is dedicated to the cult of Diana. Both Laurie Maguire and Randall Martin discern in the Ephesus of *Errors* a tension between Christian/patriarchal and Amazonian/emancipatory models of womanhood.[76] In *Pericles*, such tensions have largely dissolved, and Ephesus has become instead a kind of messianic theme park, a center of holy tourism that uses romance landscaping to harmonize, mask, or defer interreligious hostility. *Pericles* bathes a largely pagan landscape in an emergent Christian light through references to spaces shared by Jewish and

74. Randall Martin notes the complexity of the account of marriage presented in the Letter to the Ephesians and the degree to which the sisters in *Errors* test that complexity through their differing positions, "Rediscovering Artemis in *The Comedy of Errors*."

75. Apollonius of Tyana, *Letters* 67, cited by Murphy-O'Connor, *St. Paul's Ephesus*, 21. Murphy-O'Connor refers to the "ecumenical character of the Temple of Artemis" (24).

76. Laurie Maguire, "The Girls from Ephesus"; Randall Martin, "Rediscovering Artemis."

Christian scriptures (Jonah and Job, Paul and Priscilla). The viscous and resonant space-time of *Pericles*'s Asia Minor, not quite historical but also not fully mythic, offers sanctuary to messianism in its pluralist origins and mixed destinies.

Artemis and the Artemision bore a special relationship to the city of Ephesus: as one New Testament historian of the city writes, "Artemis Ephesia is homologous to a personification of the city"; and "Ephesus and Artemis were inseparable."[77] Some Ephesian coins feature a woman holding a model of the temple, while other coins depict a woman wearing a "mural crown," a representation of the city's defenses. In the Acts of the Apostles, the silversmith Demetrius sells "silver Temples" to tourists, miniature images of the city's most iconic building, like the Empire State buildings hawked on Manhattan street corners today (Acts 19:24; Geneva Bible).[78] These various representations identify city, building, and cult in a linked set of branding and placemaking efforts.[79] One of Ephesus's most famous governors was named Lysimachus, who flooded the city in order to relocate its residents from lower to higher ground; the historical Lysimachus was the Robert Moses of Ephesus, what we would now call a city planner.[80] Ephesus hosted diverse communities that administered their own affairs: the Jewish community at Ephesus, for example, was probably constituted as a *politeuma*, "a recognized, formally constituted corporation of aliens enjoying the right of domicile in a foreign city and forming a separate, semiautonomous civic body."[81] Paul (or his follower), who would have

77. Strelan, *Paul, Artemis, and the Jews of Ephesus*, 46.

78. The Geneva Bible provides the following gloss: "These were certaine counterfeit temples with Dianas picture in them, which they bought that worshipped her;" *Annotated New Testament, 1602 Edition.*

79. On the coins, see Murphy-O'Connor, *St. Paul's Ephesus*, 21. Murphy-O'Connor remarks that Demetrius really made statuettes of the goddess, and not temple figurines (94).

80. In 294 BCE, "Lysimachus 'at Ephesus founded the modern city which reaches to the sea' (Pausanias, 1.9.7)," (Murphy-O'Connor, *St. Paul's Ephesus*, 19). A Macedonian by birth, Lysimachus employed pirates to help him conquer the city.

81. Murphy-O'Connor, *St. Paul's Ephesus*, 82.

recognized the civic affordances of such mixed jurisdictions from the Jewish communities at Tarsus and elsewhere, draws on similar language to describe the early church at Ephesus: you are "no more strangers and foreigners, but citizens with the Saints, and of the household of God . . . in whom all the building coupled together, groweth into a holy Temple in the Lord. In whom ye also are built together to be the habitation of God by the Spirit" (Eph. 2:19–22; Geneva Bible).[82] "Temple" here may refer simultaneously to the Temple of Solomon in Jerusalem and the Temple of Artemis in Ephesus, while also refiguring the messianic *ecclesia* as a pluralist congregation of Jews and gentiles who create through their collective witnessing a new dwelling place for God.

In her study of *Pericles* and the politics of place, Constance Relihan avers that *Pericles*'s Ephesus "is a land of lethargy and resignation, a location that encourages Thaisa to recoil from her responsibilities just as we repeatedly see Pericles reject his role as governor."[83] I would argue to the contrary that Shakespeare identifies Ephesus with both cosmopolitan social arrangements and women's associational energy. On the cosmopolitan side, the Ephesus of *Pericles* dissolves tensions between Catholic and Protestant, Jewish and Christian, and Judeo-Christian and Greco-Roman traditions into a single harmonious if ultimately incoherent universalizing stream (not so much weak messianism as Muzak messianism). Female figures play a major role in mediating these tensions: Thaisa combines Diana and Mary, while Marina reconciles Agnes, Paul, and Persephone. According to one feminist New Testament scholar, the Artemision, served by cohorts of women, "stamped this city more than others as 'the bastion and bulwark of women's rights.'" The same scholar notes that the cult dominated city life through temple rites, sacred dramas, civic celebrations, and tourism.[84] In *Errors*, Emilia's sojourn in the abbey involves both medical and pastoral care. In the

82. On Paul's multiple citizenships, see Lupton, *Citizen-Saints*, chap. 1. On multiple jurisdictions in Shakespeare, see Cormack, *A Power to Do Justice*.

83. Relihan, "Liminal Geography," 289.

84. Gritz, *Paul, Women Teachers, and the Mother Goddess*, 43, 41–42.

highly urbanist 2011 production of *Errors* at the National Theatre in London, the abbey becomes "the Abbey Clinic," an East London ministry for addicts and immigrants.[85] Pace Relihan, can we attribute civic virtue to Thaisa? When Thaisa first awakes in Ephesus, she seeks her bearings in the manner of *Hercules Furens*: "Where am I? Where's my lord? What world is this?" (12.103). Two scenes later, she decides to assume "a vestal livery," at which point Cerimon recommends "Diana's temple" (14.9, 12). The language of retreat and withdrawal, not without a Catholic cast,[86] does indeed shadow Thaisa's movement into sacred space. But sacred need not mean private; in a messianic mood, we might imagine that *the sanctuary Thaisa seeks for herself* after surviving childbirth and tempest becomes *sanctuary that she extends to others* in her years of temple service. She is certainly prepared to appear in public when Pericles and company assemble at Ephesus in the final scene. The Temple of Diana is both the opposite of Marina's leafy shelter (monumental rather than temporary; built out of stone, not branches; situated in the hills rather than on the coast) and its counterpart, insofar as both are places for sanctuary, edification, and the practice of female citizenship.

The Artemision's legal status as a sanctuary for persons extended to its curatorial function as a depository for things. The temple was the site of votive offerings: the bringing of gifts in honor of a deity, whether to express thanks, make a wish, or mark a transition.[87] One historian of Ephesus writes of votive offering, "In contrast to sacrifice, which destroyed the offering, the deposition in a sanctuary of something enduring both removed it from the owner and gave it to the god. . . . It often marked the passage from one stage of life to another. Thus children dedi-

85. Martin refers to the "ecumenicism" of Emilia's vocation, which combines elements of Christian and pagan service in "Rediscovering Artemis," 368.

86. She is later referred to as a nun (22.35).

87. "Craftsmen often dedicated their tools to a god or goddess upon retirement. . . . The unforeseen and perhaps unintended result was that the temple of Artemis also functioned as a museum for objects of cultural significance" (Murphy-O'Connor, *St. Paul's Ephesus*, 49).

cated toys, retiring priests or priestesses a statue, and retiring craftsmen their tools."[88] Demetrius's silver figurines in Acts were probably marketed as votive offerings as well as souvenirs. Many famous statues and paintings were housed at the temple, including Apelles's *Heracles with Face Averted*, as attested by Pliny the Elder.[89] (Wilkens's and Shakespeare's play could be called "Pericles with Face Averted.") Votive offerings were protected by the rights of sanctuary, transforming temples into banks and museums. In "The Crisis in Culture," Arendt acknowledges the different institutional forms taken by the act of setting aside objects from use:

> It does not matter whether this protection takes the form of their being set up in holy places, in temples and churches, or placed in the care of museums and the keepers of monuments, although the place where we put them is characteristic of our "culture," that is, the mode of our intercourse with them.[90]

Libraries, museums, and schools along with cathedrals, synagogues, and sacred burial grounds shape their commons differently, but each brokers a relationship between the preservation of culture, the judging of value, and the exercise of public speech. The practice of votive offering zoned the Temple of Diana as such a space, a sanctuary of things that cultivated habits of thought and attitudes of care toward persons and places.

In Catholic worship, votives include candles, masses, and endowments of art and architecture;[91] in a Protestant context, Lancelot Andrewes speaks evocatively of "votive repentance" as

88. Ibid., 102.

89. Ibid., 111. See Pliny: "The Herakles with averted face, in the temple of Diana, is also attributed to Apelles; by a triumph of art the picture seems not only to suggest, but also to give the face." In E. Sellers, ed., and K. Jex-Blake, trans., *The Elder Pliny's Chapters on the History of Art*, 131.

90. Arendt, *Between Past and Future*, 218.

91. Catholic votive practices are described at great length and in largely positive terms by Orazio Torsellino, *The History of Our B. Lady of Loreto* (1608). *Catholic* "votive masses" ("as for peace, for raine, for faire weather, for women in travaile, for those who are upon their journey") are decried as idolatry by Andrew Willet, *Hexapla in Danielem* (1610), chap. 24.

the act of "sequestering our selves" in a "retired place" and in a "vacant time" in order to effect "*renewing*, as from decay" and "*refining*, as from drosse."[92] A recurrent topos of votive offerings concerns the erection of thanksgiving memorials by survivors of shipwreck. These seaside assemblages took the form of "votive tables" or pictures as well as displays of the survivors' wet garments.[93] Seen through this votive tableau, Thaisa appears as both donor and donation. When Cerimon opens her coffin in his hospital at Ephesus, the comatose Thaisa floats at the mesmerizing threshold between hibernating life and dead charisma: "Shrouded in cloth of state, and crowned / Balmed and entreasured with full bags of spices" (21.62–63). When she awakens, her returning vitality continues to borrow its magnificence from art: "Behold, / Her eyelids, cases to those heavenly jewels / Which Pericles hath lost, / Begin to part their fringes of bright gold. / The diamonds of a most praised water / Doth appear to make the world twice rich" (12.95–100). In the final scene, Cerimon says that he "placed her / Here in Diana's temple" (22.43–44): she has been "placed" as a refugee in a space of sanctuary, but she has also been "placed" as a votive offering, a donation offered up in thanksgiving for survival from the sea. In the final scene, Cerimon informs Pericles that he found "rich jewels" in her coffin; these precious things, he says, "shall be brought to my house, / Whither I invite you" (22.43–47). His statement implies that the jewels have been deposited for safekeeping in the Temple of Diana along with Thaisa, manifesting the sacred precinct's overlapping affordances as sanctuary, treasury, and archive.

In *The Winter's Tale*, Shakespeare rezones Diana's temple as the

92. Lancelot Andrewes, *XCVI. Sermons*, 211.

93. Examples include Thomas Watson, *Hekatompathia* (1582), where "votive tables" (pictures) are offered up to "*Cupids* Church" after surviving emotional shipwreck. The survivor of shipwreck also hangs up his "wet garments on the wall" (54). Shipwreck votives are mocked in an apothegm attributed to Diogenes: "To one that admired the multitude of votive offerings in *Samothracia,* given by such as had escaped shipwrack: *There would have been far more,* saith he, *if those who perished had presented theirs*"; quoted in Stanley, *The History of Philosophy in Eight Parts* (1656), 24. This commonplace crops up frequently as a critique of superstition; e.g., Jeremy Taylor, *Eniatos*, 215.

gallery-chapel of Paulina. Emilia, Thaisa, and Hermione form an Ephesian series characterized by several linked characteristics, including a sheltering cloud of Pauline allusions; built environments that afford both human sanctuary and the curation of things;[94] an affinity with shipwreck; and gynocratic priesthoods organized around rites of birth and confinement.[95] Of these three sequestered mothers, Emilia appears most actively engaged in pastoral care, while Hermione seems the most constrained and passive, implying a falling off in women's civic compass as we move from the earlier, highly urban, Plautine comedy to the later, more diffusely landscaped romances. If Thaisa appears more retiring than Emilia, her daughter Marina is both Machiavellian and messianic in her ability to seize occasion by the forelock.[96] Whereas Relihan's Thaisa suffers from Ephesian "lethargy and resignation,"[97] my Thaisa is mother to Marina insofar as both women foster female piety, poetry, and fellowship within distinctive architectural and civic spaces. This more resilient and participatory Thaisa resides in a cosmopolitan Ephesus populated by urban gentiles, house-church Christians, civil-society Jews, and tent-making missionaries. The forms of social work they supervise identify the action of romance with the slow and painful process of reintegrating knowledge and action through a renewed attention to setting and situation.

It would be interesting to think of the late plays in general as moving from a *sacrificial economy* (where persons and things get killed, destroyed, or consumed in order to renew the social body) to a *votive economy*, which strives to maintain multiple historical moments and possibilities within a fluid dramatic-symbolic space. Certainly messianism in its Christological formulation is sacrificial, but messianism houses a votive dimension as well, an

94. The goldsmith plot in *Errors* alludes to the role of Demetrius the souvenir maker in Acts and is thus linked to the votive economy of historical Ephesus.

95. See Caroline Bicks, "Backsliding at Ephesus," on Reformation controversies concerning women's confinement and churching rituals in the play.

96. On Machiavelli and messianism, see Graham Hammill, *The Mosaic Constitution*.

97. Relihan, "Liminal Geography," 290.

impulse to preserve, collect, analogize, and repair. A votive mood infuses the romances, whose forms of *philia* encompass love for places, things, and times as well as for persons. Pericles's elegy for Thaisa delivers images of humming water and simple shells as a "priestly farewell" (11.62–68) to his dead wife; his underwater seascape posits a world of things both lost and found, mute and resonant, forever scattered on the ocean floor but also newly ingathered in the music of his words. The same votive impulses return in the pearl eyes and coral bones chanted into consciousness and history by Ariel in *The Tempest*. Dissolving grace in place, these romance lyrics, not unlike Eliot's "Marina," catch loss and peril in the translucent amber of affect and allusion.

The refusal to let characters die belongs to the late plays' votive tendencies, and can feel timid and even disingenuous after the sacrificial extremities of *Lear*. Even in their shortcomings, these plays' gestures of conservation tender themselves as worthy of our keeping. In his opening chorus, Gower announces that "lords and ladies in their lives / Have read [this story] for restoratives" (1.7–8). A restorative is a medicine that boosts health, mood, or memory; poetry is such a restorative, Gower claims, especially when "sung at festivals" (1.5), or savored in the shared space of the theater. No art can restore the relationships and capacities eroded by age and fortune or destroyed by betrayal, abandonment, and injustice. Yet the very imperfection of repair, a major theme in all of Shakespeare's romances, can itself become the occasion to acknowledge our dependencies on other people as well as our capture within surroundings beyond our control, but not impervious to our care. Thaisa's questions upon awaking—"Where am I? Where's my lord? What world is this?"—frame the play at large as a messianic investigation into dwelling.

4

Nativity and Natality in *Cymbeline*

The miracle that saves the world, the realm of human affairs, from its normal, "natural" ruin is ultimately the fact of natality, in which the faculty of action is ontologically rooted. It is, in other words, the birth of new men and the new beginning, the action they are capable of by virtue of being born.
«HANNAH ARENDT, *The Human Condition*[1]»

Your furniture is not dead.
«JACK WHITE, musician and former upholsterer[2]»

It is a commonplace in *Cymbeline* criticism that Shakespeare chose to set his play during the unremarkable reign of King Kymbeline because Jesus Christ descended into "fleshy slime," as Spenser put it, during those years.[3] Those same critics, however, also note the displaced or deferred character of the Nativity in *Cymbeline*: there is no miraculous babe as in *The Winter's Tale*, no mysterious redemptive pregnancy as in *All's Well*, no Epiphany

1. Arendt, *Human Condition*, 247.

2. From interview with musician Jack White on his early career as a furniture upholsterer, in *The Believer*, May 2003, http://www.believermag.com/issues/200305/?read=interview_white, accessed December 25, 2011.

3. See Moffet, "*Cymbeline* and the Nativity"; Simmonds, *Myth, Emblem, and Music in Shakespeare's "Cymbeline,"* 147, 132; and Arbery, "The Displaced Nativity in Cymbeline."

kings as in *Othello*.[4] In lieu of shepherds we have cave-dwelling hunters, while the play's scriptural motifs gravitate more toward passion, repentance, and resurrection than toward advent and parturition. It is as if Shakespeare had chosen Cymbeline's reign because of the Nativity, but then, on those same grounds, rigorously suspended direct reference to Bethlehem in order to acknowledge the multiple sources of messianism's pregnant beforetime. *Cymbeline*, I would like to argue, is "messianic" not only because it is set in the period of Christ's birth, but because in this play Shakespeare strives to imagine the resonance, openness, and creativity of that moment not as mere shadow or waiting, but as itself charged with the invitation to act in the present, on the grounds of that moment's perilous incompleteness and undisclosed urgencies. Whereas Glenn Arbery's thoughtful account of "displaced nativity" focuses on a single messianic outcome, "the historical importance of the birth of Christ,"[5] I press *Cymbeline* for a wider messianism. Like *Pericles*, *Cymbeline* makes room for humanist virtue discourses and, like *The Winter's Tale*, pays homage to Hebrew paradigms of faith and covenant. In the syncretic and semantic density of *Cymbeline*, mythological allusions and scriptural allegories coexist with more concretely embodied and naturalistic *figurae*, in Auerbach's sense of actors who retain their historical character even when their deeds imply later happenings that deliver their true meaning.

Cymbeline's central birth involves not a baby boy but an adult woman, in the form of Innogen's successive achievement of new forms of public identity. She accomplishes these victories through speech and action after states of dormancy and error, and she suffers labor pains manifested in her ongoing relationship to dwell-

4. There is a trace of the Annunciation in Iachimo's visit to Innogen's bedchamber. Peggy Muñoz Simmonds writes that the Nativity is "the absent center of the play" (132), a formulation that echoes Robin Moffet's characterization of *Cymbeline* as "a play whose 'centre' is something not stated or presented and an action whose climax and justifying event is not shown but assumed as shortly to take place" (219). Glenn Arbery writes, "To read the play in terms of its displacements [of nativity] means thinking in near-repetitions and variations" (158).

5. Arbery, "Displaced Nativity," 158.

ing's curation of creatureliness. Whereas Posthumus's rebirth is accompanied by a prophetic dream and thus explicitly enlists a transcendent dimension, Innogen becomes herself through primarily human means, acting in concert with other persons and in response to the teeming world and her own creaturely estate. She is thus less a figure of *nativity* than of *natality*, in Hannah Arendt's sense of the new beginnings—in the form of fresh stories, relationships, and institutions—initiated by human beings acting in the world. Key here is Arendt's concept of courage as exodus from the *oikos*, a definition both tested and twisted by Innogen's strikingly nonleonine brand of bravery. Innogen's movement out of the enclosure of the palace through acts of election, speech, disobedience, and self-overcoming lead her to embrace new modes and arts of dwelling in the mountains. Her birth as "Innogen," retroactively achieved on the way to Milford Haven, leads to her self-baptism as "Fidele," a fidelity she practices not as an abstract mental ascription to a truth proposition, but rather as a comportment of dwelling that identifies her own will to survive with the durability and abiding interests of the world.

Cymbeline follows dwelling from the famous bedroom scenes in act 2 to the Welsh settings of primitive habitation and hospitality in acts 3 and 4.[6] The second half of this chapter considers objects, affordances, and routines in the play's phenomenological delivery of theatrical space from what James Gibson calls "the furniture of the earth," the protrusions and concavities given by topography. Over the course of the play, the routine of falling asleep shifts from the highly specialized, design-rich environment of the palace bedchamber to more impromptu settings (ground, cave, grave, corpse), manifesting the dynamism of affordances in a taskscape animated by human habits but responsive to nonhuman *données*. Building from Auerbach's *figura* and *creatura* in the first two sections below, I suggest a new coinage, *furnitura*, in the third section, a word intended to grasp the direc-

6. For a compelling account of dwelling as sojourning in *Cymbeline*, see Dubrow, "'No place to fly to': Loss of Dwellings," in *Shakespeare and Domestic Loss*.

tionality, tendentiousness, and coactive character of the objects we live with and the places they make. In the final section, I connect Innogen's capacities for action with the virtue of resilience, associated in contemporary discourse with the ability of both environments and individuals to adapt to privation, insult, and abuse. *Cymbeline*, I argue, tests human capacities for action, survival, renewal, and covenanting within environments of risk and obligation that draw on Hebrew, classical, and humanist as well as Christian paradigms.

Creatura *and* Figura

In act 3, scene 4, Pisanio and Innogen have fled the court. She bursts onto the scene eager to join Posthumus at Milford Haven: "Thou told'st me when we came from horse the place / Was near at hand. Ne'er longed my mother so / To see me first as I have now" (3.4.1–3). She compares her ardent anticipation to see her husband to her mother's desire to give birth to her. Since her mother is dead, we might surmise that this delivery was a difficult, even fatal one, presaging the difficulties of the scene ahead.[7] The pregnant figure implicitly compares Posthumus to the unborn child and Innogen to his mother, who also died in childbirth. Indeed in some sense Innogen does give birth to Posthumus, by allowing him to err, repent, and be forgiven in his own eventful journey toward recovenanting with her.[8] Yet the real labor of this scene is the process by which Innogen gives birth, posthumously, to herself, by both avowing the courage of her earlier deeds and by pulling herself out of the temptation to martyrdom and into the next phase of the drama's action.

At a key moment in the scene, Innogen directly addresses the absent Posthumus:

7. The boys were stolen twenty years before the beginning of the play, and the oldest of the two was three years old. I am assuming that Innogen is the youngest of the siblings. In any case, childbirth may have taken their mother.

8. Sarah Beckwith's reading of the play focuses on the drama of Posthumus's confession (*Grammar of Forgiveness*, 104–26).

And thou, Posthumus,
That didst set up my disobedience 'gainst the King
My father, and make me put into contempt the suits
Of princely fellows, shalt hereafter find
It is no act of common passage but
A strain of rareness; and I grieve myself
To think, when thou shalt be disedged by her
That now thou tirest on, how thy memory
Will then be panged by me. *(To Pisanio)* Prithee dispatch.
The lamb entreats the butcher. Where's thy knife?
Thou art too slow to do thy master's bidding
When I desire it too. (3.4.87–98)

Recounting her past life with an eye to shaping Posthumus's evaluation of her, Innogen recognizes, perhaps for the first time, that her choice of Posthumus as her husband separated her from the household and established her ethical freedom by exercising "disobedience" and "contempt." If marriage and the sexual act merge partners in one flesh, the elective and self-determined love that runs through Shakespearean drama also has the capacity to distinguish them from each other, as Paul Kottman has argued in his iconoclastic reading of *Romeo and Juliet*.[9] Innogen's decision may have been "no act of common passage," but it was most certainly *an act*, a life-changing deed exercised in concert with another in a fraught social and legal scene. This deed revealed her "strain of rareness" by putting her virtuous capacities to the test—by straining or stretching them into the shape of a supple and commodious personhood. Three times earlier in the play, the word "election" had been used of Innogen's choice, highlighting her definitive role in bringing about the marriage. As Bonnie Lander argues, Innogen's story is a drama of personhood: although Innogen blames Posthumus for "setting up" her disobedience, she insistently highlights her own moral energy and demands that she be recognized for what she has risked.[10]

9. See Paul Kottman, "Defying the Stars."

10. Although Lander does not mention Arendt, her insightful dramaturgical analysis of the play is everywhere concerned with the relationship between speaking, action,

Indeed, editor Roger Warren is almost embarrassed by her willingness to "praise herself"; earlier, however, she had in rebuffing Cloten already noted her ability to "forget a lady's manners/ By being so verbal" (2.3.102–3). This is a girl who becomes a woman by learning to speak.

Innogen practices the civic virtue of courage, a strength she explicitly dons along with men's clothing at the end of the scene, when she exits wearing the "waggish courage" (3.4.158) and "prince's courage" (3.4.185) of a humanist as well as masculine *virtù*. Arendt defines courage:

> To leave the household, originally in order to embark upon some adventure and glorious enterprise and later simply to devote oneself to the affairs of the city, demanded courage because only in the household was one primarily concerned with one's own life and survival. Whoever entered the political realm had first to be ready to risk his life, and too great a love for life obstructed freedom, was a sure sign of slavishness. Courage therefore became the political virtue par excellence, and only those men who possessed it could be admitted to a fellowship that was political in content and purpose and thereby transcended the mere togetherness imposed on all—slaves, barbarians, and Greeks alike—by the urgencies of life.[11]

Arendt identifies courage with the act of leaving the household by risking public speech. The "life" disdained by speech is not only physical survival, but also one's way of life, the routines of daily sustenance and shelter supported by the *oikos* as well as the given or inherited relationships that run through those routines. Pocock defines Machiavellian *virtù* as "the skill and courage by which men are able to dominate events and fortune."[12]

---

courage, and the affirmation of personhood. Lander tracks Innogen's active eloquence in the 1988 performances of the role by Harriet Walter at The Other Place and Geraldine James at the National Theater ("Interpreting the Person," 156–84).

11. Arendt, *Human Condition*, 36.

12. Pocock writes that *virtù* conceived this way could "lose its Christian and ethical meaning altogether; but as long as it appeared that *virtù,* in the policy sense, was best practiced by the concurrence of citizens in a republic, it could not lose its association with the social virtues, which were still best described in Christian terms" (*The Machiavellian Moment*, 92).

To choose one's love partner may seem far from the epic and civic horizons courted by Arendt and Pocock, but the egalitarian character of Innogen's choice, its consensual and contractual character, its "disobedient" edge, and its solicitation of speech lift her act above the merely personal. Her choice of Posthumus is not new to romance; in Boccaccio, a noble heroine's election of a lesser lover both acknowledges his merits and establishes her *virtù*. These precedents do not eclipse the radical character of this act *for Innogen*, its momentousness rendered into life story in her exchange with Pisanio. Her love choice, the stuff of *Romeo and Juliet* and *All's Well That Ends Well*, had occurred before the play began; it is the re-cognitive process of coming into a hard-won relationship to that action in the presence of new audiences and witnesses that interests the author of *Cymbeline*.

Anger at Posthumus has led Innogen to avow her own courage; in this phase of the drama, righteous anger plays midwife to her self-birth. Aristotle, citing Plato, associates anger with the heart.[13] Courage also comes from the *coeur* or heart, and its peculiar rousing to action can be stimulated by anger as well as love. If Innogen had already begun to separate from Posthumus in the act of electing him, her righteous anger at her husband in this scene lays claim to that differentiation as the core of her personhood, a *coeur* of radiant connectivity rather than reified interiority. In other words, romantic love can issue in natality in the sense developed by Arendt:

> Labor and work, as well as action, are also rooted in natality in so far as they have the task to provide and preserve the world for, to foresee and reckon with, the constant influx of newcomers who are born into the world as strangers. However, of the three, action has the closest connection with the human condition of natality; the new beginning inherent in birth can make itself felt in the world only because the newcomer possesses the capacity to begin something anew, that is, of acting. Moreover, since action is the political activity par excellence,

13. Emido Campi and Joseph C. McLelland, eds., *Commentary on the Nichomachean Ethics*, 315.

> natality, and not mortality, may be the central category of political, as distinguished from metaphysical, thought.[14]

Natality encompasses both physical birth (that "act of common passage" that we all undergo in exiting the womb) and the other kinds of birth that succeed and differ from parturition. Native to the *oikos*, children are also "strangers" to it insofar as their developmental prematurity poses dangers to both themselves and their environment. As every new parent, aunt, and nanny knows, children are both *heimlich* and *unheimlich*, the most at home and the most uncanny of creatures. Born to the *oikos* are children; the objects, goods, and routines fashioned and managed by human art and skill in order to protect children and other beings; and "the world" as a contexture of objects, spaces, stories, and routines that must survive as well as accommodate those children.[15]

Action enters this scene of parturition, sustenance, and early education as a venture different from work and labor: associated with "the new beginning inherent in birth," it concerns "the capacity to begin something new." Action attaches to what is strange and potentially violent in the child: the contingency and variability of the *child's actions* are what the *oikos* must defend itself against. Arendt often emphasizes the affirmative and initiatory character of action, but she is also attuned to its unpredictable and hazardous edge: action "always establishes relationships and therefore has an inherent capacity to force open all limitations and cut across all boundaries. . . . The boundlessness of action is only the other side of its tremendous capacity for establishing relationships."[16] If work and labor are fundamentally conservative, action's greater contingency endows it with destructive as well as creative potential. Although the births that action gives rise to are in some sense metaphorical (birth into speech, personhood, recognition, or public life), the fact of being born

14. Arendt, *The Human Condition*, 9.

15. On the strategic conservatism of education, in which the teacher takes responsibility for the world, see Arendt, "The Crisis in Education."

16. Arendt, *The Human Condition*, 190–91.

is never stripped from the actor, who remains a living being capable of reclaiming her initial strangeness as the essence of her own creatureliness. Both the initial birth into the laboring world of the *oikos* and its escape and recapture as action intertwine the embodied and the re-cognitive dimensions of life. The word "natality" indicates that what is at stake here is not a movement from the somatic to the symbolic, but rather a reconfiguration of their connate bundling.[17] Physical birth, which belongs to dwelling yet also inserts a foreignness into the domesticating operations of the *oikos*, also models action as an exit from dwelling.

Auerbach's notion of *figura*, in which one event receives new meaning from a later event without losing its own historicity, draws birth imagery into its recursive architecture:

> It was directly from its general meaning as "formation," "forming," and "shape" that *figura* proceeded to acquire its new meaning. Indeed, the use of the term by the very oldest of the Latin ecclesiastical writers suggests this, as when individuals or events in the Old Testament are often described as being *figuram Christi* (*eccesiae, baptismi*, etc.) *gerunt* or *gestant* [providing or giving birth to a figure of Christ, of the church, of baptism, etc.].[18]

In the typological imagination sketched by Auerbach, the initial Old Testament action (the unexpected birth of a baby, as Samuel for Hannah or Isaac for Sara) is pregnant with a future parturition (the birth of Jesus). If *nativity* as incarnational theme is the specific outcome of these typological transfers, *natality* as the potentiality for future action infuses both *figura* and *creatura* with a significance both dependent on Christian historiography and flowing from non-Christian (Jewish and classical) sources into post-Christian futures. Thus Auerbach discovers within *figura*'s "dynamic, concrete historicity" the possibilities, quintessentially

17. In Miguel Vatter's formulation, Arendt uses the concept of natality in order to "reconnect the essence of human freedom to biological life so as to gain a new aim for politics," a politics that concerns "the freedom of life itself" ("Natality," 137). On the theological origins and significance of natality in Arendt's writings, see John Kiess, *Hannah Arendt and Theology*.

18. Auerbach, *Selected Essays*, 90.

Renaissance in imagery and impulse, for "a new beginning and a rebirth of creativity."[19] In *Mimesis*, Auerbach suggests that Shakespeare's own figural imagination unfolds in response to the loosening of the Christ event as the signifying punctum for world history, unleashing figural energies across a wider, more varied, and more agitated landscape that he associates with "the creatural view of man."[20] Both *figura* and *creatura* bear the *-ura* of the future active participle (meaning "intending to," "going to," or "about to"), which is in turn built out of the perfect passive participle, and thus condenses past and future as well as active and passive into its vibrant verbal tail. Auerbach writes that the direct attachment of the ending to the root in *figura* "expresses something animated and lively, open-ended and playful."[21] Auerbach's interest in creatureliness as a specific bequest of medieval Christianity to Western literature reflects the affinity between *figura* and *creatura* in his thought. In *Mimesis*, he defines "the creatural picture" as the scenario of "man living in reality which the Christian mixture of styles has produced," and he speaks throughout the book of a "creatural realism" that mingles suffering and a sense of becoming with an acute attention to sensory experience.[22] Whereas *figura* links Old Testament and New Testament in such a way as to confer ongoing significance to Israel's history, *creatura* collates life on earth with divine order to render ordinary existence worthy of portrayal.[23]

19. Ibid., 98.

20. "The dissolution of medieval Christianity, running its course through a series of great crises, brings out a dynamic need for self-orientation, a will to trace the secret forces of life. . . . The great number of moral phenomena which the constant renewal of the world as a whole produces, and which themselves constantly contribute to its renewal, engenders an abundance of stylistic levels such as antique tragedy was never able to produce" (*Mimesis*, 324–25). *Mimesis* is substantially later than "Figura," published in the same decade as *The Human Condition*.

21. Auerbach, *Selected Essays*, 65.

22. Auerbach, *Mimesis*, 248, 261.

23. "'Creaturality' necessarily implies such a relation to the divine order: it is constantly referred to; furthermore, the fifteenth century is precisely the great epoch of the passion play. . . . However, there has been a shift of emphasis, it now falls much more strongly upon life on earth. . . . Graphic portrayal is now much more immediately in

Through its links to politics, the concept of natality is primarily humanist for Arendt, yet enters her thinking from scriptural sources. In *The Human Condition*, she explicitly links natality to nativity:

> The miracle that saves the world, the realm of human affairs, from its normal, "natural" ruin is ultimately the fact of natality, in which the faculty of action is ontologically rooted. It is, in other words, the birth of new men and the new beginning, the action they are capable of by virtue of being born. Only the full experience of this capacity can bestow upon human affairs faith and hope, those two essential characteristics of human existence which Greek antiquity ignored altogether, discounting the keeping of faith as a very uncommon and not too important virtue and counting hope among the evils of illusion in Pandora's box. It is this faith in and hope for the world that found perhaps its most glorious and most succinct expression in the few words with which the Gospels announced their "glad tidings": "A child has been born unto us."[24]

Emphasizing the worldly quality of nativity, she calls our attention not to Christ's incarnation but rather to the fact of being born. Birth is a "miracle" not because God makes it possible but because every human birth introduces contingencies that make exception the rule. Elsewhere Arendt reads natality through Augustine, the subject of her dissertation and an ongoing source for her thinking about the politics of historical renewal. She ends *The Origins of Totalitarianism* by quoting Augustine: "Beginning, before it becomes a historical event, is the supreme capacity of man; politically, it is identical with man's freedom. *Initium ut esset homo creatus est*—'that a beginning be made man was created.'"[25] Birth

the service of earthly events; it enters into their sensory content, it seeks their sap and savor, it seeks the joy and torment which flow directly from life on earth itself" (*Mimesis*, 258–59).

24. Arendt, *Human Condition*, 247. On this passage as an example of Arendt's worldly, and Jewish, messianism, see Susannah Young-Ah Gottlieb, *Regions of Sorrow*, 135–40.

25. Arendt, *The Origins of Totalitarianism*, 479. Arendt's 1929 dissertation, written under the direction of Karl Jaspers, was on Saint Augustine; she later reworked it in English (1958–64), the language in which it was published as *Love and St. Augustine*.

is creaturely because "inter faeces et urinam nasciumur"[26]; birth is also creaturely because we do not choose our parentage or our birthday. As Miguel Vatter argues, the condition of createdness in Arendt's Augustine dissertation places man's essence outside his existence, at the hands of the Creator; Arendt's later work, which largely sheds its theological origins, absorbs createdness into natality as the this-worldly contingency of birth.[27]

Auerbach and Arendt, German Jewish émigrés to America born within ten years of each other, share an appreciation of Augustine's energetically temporalized sense of language and history, and they each link that dynamism to the novelty exercised in human action and embodied in gestation as a simultaneously somatic and signifying, creatural and figural, process.[28] Each acknowledges the Christian tenor of Augustinian thought, but also links humanity's initiatory capacities to both the Hebrew Bible and classical humanism. For Arendt, theologically circumscribed nativity is pregnant with the truth of a broader existential natality, just as biological birth, in its unwilled and creaturely character, predicts the contingency of a political action unguided by foundationalist signposts. To gloss Arendt using Auerbach: Judeo-Christian nativity operates as a *figura* for humanist and historiographical natality, just as biological birth into the *oikos* is a *figura* for later actions that lead out of the *oikos*. In each case, we are dealing with actualities "separate in time" and "l[ying] within time as real events"; each pole, that is, retains its lived and historical specificity.[29] Enlisting a historical moment fraught with classical, Jewish, and Christian potentialities and harboring landscapes alive with creaturely ache and glow, *Cymbeline* hosts a world in which nativity and natality converge.

26. "We are born between piss and shit"; proverb attributed to Augustine; cited by Bataille, *The Accursed Share: Consumption*, 62.

27. Miguel Vatter, "Natality," 141.

28. Auerbach was born in Berlin in 1892 and died in Wallingford, Connecticut, in 1957. Arendt was born in Hannover in 1906, grew up in Königsberg and Berlin, and died in New York in 1975. Auerbach delivered what would become the Gauss Seminars in Criticism at Princeton in 1949; Arendt contributed to the same series in 1953.

29. Auerbach, *Selected Essays*, 96.

Akedah

We might expect to encounter a wealth of natal figures in a play energized by the word "posthumous." Innogen, however, not her husband, is *Cymbeline*'s most powerful enactor of the umbilical knot connecting nativity and natality. If Christian charisma halos her special personhood, her deeds and comportment also recall Hebrew heroes such as Job, Abraham, Isaac, and Jacob, familiar founts of dramatic action in other Shakespearean plays. A strain of Job colors Innogen's righteous anger at Posthumus and her insistence on her own integrity, while the wager scene itself reaches back to the Book of Job's dramatic prologue in Heaven, as Arbery notes; meanwhile, the female Job passes into European literature through Griselda, who endows Shakespeare's heroines not only with exemplary patience, but also with a capacity for self-disclosing speech.[30] Imitating the Book of Job, some medieval versions of the sacrifice of Isaac also include a wager scene in which Satan dares God to test Abraham.[31] Auerbach called the Abraham and Isaac story "one of the most famous examples of realistic figural interpretation" and gave it extended analysis in "Odysseus's Scar," the stunning inaugural chapter of *Mimesis*.[32] The sacrifice of Isaac, known in the Jewish tradition as the Akedah or Binding, lights up Shakespeare's wrestling with the Hebrew testament.

Before she can adopt the explicit mask and role of courage, Innogen must overcome the temptation to martyrdom. The thought of Posthumus's own psychic pain upon recognizing his error ("I grieve myself / To think . . . how thy memory / Will then be panged by me") quickens rather than retards her desire for death: "The lamb entreats the butcher. Where's thy knife?" There are echoes here of Antonio in *The Merchant of Venice*, and within and behind Antonio, of Abraham and Isaac.[33] Like Antonio de-

30. Arbery, "Displaced Nativity," 160.

31. Berman, *The Akedah*, 74–75.

32. Auerbach, *Selected Essays*, 84; *Mimesis*, 8–16.

33. On Abraham and Isaac in *Merchant of Venice*, see, e.g., Jackson, *Shakespeare and Abraham*, and Kietzman, "Performing Biblical Stories in *Titus Andronicus* and *The Mer-*

siring that Bassanio witness his execution, Innogen, imagining Posthumus's regret at her death, briefly samples masochism's melancholic cocktail of narcissism, fantasy, and violence.[34] What an anger-prompted courage had delivered in one moment—a sense of agency and moral worth rooted in humanist virtue—is threatened in the next by a *Schadenfreude* that enters under the cover of religious sentiment. To call Pisanio her "butcher" is both to discredit and to brutalize the end she wishes upon herself; the same word appears in Brutus's desire to script the conspirators as "sacrificers, but not butchers" in *Julius Caesar* (2.1.166).[35] The appearance of "butcher" in Innogen's request reveals the retributive edge of her death wish. It is an inherently "posthumous" fantasy whose special satisfactions—its rebounding "pang"—require that she die in order to inflict the most harm on her husband. The same anger that fuels her sense of self-worth also threatens not only to destroy her physical being but also to disable her subjective gains.

In *Merchant*, the always canny Portia recognizes Antonio's desire for martyrdom for what it is: a passive-aggressive bid to undermine her marriage. Her task in the trial scene, as Harry Berger Jr. has argued, is not to overcome Shylock so much as to vanquish Antonio, by denying him his martyrdom and thus derailing his emotional usury.[36] Aryeh Botwinick has interpreted *Merchant*'s trial scene as an interrupted Akedah, in which Antonio's absolutist Christological fantasies are ultimately stymied by Portia's Jewish administration of equity:

---

chant of Venice." Kietzman also addresses Jacob's struggle with the angel as a proof text for *Merchant*. On this theme, see also Tracy McNulty, *Wrestling with the Angel*.

34. On melancholy and masochism in *The Merchant of Venice*, see Daniel, *The Melancholy Assemblage*, 104–19.

35. *Julius Caesar* cited from the *Riverside Shakespeare*. In James Maxwell's quasi-dramatic commentary on the life of Abraham from 1611, he imagines a less obedient patriarch *not* posing the following question to God: "must I, and none other but I be the butcher of [my son's] body, the spiller of his blood, and the burner of his bones?" (*Mirrour*, 8).

36. Berger, *A Fury in the Words*, 59–65.

> The ultimate visual symbol for the Judaization of Christianity in *The Merchant of Venice* is the binding of Antonio, which recapitulates the binding of Isaac in the Hebrew scriptures and the crucifixion of Jesus in the Christian scriptures. Under Shakespeare's auspices, this time around the Christians do it "right." The life of the bound person is spared. He is not crucified. It this Jewish revitalization of Christianity that makes modernity possible.[37]

Whereas classic typological readings of *The Merchant of Venice*, whether celebrated (Lewalski) or condemned (Adelman), see the play as inexorably replacing Judaism with Christianity, Botwinick argues for a different kind of settlement: by incorporating Jewish persons (Jessica and Shylock) along with Hebrew legal, economic, and exegetical instruments into a rapidly modernizing Venice, the play announces the "Enlightenment dream and project" of a "Judaically softened and modulated Christianity, as the state religion that even a Jew can live with."[38] When Jews become Christians, Botwinick argues, Christian institutions become just a little bit Jewish. Choosing *akedah* (suspended sacrifice) over crucifixion (achieved sacrifice) allows the particular easements harbored by the Jewish moment to liberalize and secularize the Christian playing field. These Jewish resources include an unrepresentable God whose distance permits human affairs to unfold; a pragmatic legal order based on contract and covenant; an adaptive exegesis; and a willingness to settle for substitutes.

Whereas *Merchant* fixates on the posture of binding and cutting, *Cymbeline*, in keeping with romance meandering, revisits the topography of the Akedah, including the journey from home accompanied by beasts (the ass in Genesis, the horses in *Cymbeline*) and the arrival at a mountain where a murder is supposed to take place, but doesn't.[39] Like Abraham, Pisanio travels bur-

37. Botwinick, "Shakespeare in Advance of Hobbes," 155.

38. Ibid., 158.

39. Here as in Genesis, the place of averted sacrifice appears to be a mountain; thus we later learn that Pisanio showed her Milford "from the mountain-top" (3.6.4). It is worth noting Shakespeare's divergence from Boccaccio, whose far more desultory

dened with knowledge while Innogen, like Isaac, enters innocent of their errand. In the Torah the pair is accompanied by two servants, identified by the rabbis with the steward Eliezer ("God's Help") and Isaac's half brother Ishmael.[40] In *Cymbeline* the two travel alone: Pisanio combines aspects of Abraham—a father figure tasked with his master's bitter order to destroy a young person—and Eliezer, the patriarch's household manager and representative. Posthumus's letter to Pisanio, like God's command to Abraham, frames the order as a test of his servant's faith, delegated to represent a distant power: "That part thou, Pisanio, must act for me, if thy faith be not tainted with that breach of hers" (3.4.25–26). Like Isaac in some retellings and like Antonio in *The Merchant of Venice*, Innogen urges Pisanio to complete the deed: "Do thou thy master's bidding. When thou seest him, / A little witness my obedience" (3.4.65–67). Choosing Isaac over Jesus, type over fulfillment, she is ultimately able to exit the sacrificial scenario, "almost / A man already" (3.4.167–68).

The symbol of suspended sacrifice in *Cymbeline* is the bloody cloth, which stands in for the ram in the thicket in the Akedah. Mary Jo Kietzman glosses the ram as "a figure for [Abraham] himself and all he offered up in suffering the ordeal, while trusting God to provide a substitute."[41] As in the Pyramus and Thisbe story, the blood itself likely comes from some animal, and thus suggests the vital link among sacrificial protocols. In some accounts of the Akedah, Isaac is lightly wounded by Abraham's overzealous blade; either scarred (at the neck) or limping (from a wound near the groin), he disappears into a therapeutic seclusion until his marriage with Rebecca, a union brokered by the same steward Eliezer who had waited at the base of the mountain for father and son to

---

retainer chooses "a very deep ravine, a lonely spot with precipitous crags and trees all around" as "the ideal place" to carry out his master's command (*The Decameron*, 170). The mountain may also be lonely, but its exposed character makes it the appropriate site for an act that takes on a public character.

40. Rashi identifies the two servants with Eliezer and Ishmael (*Chumash with Rashi's Commentary*, 94).

41. Kietzman, "Performing Biblical Stories," 11.

return.[42] In *Cymbeline*, the bloody cloth and Innogen's subsequent sickness signify the creaturely continuum among physical birth, its replay as action, and postpartum healing.[43]

As many critics have noted, Innogen responds to Posthumus's slanderous letters in markedly religious terms: "The scriptures of the loyal Leonatus, / All turned to heresy?" (3.4.81–82). "Heresy" is a fighting word, the exorbitance of the accusation suggesting the play's irenic desire to resolve schism in a covenantal settlement that might honor the different sources and itineraries of the sacrificial scene.[44] When the spouses restore faith at the end of the play, their passage through separation and divorce as well as attempted murder and resisted martyrdom will have stretched their faith into a new, more resilient *religio*. This new binding honors courage as well as suffering, doubt and anger as well as love and trust, and Isaac unbound as well as Christ crucified. Innogen's dark consciousness and typological being is hedged about by images of sacrifice and suicide (Lucrece, Philomel, and Juliet as well as Jesus and his saints), and it is one task of the play to move her through and beyond those scenarios toward a fidelity that affirms life and overcomes schism.

In section 3 of "Figura," Auerbach lays out the complex contribution of Paul to the drama of European literature. Paul, he argues, developed biblical typology out of the techniques of prophetic Judaism in order to wage a polemic against Jewish Christians, installing an element of anti-Judaism into figural interpretation.[45] In a second, later battle, however, between the radically

42. Spiegel, *The Last Trial*, 7.

43. On the primal link between the Akedah and circumcision, see Berman, *The Akedah*, 178. The circumcision of Isaac is one of the scenes featured in the Hampton Court tapestry cycle on the life of Abraham acquired by Henry VIII; I analyze the image's implications for dwelling as well as sovereignty in "Soft *Res Publica*."

44. In the assessment of Thomas Betteridge, Shakespeare's effort in the late plays "to rescue devotional words such as 'grace' and 'forgiveness' from confessional contamination is radical and expansive, not containing and moderate" ("Writing Faithfully in a Post-Confessional World," 228).

45. Auerbach writes, "What for him had been a book of the Law and of the history of Israel was now transformed into a single great promise, the prehistory of Christ. . . .

Pauline Marcionites, who wanted to purge Christianity of the Old Testament, and those church fathers who wanted to preserve the historical authority of Israel, Paul ended up ensuring a place for the Old Testament in the ongoing development of Western historical consciousness. Paul is thus Janus-faced with respect to the Jews, canonizing both Jewish and anti-Jewish attitudes at the heart of Western historical thought. This Pauline spiral of aversion and inclusion as well as anticipation and recollection cuts through the layered landscape of *Cymbeline*. The play's easy, open syncretism is Hellenistic. The play's typological attitude toward the Law, in the figure of the jealous and vengeful Posthumus, is incipiently anti-Jewish (and anti-Catholic).[46] The tapping of Old Testament figures such as Abraham, Isaac, and Job passes largely unmarked, in the manner of the medieval cycles, and speaks to a preconfessional Christianity nested in a Judeo-Christian matrix. Finally, *Cymbeline*'s juxtaposition of modern Europe with ancient Rome implies the heightened historical consciousness of the Reformation. Innogen is ultimately faithful to a Christian unity that embraces the Catholic present and past in its inclusive pax. The Hebrew proof text binds nativity and natality within a messianic space that reveals its striation by multiple inputs and uncertain outcomes. These Abrahamic undercurrents never crest into conscious allusion, but they do belong to the larger world of Shakespearean drama, especially the Venetian plays, which share with *Cymbeline* the tension between sacrifice and murder, the courage of mixed marriage, the specter of a God whose name is Jealous, and the bloody signatures shared by marital, natal, and national covenants.[47] The elastic *religio/Akedah* of the late plays is

---

This was how Paul, in whom the practical and the political combined in exemplary fashion with a faith endowed with a high level of poetic creativity, managed to transform the Jewish idea of the resurrection of Moses in the Messiah into a system of historically real prophesy" (94–95).

46. Lila Geller associates Posthumus with "the Old Law": "Like the Old Testament covenant of works, valuable and necessary in itself, but obsolete without the addition of faith, Posthumus is of a line now dead" ("*Cymbeline* and Covenant Theology," 248, 249). In this account, "Posthumus" means "Old Testament."

47. I address these motifs in *Citizen-Saints*.

generous enough to incorporate humanist *virtù* and to take stock of Hebrew debts and affinities, those "strains . . . more rare" that animate both Arendt's politics and Auerbach's *Weltliteratur*. If James's irenic policies provide an immediate occasion for these explorations, topical incitement allowed Shakespeare to touch upon existential themes that endow the play with its unexpected reach and heft.[48]

Furnitura

In the Welsh scenes, the courage evinced by Innogen's exit from the sheltered dwelling of the court is matched by the ingenuity and care with which she enters into new, more provisional and itinerant conditions of dwelling. Perhaps more than in any other Shakespeare play, furniture plays midwife to action in *Cymbeline*. Innogen's image-rich bedchamber resembles that of Bess of Hardwick, who used soft goods to create what Agnès Lafont calls a "mythological house" with the cult of Diana at its center.[49] Susan Frye describes Innogen's textile collection as a means for her to "express her identity and exercise her agency,"[50] techniques of self-fashioning that Innogen shares with real-life female curator-patronesses such as Bess of Hardwick, Elizabeth Tudor, and Mary Stuart. In act 2, Innogen's furniture approximates Gibson's definition of affordances as "value-rich rich ecological objects," whose real and imagined presence takes shape in the feedback loops that connect domestic function, iconographic meaning, social and somatic routine, and the production of mood and atmosphere. In act 3, affordances float free from designed objects by inhering in routines such as bedtime, housekeeping, and hospitality, arts of dwelling that Innogen carries with her

48. Frances Yates, *Shakespeare's Last Plays*.

49. Lafont, "Political Uses of Erotic Power," 52. On Innogen's objects, see especially Simmonds, *Myth, Emblem and Music*; R. Olson, "Before the Arras," 45–64, an essay that helpfully considers the role of actual hangings on stage; and Susan Frye, *Pens and Needles*.

50. Frye, *Pens and Needles*, xix.

into the Welsh mountainside. The play's work with affordances exploits the affinities between manufactured things and ecological *données* and employs theater as that experimental space where those affinities are brought forward for phenomenological and ethical consideration.

We tend to associate "furniture" with the mute, brute existence of chairs, tables, and couches, but its early meanings were more dynamic and agential. The first definition of "furniture" given in the *OED* is "the action of furnishing; the action of fitting out or equipping." Its Germanic roots include *vrümmen*, "to further, promote, accomplish, supply," and *frum-*, meaning forward.[51] Furniture carries a directionality and momentum, a tendency or tendentiousness, that my coinage *furnitura* is designed to highlight, on the model of *figura* and *creatura*. Through both its actions with objects and its language about environments, theater bids furniture to manifest its dynamism. Hamlet's description of funeral baked meats "furnish[ing] forth" the wedding table (1.2.180–81) suggests the way in which ceremonial foods make their own appearance as actors on the festive boards, shaping mood and cuing behavior. In *As You Like It*, to be "furnished like a hunter" (3.2.245) is to be equipped or provisioned for the taskscape of the forest. Hunting requires horses, and horses require furniture: saddles, spurs, and bridles are sensitive communication devices that support the rider's interaction with the animal.[52] And in *Cymbeline*, Giacomo praises Innogen's beauty as "out of door most rich" and then wonders if she is "*furnished* with a mind" equally rare (1.6.15–16). The architectural metaphor supplies the mind as the interior's furnishing, taken not as passive decor but as virtuous equipment; these words are delivered, moreover, in an architectural space—the theater—in which every doorway, floorboard, stool, and chair is tested for its action cues and symbolizing potential.

Innogen's bedroom, entered in act 2, scene 2 and then recalled

51. "furniture, n.," *OED Online* March 2016.

52. E.g., *All's Well*: "I'ld give bay Curtal and his furniture" (2.3.59).

through ekphrasis in act 2, scene 4, may be the most richly furnished chamber in all of Shakespeare. Whereas the recollection in Rome highlights the semiotic richness of the room's furnishings, the first scene is more concerned with their affordances. Editors have deduced from the uneven distribution of detail between the two scenes that little elaborate furnishing would have actually appeared on stage. Instead, Giacomo uses the resources of dramatic poetry to decorate Innogen's chamber retroactively, the bareness of the stage facilitating the loading of theater's special cognitive space with luxury goods.[53] Among the actions that bedchambers supported, from female conversation, hygiene, prayer, and study to birth, death, child-rearing, and conjugal duty, this scene revolves around the ritual of bedtime as somatic state and social process.[54] Sleep, as we saw in *Macbeth*, orchestrates an assemblage of home furnishings and linguistic ritual (here, bedtime reading followed by a brief prayer) that loosen consciousness and dissolve the sleeping subject into her soft surrounds.[55] In Renaissance softscapes, rich fabrics not only draped the bed to create a room within the room, but also warmed the walls, absorbed sound, and boosted ambient illumination through metallic threads. Emphasizing ambience, Giacomo's inventory is replete with objects designed to adjust sound, light, and temperature: windows, canopies, tapestries, sheets, candle, andirons, and fireplace all contribute to the room's climate, as do the rushes that Giacomo draws into our auditory consciousness from the story of Lucrece: "Our Tarquin thus / Did softly press the rushes ere he wakened / The chastity he wounded" (2.2.12–14). In an ambient

53. Rebecca Olson associates "arras" with physical properties tapped for their theatrical affordances of revealing and concealing, while "tapestry" is more often the occasion for mythographic description and the display of offstage wealth ("Before the Arras," 52). Leonard Barkan notes that the second scene "stages the drama of cultural absence and poetic recuperation in the spaces that separate picture from word and Italy from England" ("Making Pictures Speak," 344).

54. On women's bedchambers as scenes for politics, see Dolan, "Gender and the 'Lost' Spaces of Catholicism." See also Ziegler, "My Lady's Chamber."

55. On sleep and romance from a phenomenological point of view, see Sullivan, *Sleep, Romance and Human Embodiment.*

mapping of *mulier* as "tender air," Giacomo builds the impression of atmosphere when he declares, "'Tis her breathing that / Perfumes the chamber thus" (2.2.18–19). Giacomo's comparison of her eyelids to canopied windows (2.2.21–22), Warren notes, refers to wooden shutters with curtains drawn; the metaphor uses light technologies in order to melt Innogen's self-abandonment into the dusky quiet of the room. The Cleopatra tapestry threatens to dissolve completely into mood and setting: "it was hanged / With tapestry of silk and silver; the story / Proud Cleopatra when she met her Roman, / And Cydnus swelled above the banks, or for / The press of boats or pride" (2.4.68–72).[56] Revisiting a similar set of environmental exchanges in *Antony and Cleopatra*, the argentine weaving becomes one with the waters of the Cydnus it depicts, each subject to billowing flow; the poetry itself is silky with sibilants.

Giacomo's inventory builds a contexture of things, surfaces, and routines that sustain sleep as a bodily, cognitive, and environmental process. The Folio stage direction reads, "Enter Innogen, in her Bed, and a Lady"; the serving woman, embodying the overlap between theatrical and domestic labor, belongs to a world in which dressing and undressing required assistance.[57] Warren suggests that the bed would have been "pushed out" or "put forth" from the discovery space (128); Shakespeare's dramaturgy pulls room-like furniture out of a furniture-like room, allowing fictive and theatrical spaces to infuse each other. When Innogen puts down her book with the declaration that "Sleep hath seized me wholly," she imagines slumber not as an internal state but as an external force that takes her up in its cradling embrace (2.2.7).

56. Scholars find parallels between Innogen and Cleopatra, but Shakespeare seems attracted rather to the affective affordances of fabric in its shimmering, billowing capacities. The same affordances interest him in the parallel scene in *Antony and Cleopatra*, as I note in "Hospitality," 438, 440; and as Colby Gordon notes in his account of the scene in "Shakespearean Futurity."

57. On assisted undressing and its implications for Renaissance theater and life, see Stallybrass, "The Mystery of Walking," 574.

Giacomo remarks, "How bravely thou becom'st thy bed" (2.2.15): in sleeping we indeed "become our beds," merging with our nocturnal environment.

For Arendt, the most distinctive feature of objects is their durability, "which gives the things of the world their relative independence from men who produced and used them, their 'objectivity' which makes them withstand, 'stand against' and endure, at least for a time, the voracious needs and wants of their living makers and users."[58] Arendt contrasts the objects made by human work to more transient products for consumption such as foodstuffs. Although the chair "will again become wood, and the wood will decay and return to the soil" if not properly taken care of, the chair does not reenter the ecosystem with the same inevitable immediacy as our daily bread. The very practices of care that ensure the longevity of the chair include its eventual replacement by another chair in a maintenance schedule that identifies the durability of a world with something more than the lifespan of its contents. Objects that receive care and upkeep in a pattern that acknowledges mutual dependencies give "the human artifice the stability and solidity without which it could not be relied upon to house the unstable and mortal creature which is man."[59] In Roman law, the curator is the guardian of the estate and physical well-being of his charge. Curation, unlike ownership, attributes something like rights to objects: the right to be cleaned and repaired, the right not to be thrown away. Consumerism treats durable objects like disposable comestibles: "we must consume, devour, as it were, our houses and furniture and cars as though they were the 'good things' of nature which spoil uselessly if they are not drawn swiftly into the never-ending cycle of man's metabolism with nature."[60] Innogen's chamber resembles a museum or temple, where objects of beauty are removed from use,

58. Arendt, *Human Condition*, 137.
59. Ibid., 136.
60. Ibid., 126.

offering "its space of display to those things whose essence it is to appear and be beautiful."[61] Growing up in such a space, Innogen becomes its curator, "trusted to tend and take care of a world of appearances whose criterion is beauty."[62]

The world of things composes the environment for action; care for the world, in the form of physical cultivation and housekeeping as well as written inventories and testaments, is thus care for the conditions of action.[63] Bonnie Honig links the world-building capacities of things in Arendt to Winnicott's transitional objects, embodied by soft goods like the teddy bear and the security blanket: "the child's blanket has a stubborn existence and this is how the child learns non-mastery: there is a world that can survive her rage and also her love."[64] Security blankets and teddy bears allow the child to move from nativity as the sheer fact of birth to natality as the possibility for action. Honig identifies the kind of permanence that children borrow from objects with the virtue of resilience: "in loving them, we acquire some of that resilience. It rubs off on us, as it were.[65] When Arendt speaks of the world of things as "withstanding" and "enduring," her language reveals resilience as a virtue sustained by the sharing of services and attributes among people and their possessions in what Winnicott calls "the holding environment" in which we come to know objects and apprehend their permanence.[66]

Innogen's bedchamber may function as such a "holding environment." We know that she reads in this room, and that her reading material is continuous with the mythographic and

61. Arendt, "The Crisis in Culture," 218. What makes Innogen's chamber different from a museum is its largely private character, though it would have a place for the gathering of women.

62. Ibid., 219.

63. In Honig's gloss, "Things provide us a world in which to move and they provide the friction of finitude that limits or thwarts but also drives human care for the world" ("Arendt's Object-Relations," 310).

64. Honig, "Resilience," 3.

65. Ibid.

66. Honig citing Winnicott, "Arendt's Object-Relations," 309.

iconographic displays of eros, chastity, and power depicted in her objets d'art. Her book zones the bedchamber as a *studiolo*, like the humanist retreat of Isabella d'Este.[67] Her codex affords multiple reading sessions, since she has turned down the leaf "Where Philomel gave up" (2.2.45–46): the *Metamorphoses'* stories of endless change themselves obtain a certain consistency thanks to the reliability and durability of printing and book binding. "A poem," writes Arendt, "is less a thing than any other work of art," yet it can be "written down and transformed into a tangible thing among things"; a book resting on a bedside table asserts its character as such a thing.[68] An edifice for edification, this meaning-padded, climate-controlled bedchamber externalizes Innogen's fears and imaginings as well as her academic understanding of virtue. It is a place to think with, not only a memory palace for Giacomo, but also a princess diary for the young woman who retreats to this humanist environs for study and repose. Object lessons abound: the cupid andirons, "each on one foot standing, nicely / Depending on their brands" (2.4.88–91), figure the propping of human actions on the world of things.[69] Standing pertly on one leg, the cupids maintain their balance by leaning on their torches, which in turn only do their illuminating work by virtue of their human holders. (Recall Romeo as torchbearer in chapter 1.) Cradling the burning logs, this fireplace furniture both aerates and holds back the fire in the hearth, guarding the limen between inferno and *Gemütlichkeit*. The Queen had earlier belittled Pisanio for being a "depender on a thing that leans" (1.5.58); embracing such forms of dependency is one way of understanding the play's environments of action, what Randall Martin calls the play's "eco-cosmopolitanism."[70] The appliances'

67. On Isabella d'Este as art collector, especially of smaller decorative items, see Juan, "The Court Lady's Dilemma." On reading and writing in bed in medieval romance, see also Mary Carruthers, "Mystery of the Bed Chamber."

68. Arendt, *The Human Condition*, 170.

69. Ziegler associates the andirons with "the loyalty of marriage" (82).

70. Martin, *Shakespeare and Ecology*, 94.

boyish bodies aglow with flickering firelight communicate permanence in change and a posture of propping in a manner that affirms Innogen's upcoming experiments with fidelity.[71]

When she falls asleep, this room remains, reassuringly weighted with its sculpted objects and storied surfaces, "because remembrance and the gift of recollection, from which all desire for imperishability springs, need tangible things to remind them, lest they perish themselves."[72] Innogen's bedtime prayer acknowledges the risk of sleep: "To your protection I commend me, gods. / From fairies and the tempters of the night / Guard me beseech ye" (2.2.8–10).[73] Winnicott associates "an infant's babbling and the way in which an older child goes over a repertory of songs and tunes while preparing for sleep" with the comfort of transitional objects.[74] The room itself is a kind of prayer, its magnificent clutter, textile membranes, and cherubic ceiling shored up against bad dreams, nocturnal invaders, and the dissolution of the baseless fabric of the world itself. Giacomo's action belies her prayer by turning the precious objects of her world into evidence against her chastity. As he prepares to remove her bracelet, Giacomo delivers his own antiprayer: "O sleep, thou ape of death, lie dull upon her, / And be her sense but as a monument / Thus in a chapel lying" (2.2.31–33). Under his calculating gaze, the soft architecture of the bed hardens into the stony architecture of a funerary monument, pure silhouette without hope of shelter. If sleep "lies dull upon her," this is because palace life has accustomed her to a *heavy* sleep, a repose knitted out of textiles, devices, images, texts, and servants. The very softness of the furnishings contributes to a kind of hardness: not a moral

71. The "golden cherubins" that fret the ceiling and are introduced just before the andirons are also infantile in aspect (2.4.88).

72. Arendt, *The Human Condition*, 170.

73. Her prayer, Warren notes, echoes "the Third Collect for Evening Prayer in *The Book of Common Prayer* (1559): 'defend us from all perils and dangers of this night'" (*Cymbeline*, 129n). For an evocative reading of the "porous self" implied by evening prayer in response to "material and spiritual dangers," see Oldridge, "Something of the Night."

74. Winnicott, *Playing and Reality*, 3.

hardness surely, but a thickness and naïveté—the untested "innocence" of her name—that accompanies being enclosed in a room such as this.

Bonnie Lander speaks of Innogen's entrapment by "static and superficial images" that ultimately give way to more ironic and supple models of subjectivity, fidelity, and action.[75] The very splendor of Innogen's surrounds, participating in the soft power of courtly ideology, contributes to her initial willingness to give credence to Giacomo's misdirections. Take, for example, the image of Diana in the chimney piece, a favored emblem of female virtue and power for royal women of the Renaissance, from Diane de Poitiers to Bess of Hardwick.[76] Her own identification with Diana comes with the courtly territory, while the audience easily supplies Giacomo as Actaeon, voyeuristically invading the sanctuary of the virgin goddess. In her interview with Giacomo, however, Innogen inadvertently reveals her kinship with Actaeon. When she begs Giacomo to explain his lewd insinuations, "You do seem to know / Something of me, or what concerns me. Pray you . . . discover to me / What both you spur and stop" (1.6.93–99), Innogen plays Othello to Giacomo's Iago. Shocked by her own willingness to entertain a corrupted image of Posthumus, she then too quickly accepts Giacomo's hyperbolic praise of her husband as a "descended god" (1.6.169) and rashly agrees to house his trunk in her room. Giacomo praises her "great judgement / In the election of a sir so rare" (1.6.174–75), but judgment is precisely what innocent Innogen lacks. Or rather, we watch her beginning to exercise judgment, using the art in her room as a guide, but her discretion is hampered by received meanings and the brittle tyranny of good manners. It is not that she has the wrong pictures, books, or andirons in her room, but rather that learning how to apply them will take a different kind of education.

If home decor both educates and constrains the heroine as moral agent, furniture aids what Giacomo calls his "design"

75. Lander, "Personhood," 177.

76. Agnès Lafont, "Political Uses of Erotic Power."

(2.2.23).[77] Considered dramaturgically, the most affordance-rich object in the scene is the trunk. Likely placed over the trapdoor, the trunk sucks the hidden extensions of theatrical space into its own capacities for hiding, peering, and disclosing.[78] Not unlike the cupids with their andirons or Romeo with his torch and his crowbar, Giacomo forms a composite with the trunk, becoming a veritable "Jack in the box," complete with a spring: "To th' trunk again, and shut the spring of it" (2.2.47).[79] The chest is also a *camera* for viewing; in the BBC film of 1982, Robert Lindsay's Giacomo isolates and manipulates this peephole function by using Innogen's purloined bracelet as a viewing device through which he spies and frames her telltale mole.[80] Colby Gordon has compared Giacomo's trunk to Italian wedding *cassoni*, which, filled with soft goods, were carried from the bride's home to her husband's house as part of the marriage procession; they were often painted with stories related to love and marriage, including scenes from Boccaccio.[81] Disassembled from their original casing and hung on museum walls, *cassone* paintings are now encountered as iconographic exercises, yet they originally belonged to action-nourishing Renaissance *furnitura* as a composite of affordances,

77. Colby Gordon writes of his use of the word, "The multiple, labile definitions of disegno are layered and blended in Jachimo's sketch, which mobilizes the full range of meanings attributed to design: a plastic art, a rough schematic of a location, a graphic representation, a narrative, a surface-level embellishment, and a long term plan" ("Shakespeare's Landscape Futures," 43).

78. Warren notes that the trunk may have been "pushed up through the trap" at the same time as the bed is put forth from the discovery space; in both cases, furniture relates dynamically to the architecture of the stage.

79. The *OED* dates the toy to 1702, but the expression, as "the name for a sharper or cheat," to 1570. The phrase was also used contemptuously of the consecrated host. Antonia Fraser notes that this typically Victorian toy has a sixteenth-century name (*A History of Toys*, 159).

80. *Cymbeline*, dir. Elijah Moshinsky (1982).

81. Katherine Duncan-Jones suggests that Shakespeare may have seen *cassone* paintings at the estates of either Southampton or Burghley. *Shakespeare: An Ungentle Life*, 89. On *cassoni* as part of civic marriage ritual, see Bruccia Witthoft, "Marriage Rituals and Marriage Chests." Warren reproduces a *cassone* panel illustrating *Decameron* 2.9, the source of *Cymbeline* (29).

meanings, and routines.[82] As objects designed for transport and transmission, chests contributed to the kind of resilient world-building that Arendt sees as the ultimate affordance of objects.

Giacomo's entry out of the trunk dramatizes the natal character of all theatrical entrances, as actors pass from the choric backstage into the region of individuating publicity. This is, moreover, the scene in *Cymbeline* in which nativity in its biblical sense is perhaps most tangible. In their interview, Giacomo had praised Innogen in an abbreviated *Ave Maria* ("Blessèd live you long, / A lady to the worthiest sir" [1.6.159–60]), a reference carried into his exorbitant praise of Posthumus as a "descended god" (1.6.169). Arbery analyzes the bedroom scene as an "inverted Annunciation," in which Giacomo is a bad angel who spirits himself into the private room of a blessed *mulier* in order to perform a chaste rape.[83] Overshadowed by advent, Innogen's richly furnished bedroom becomes the Virgin's private quarters, as depicted in Netherlandish genre paintings such as the Merode Altarpiece, with its candle, books, screened casements, carved mantelpiece, and fire screen; or the many paintings in which the Annunciate appears reading scripture beside a curtained bed; or in genre scenes and birth trays depicting Mary's own nativity in the house of her parents Anne and Joachim.[84] Such scenes gather a world of *furnitura* along with human and angelic messengers as witnesses and midwives supporting the fact, act, and promise of birth.

82. Catherine Richardson writes of chests in the lives of both women and men that they embodied "domestic objects' perceived ability to carry and transfer identity" across locations and generations. *Domestic Life and Domestic Tragedy*, 72–73.

83. Arbery, "Displaced Nativity," 163–64.

84. The Merode Altarpiece (attributed to Robert Campin or Master of Flemalle, ca. 1425, Metropolitan Museum of Art, Cloisters Museum), has been most famously interpreted by Erwin Panofsky, *Early Netherlandish Painting*, 173–77. For Mary in her bedroom, see, e.g., Rogier van der Weyden's Louvre *Annunciation*, which includes a book, bed, hearth, candelabra, window shutters, and luxurious textiles. Another Annunciation by van der Weyden at the Metropolitan features a window seat/chest. For the birth of the Virgin, see the richly detailed interior by Vittore Carpaccio, ca. 1505–6, Accademia Carrara.

Innogen admits the chest into her room because Giacomo presents Posthumus and himself as "partners in business." She eagerly agrees to house the trunk: "Willingly, / And pawn mine honour for their safety; since / My lord hath interest in them, I will keep them / In my bedchamber" (1.6.193–96). She accepts the chest as a proxy for her husband's international business connections as well as his exilic precarity. Although Innogen's willingness to house this Trojan horse is an error in judgment (she is indeed "pawning her honour"), allowing this most mobile of movables into her chamber eventually leads to her own exit from the thickness of things, and thus into a new kind of environmental education. The trunk harbors action possibilities that include the immediately physical (a portable place for storing plate and hiding persons), the economic-transactional (the favor of a hostess, a gift for an emperor, the hollow trick of the bad guest), the dramaturgical-architectural (a room within a room that bears alternative routes of entry and exit into the theatrical scene), and the symbolic and typological (as womb, tomb, ark, and hell).

Modern productions of *Cymbeline* often deploy the trunk in as many ways as possible in order to dramatize the affordance character of all objects put to work on stage.[85] In the semiotic approach to stage props, a chair is always also a representation of a chair. In an affordance orientation, citational self-doubling is less interesting than the multiple avenues for action that objects make available, what Teemu Paavolainen calls the "field of potential affordances" carried by the material reality of the stage.[86] The implications are technical, and not only in a narrow sense, since actors' training in a range of physical and expressive traditions affect their approach to scenographic affordances. But the implications are also existential, since our relationship to things (possessive, dependent, beholden, entangled, mutual, agonistic, and so

85. E.g., Fiasco Theater's production of *Cymbeline*, 2011, discussed below, dir. Noah Brody and Ben Steinfeld; chest designed by Jacques Roy. http://www.fiascotheater.com/cymbeline/, accessed July 22, 2017.

86. Paavolainen, *Theatre/Ecology/Cognition*, 33–37. On personal knowledge, see Michael Polanyi, *Personal Knowledge*.

on) shapes our response to other persons and our sense of world. Glossing Arendt, Honig writes, "We vest Things with meaning, but Things also do the same for us: they anchor, limit, and orient us."[87] Theater investigates both dimensions in the glamour and friction of their exchange.

Resilience and Fidelity

Innogen's palace furnishings both support and constrain her birth into action. Her existence among a profusion of things endows her with a more durable sense of world than that met, say, by the orphan Posthumus, who, having been made "of [the king's] bedchamber" (1.1.42), enjoyed the intimacies of courtly life to the extent of jeopardizing his own uncertain place in that world. Then as now, social position helps determine whether the agent learns permanence or precarity from the objects he handles. When Innogen slips away from the court, she leaves her furnishings behind but brings her routines of living with her, building what modern observers might call her resilience. Resilience gained currency in systems ecology in the 1970s, where it referred to the ability of environments to absorb trauma; since 2000, it has become a liberal and neoliberal buzzword for the capacity of individuals, communities, and locales to withstand shocks ranging from tsunami, recession, and terror to the displacements of gentrification and the insecurity of just-in-time labor practices. Countering the term's neoliberal repurposing, Honig derives resilience as a specifically democratic virtue from the forms of permanence and durability passed between things and persons in Arendt and Winnicott.[88] In his reading of *Cymbeline*, Randall Martin returns the term to its ecological origins in order to discern the romances

87. Honig, "Arendt's Object-Relations," 310.

88. Honig writes, "Winnicott says it is through object use and play that we come to apprehend the idea of worldly permanence and come to acquire some of it ourselves. In his account of object relations, resilience is a key trait of both objects and the subjects who use them" ("Laws of the Sabbath," 471). On the recent history of resilience, see Walker and Cooper, "Genealogies of Resilience," 145.

as modeling biodiversity.[89] Resilience contributes to dwelling by laying out a path among environmental, object-oriented, and civic-humanist domains. In *Cymbeline*, resilience helps account for the repurposing of courage from its classical political meaning, as exit from *oikos*, to its implications for dwelling under duress. In the wilderness, courage requires an attitude of ingenious and respectful response to a demanding taskscape that harbors its own adaptive ratios and immunological feints. The alternative *oikos* established in such a setting both opposes the august household of the court and reinstitutes its rhythms in order to sustain techniques of permanence. The play's movement from the palace to the countryside not only shifts focus from designed things to geological formations—what Gibson calls "the furniture of the earth"—but also from affordances as inhering primarily in objects to affordances as part of an "intentional repertoire" composed of human habit and enskillment.[90]

Innogen enters act 3, scene 6, delivering a roving speech that expresses her own wavering state in response to a beckoning environment given dramaturgical reality by her words and gestures:

> I see a man's life is a tedious one.
> I have tired myself, and for two nights together
> Have made the ground my bed. I should be sick,
> But that my resolution helps me. Milford,
> When from the mountain-top Pisanio showed thee,
> Thou was within a ken. O Jove, I think
> Foundations fly the wretched—such I mean,
> Where they should be relieved. Two beggars told me
> I could not miss my way. Will poor folks lie,
> That have afflictions on them, knowing 'tis

89. Randall Martin applies ecological resilience to the world of the romances, which "create analogies for resilience-building biodiversity, and therefore help audiences imagine appropriate social and cultural responses to today's environmental dilemmas" (*Shakespeare and Ecology*, 191).

90. Paavolainen, "From Props to Affordances," citing Harry Heft, 33. Philosopher John Sanders defines affordances as "analytical units of embodiment" in which the agent's environment encompasses "the entire universe of potential action" implied by her skills, habits, and intentions ("Affordances," 135).

> A punishment or trial? Yes; no wonder,
> When rich ones scarce tell true. To lapse in fullness
> Is sorer than to lie for need, and falsehood
> Is worse in kings than beggars. My dear lord,
> Thou are one o'th' false ones. Now I think on thee
> My hunger's gone, but even before I was
> At point to sink for food. But what is this?
> Here is a path to't. 'Tis some savage hold.
> I were best not call; I dare not call; yet famine,
> Ere clean it o'erthrow nature, makes it valiant.
> Plenty and peace breeds cowards, hardness ever
> Of hardiness is mother. Ho! What's here?
> If anything that's civil, speak; if savage,
> Take or lend. Ho! No answer? Then I'll enter.
> Best draw my sword; and if mine enemy
> But fear the sword like me, he'll scarcely look on't.
> Such a foe, good heavens! (3.6.1–27)

If every entry onto the stage hatches the birth of actor into character, character into action, and one setting into another, this entrance is natal in all these senses, as Innogen enters dressed as a boy, rezones the stage as cave-side clearing, and assumes the forms of virtue required by this new situation. Her first line, "I see a man's life is a tedious one," often earns a laugh in modern productions.[91] Although "tedious" can mean boring (e.g., "tedious homily of love" [*As You Like It*, 3.2.142]), the primary sense here is exhausting or wearying, as when the Player King in *Hamlet* wants to "beguile / The tedious day with sleep" (3.2.226–27). Indeed, sleep is very much on Innogen's mind, as she goes on to say: "I have tired myself, and for two nights together / Have made my ground my bed." The ground is more basic than the "furniture of the earth" in Gibson's sense, concerning not the convexities and concavities that articulate shelters and lookout points, but rather "the earth-air interface" itself, "the most important of all surfaces for terrestrial animals . . . the ground of their perception and

91. On the dramatic affordances of this line, see Lander, "Interpreting the Person," 183.

behavior . . . their surface of support."[92] To make the ground her bed is to take this fundamental support and reencounter it as *furnitura*, to pull out and acknowledge its most minimal capacities for dwelling. Perhaps like Hermia, she sought out some gentle incline ("Find you out a bed, / For I upon this bank will rest my head"), or like Lysander found some grassy softness ("One turf shall serve as pillow for us both"; 2.2.39–41). If so, she doesn't tell us, instead identifying the austerity of her circumstances with the hard flatness of the stage itself, which provides the "surface of support" for most theatrical work.

"A man's life" in this circumstance entails "leaving the household, originally in order to embark upon some adventure."[93] Yet her travails expose her to physical want and thus take on a creaturely valence: it is not only "a *man*'s life" but "a man's *life*" that she finds herself suddenly saddled with. Having left the protections of dwelling, she experiences the pressures to which dwelling responds and thus must draw on dwelling's arts with new urgency and ingenuity. We could call courage with respect to survival *resilience*, "that trait by which persons or systems manage to survive a test or even catastrophe."[94] The word itself does not appear in Innogen's speech (or anywhere in Shakespeare);[95] she speaks instead of the relationship between privation and stamina, first averring, "I should be sick, / But my resolution helps me," and then nominating "hardness" as the "mother" of "hardiness." The first formulation implies an agon between perseverance and creaturely challenge, while the second formulation attributes to hardship itself the ability to nurture moral character. "Hardiness," meaning both boldness and daring (*OED*, 1) and physical or mental endurance (*OED*, 3), occupies some of the same range as "resilience," including its extension to a variety of creatures.

92. Gibson, *Ecological Approach*, 16.

93. Arendt, *Human Condition*, 36.

94. Honig, "Resilience," 1.

95. The *OED* attributes the first use, in the sense of "the action or an act of rebounding or spring back; rebound, recoil," to Francis Bacon in 1626; the moral sense of robustness or adaptability doesn't come until 1857.

The link between hardiness and the hardness of the ground, moreover, has affordance implications for both mammalian life and life on stage. As Innogen walks across that stage seeking her way, her words and actions bring the setting into focus as a wilderness clearing by a cave: "But what is this? / Here is a path to't. 'Tis some savage hold." The short syntactical bursts perform way-finding as a peripatetic effort that orients the actor toward the layout and affordances of the setting.[96]

Finding the cave empty of people but provisioned with cold meat, Innogen proceeds to make herself at home. The scene recalls Odysseus in the cave of Polyphemus, helping himself to victuals while the owner tends his flocks; and Orlando in *As You Like It*, seeking sustenance in the forest and being willing to kill for it. A makeshift hospitality guides the interactions in this scene. Planning to pray, pay, and leave, she is also prepared to fight for her food if necessary ("Best draw my sword," she says, voicing another implicit stage direction). She shouts into the cave, "Ho! Who's here? / If anything that's civil, speak; if savage, / Take or lend." The sense of caution and genuine need distinguishes Fidele the uninvited guest from Innogen the overgracious hostess. This is hospitality not as the crown of civilization but as its primitive origin, a congeries of improvised maneuvers whose status as taking or lending—as expropriative or mutualistic (3.6.24)—depends on the response of the unknown host. The heroine adjusts *virtù* to *fortuna*, marshalling her own courage and ingenuity in response to available resources and the goodwill of strangers.

What settles into shape in the Welsh scenes is an impromptu form of dwelling in which persons unknown to each other establish living and working arrangements that allow them to coexist and even flourish. Both ritual and routine are instruments of resilience. By routine I mean the transfer of dwelling activi-

96. Randall Martin provides a helpful Gibsonian reading of the Welsh cave, with an emphasis on Belarius and the boys' adaptation to its features and rhythms (*Shakespeare and Ecology*, 206–7). Kevin Lynch defines wayfinding as "a consistent use and organization of definite sensory cues from the external environment" (*Image of the City*, 3).

ties from the heavily designed environment of the court to the rough-hewn furniture of the earth. Food and commensality run through these scenes as both the effortful product and the blessed reward of labor and hence a cornerstone of dwelling's arts, while routines of sleep continue to shape the play's main action. By ritual I mean the element of verbal and physical formalization that renders hospitality as both incipient theater and prototheology. Thus Innogen assures her hosts that she had not only planned to leave money for the food, but that she would also have "parted / With prayers for the provider" (3.6.50–51). Gratitude for *données* balanced by a sense of entitlement belongs to the comportment of resilience; in scenes of dearth and insecurity, mindful prayer inculcates respect for the network of dependencies that make survival possible. The cave family's ritualization of hunting and cooking—the "best woodman" is "master of the feast" while the others "play the cook and servant" (3.6.28–30)—transposes courtly hierarchy into the rustic setting while democratizing that hierarchy by making its offices transferrable.

Once Innogen finds herself in a situation of semistable routine, resilience expands to include the luxury of being sick. She has been nurse to others: "He cut our roots in characters, / And sauced our broths as Juno had been sick / And he her dieter" (4.2.51–53). Now she turns to care for herself. Her malaise is linked to the bloody cloth, which Susan Frye associates with "menstruous rags" and Desdemona's spotted linens.[97] Mixing miscarriage and menstrual distress with psychic scars and sexual *evidentia*, the bloody cloth indexes the painful birth of Innogen as she expresses anger, courts death, chooses courage, jumps genders, wanders the wilderness, and seeks rest and repair. Her sickness is a kind of Sabbath, a concerted exit from all that busy cave-keeping that readies her for future action. Thus the Queen's cordial puts Innogen to sleep, not to death. Later, when Arviragus discovers her corpse-like form, he first says that her "right cheek / [was] Reposing on a cushion" and then explains that their

97. Frye, *Pens and Needles*, 186.

guest was "o'th' floor./ His arms thus leagued, I thought he slept, and put / My clouted brogues from off my feet, whose rudeness / Answered my steps too loud." (4.2.213–16). Like Giacomo in the first scene, but for very different reasons, Arviragus does not want to wake her with the sounds of his steps. (The same motif is repeated in an even darker register at the end of the dagger speech in *Macbeth.*) What had been first called a "cushion" is very likely Innogen's own hands, "leagued" into a provisional support for her head in a curled-up position on the ground. "Becoming her bed" in a new and different sense, Innogen recreates the routine of sleeping using the plasticity and warmth of her own pliant limbs.

These redesigns of bedtime continue through the mountain scenes: Guiderius, struck by the beauty of the only apparently dead youth, exclaims that Fidele will "make his grave a bed" (4.2.217). And she does indeed make a grave into a bed when, awaking briefly from her drugged slumber to the horror of the headless man beside her, she falls back asleep upon his trunk. Lucius, the Roman general who finds her, asks, "Who is this / Thou mak'st thy bloody pillow?" (4.2.363–64). Whereas before she had used her own body for support, now she uses the corpse of Cloten to rest her heavy head. Earlier, that same Cloten had planned to murder Posthumus and then rape Innogen on *his* corpse, a motif that appears in *Titus Andronicus* as well; *furnitura* with a vengeance, the body-as-bed taps a deep affordance that interfolds maternal cradling and amorous propping with debased and morbid violence. In *Cymbeline*, beds are actions, postures, and places as much as objects, crafting sleep as an ecological assemblage that engages soundscape and softscape while oneirically breeding tableaux of violation and abuse. Anyone but Innogen would prefer curling up in her own embrace on the hard earth to lying on the softest of corpses; as Lucius notes, "nature doth abhor to make his bed / With the defunct, or sleep upon the dead" (4.2.358–59). If the gesture expresses her commitment to Posthumus, the form of fidelity she practices is closer to resilience ("resolution" and "hardiness") than to a spiritualized faith. What is most abhorrent is also most convenient, her action manifesting a survivalist's ability to find affordances in successively more difficult and tenuous scenes of sojourn.

Like Job's patience, Innogen's fidelity is tempered by indignation and an injured sense of merit. Viewing her cave hosts with a longing for belonging, she makes a brief invocation:

> Pardon me, gods,
> I'd change my sex to be companion with them,
> Since Leonatus' false. (3.6.84–86)

For a moment she imagines her cross-dressing becoming permanent, like the gender change undergone by Phillida at the end of John Lyly's *Galatea*, so that she can join the all-male family in the woods and make her life there. Like her sabbatarian sick leave, prayer offers a time of exception that strengthens fidelity by modulating and adjusting its strictures.[98] Whereas Juliet wakes up to the corpse of her husband and promptly kills herself, Innogen's sense of injury seasons her appetite for survival. Thus she awakens not only to dead Cloten but to living Lucius: her willingness to follow a new master into an uncertain destiny demonstrates her ability to substitute and sublimate. She tells him,

> and when
> With wildwood leaves and weeds I ha' strewed his grave
> And on it said a century of prayers,
> Such as I can, twice o'er, I'll weep and sigh,
> And leaving so his service, follow you,
> So please you entertain me. (4.2.390–95)

Planning for departure, she aims to perform a lightly scripted funerary rite that is environmental as well as linguistic: when she refers to "wildwood leaves and weeds," the actor might be looking around to see what's ready to hand, conjuring sylvan underbrush out of a simple searching glance. Her terms for a pious but resolute departure end with the idea of *entertaining*: both the reciprocal obligations that bind page and master and the ability

98. The word "pardon" is associated with the exception. See Bernadette Meyler, "Theaters of Pardoning."

to entertain the branching paths and replacement realities that her new service contract embodies.[99]

Innogen's fidelity is "interested," in Arendt's sense of engaging with other people through worldly concerns. Interest, as we saw in the introduction, is Arendt's pregnant word for the pivot between *work with objects* and *action in response to other persons*: "These [worldly] interests constitute, in the word's most literal significance, something which *inter-est*, which lies between people and therefore can relate and bind them together."[100] "What's thy interest / In this sad wreck?" Lucius asks Innogen (4.2.366–67). Earlier, she had taken Giacomo's trunk into her bedchamber on account of her husband's "interest" in its contents (1.6.195). Innogen's fidelity is always "interested," affectively and pragmatically caught up with the world of persons and things. This resilient fidelity solicits not her own death (like Jesus or Juliet), but rather her continued activity as a midwife of posthumous births, including her own. Recall Arendt's definition of natality as "faith in and hope for the world," a faith manifested in Innogen's commitment to living. This requires that she survive the temptation of martyrdom; in the scene with Pisanio, she rehearsed the Akedah, whereas here her dream-sick sleep followed by the affirmation of her new, covenantal name recalls Jacob's wrestling with the Angel on the road back to conciliation with Esau. In both scenes, Innogen chooses life over death by practicing a dissonant and worldly form of faith that integrates indignation, ingenuity, and interestedness into its affective ensemble. Hers is a "low fidelity" that remains close to the ground rather than a "high fidelity" that soars into the spheres.

"Interest" binds Innogen to two very different "trunks," the chest of Giacomo and the headless corpse of Cloten, each installing a vibrant suite of physical affordances and social invest-

99. *OED*, 5: "To keep, retain (a person) in one's service; to be at the charges of (a person) in return for services rendered by him." Daryl W. Palmer elucidates the etymology: "hospitality meant . . . entertainment, a term whose etymology elucidates its social function: *inter* and *tenere*, to hold together" (*Hospitable Performances*, 3).

100. Arendt, *The Human Condition*, 42.

ments at the center of *Cymbeline*'s environments of action. Visualizing the play's most wooden visual pun, Fiasco Theatre's 2011 production of *Cymbeline* designed its entire action around this play of words and things: the main stage property, created by set designer Jacques Roy, was a chest composed of a number of hinged lids and openings, allowing the box to serve as cave, throne, chest, table, stage, and more. In act 4, scene 2, his killers thrust Cloten's head into one of these openings so that the actor's body could figure a headless corpse, concatenating the two "trunks" of the play. Each trunk is a site of inventive theatrical work with affordances. Each trunk is a test of Innogen's fidelity and judgment. Each trunk is an occasion for and symbol of natality. The first, associated with Posthumus's international object relations, launches Giacomo's sprint into villainous voyeurism and Innogen's departure from dwelling. The second initiates Innogen's awakening into the next phase of her adventure, which is also *Cymbeline*'s dramaturgical birth out of and partial emancipation from the world of *Romeo and Juliet*.

It is of course Cloten's fallen trunk and its appendages that Innogen somewhat bathetically blazons ("his foot Mercurial, his Martial thigh, / The brawns of Hercules" [4.2.311–12]), putting to work the kind of humanist education embodied in the *furnitura* of her *studiolo*. Just as earlier her identification with Diana had blinded her to her affinities with Actaeon, here the mechanical application of book knowledge supports her misrecognition of Cloten as Posthumus. Innogen's blazon, however, also demonstrates her efforts to recreate and reaffirm continuities by piecing together a whole out of parts and by translating the world she has lost into the one she has found. In Bonnie Lander's analysis, Innogen "may be confused, mistaken in her assessments, mistrustful of her own perception and cognition, but from that place she experiences and enunciates the simple feeling of being physically present in the world."[101] In gestures like these, fidelity comes to mean resourceful endurance, figuring dwelling as a sustained and sustaining abiding.

101. Lander, "Interpreting the Person," 180.

Resilience in *Cymbeline* contains and coordinates the ethical, the environmental, and the dramaturgical: from Innogen's resolution, hardiness, and fidelity, to the acclimation of a range of species and inhabitants to the Welsh landscape, to the resources of the stage itself, which yields a sequence of settings through the notational work of word and gesture. *Cymbeline*'s existential dramaturgy composes and recomposes its scenes of subjective birth and somatic sleep out of object, ground, posture, prayer, and atmosphere, asking actors, audiences, and readers to think with and about the furniture of both earth and world. In the process, the play explores forms of fidelity to self, world, and other in their intricate coproduction. Read in this way, *Cymbeline* might cue our pursuit of resilience today, not as the neoliberal imperative to embrace precarity or accept the inevitability of ecological degradation, but as the cultivation of alternative economies and neglected tools that might readjust our relationships to persons, places, things, and our actions in and with them. Randall Martin's ecocosmopolitan reading of the play is exemplary; along these lines, we might access Innogen/Fidele's momentary dream of making a permanent home in the cave—a fantasy radical enough to require "pardon"—as the utopian vision of a queer family living off the grid.

Matthew Smith argues that theatrical belief should be grasped phenomenologically as a form of embodied thought and place-based action, and not as an inner state of mind. He cites John Donne: "Faith is incorporated and manifested in a body by works."[102] Fidelity as an embodied stance *is* that process of incorporation, a posture and set of behaviors far more than cognitive adherence to a truth claim.[103] And Innogen's fidelity incorporates a range of ethical moods (including disobedience, contempt, indignation, moral and rhetorical confidence, and an openness to new affiliations), stances drawn from Hebrew and

102. Smith, "Donne," 171.

103. On comportment, see Mark A. Warthall: "Comportment involves things I do or experience without an occurrent mental state in which I intend to do it or register this experience. Thus comportment includes automatic actions, for example, which reflect a responsiveness to the meaning of a situation" ("Unconcealment," 346).

classical as well as Christian virtue discourses. By allowing Innogen to compose her fidelity out of mixed sources, Shakespeare invites dispensations both ancient and modern to cohere in a heterogeneous universalism that continually footnotes its sources and flags its contradictions. My *Cymbeline* is messianic (with a small *m*) and catholic (with a small *c*), in the sense that its reach is as vast as its sources and emotional palettes are varied.

5

Room for Dessert in *The Winter's Tale*

So are the arts and humanities only auxiliary functions, icing on the cake, nice to have but not essential to the nutritional needs of society?
«DICK STANLEY, study for Council of Europe[1]»

Nowe we knowe what was done in the feast of Pentecost, namely that the holy Ghost was sent down vpon Christs disciples, and that there was a kinde of renewing of the worlde.
«JOHN CALVIN, *Sermons on Deuteronomy*[2]»

At my house, a meal for company ends with the clearing of the table and the presentation of a homemade fruit crumble, a store-bought pastry, or little bowls of dried fruits and nuts. We also bring out a beloved steel teapot and a set of glasses, the gift of a friend from Morocco who also gave me her recipe for Moroccan mint tea (fresh mint, gunpowder tea, orange blossom water, and plenty of sugar). The presence of the tea service announces that we have entered the special gift ecology of hospitality, where

1. Cited by Helle Porsdam, *Civil to Human Rights*, 138.
2. Calvin, *Sermons on Deuteronomy*, 610.

"saving room for dessert" means honoring the space for reflection and digestion that we share with others.

The great nineteenth-century chef Marie-Antoine Carême dubbed confectionary the "main branch of architecture."[3] As we move toward the promised end of this book, I take up the deep connection between architecture and dessert in order to consider afresh the art of concluding. What engages me, however, is not castles of sugar but rather the way in which dessert constitutes a final act in the sequence of the meal, opening a space in which renewed forms of social, gustatory, and environmental encounter can take place. Dessert, in its modern sense as a final course of sweet foods, often though not necessarily shared with company for a festive occasion, is defined by an act of clearing that precedes and affords the sumptuary display exercised in its name; it is this dynamic between clearing and appearing, moreover, that affiliates dessert with theater.

In *Arranging the Meal*, the great food historian Jean-Louis Flandrin argues that dessert emerged as a sweet course separate from the rest of the meal in the period stretching from the sixteenth to the eighteenth century. "Dessert," he notes, comes from *desservi*, the act of clearing the table; dessert in its first uses refers

> not to a collection of dishes . . . but to the course that came after the table was cleared (*desservi*) for the first time since the start of the meal. Up to that point, dishes from the preceding course were simply removed (*relevé*), that is, replaced one at a time by the dishes of the next course, the table never being left bare. For this last stage, all dishes were cleared from the previous course. It was long the practice even to take away the top tablecloth as well, the dessert dishes then being set on the second tablecloth beneath.[4]

3. See Krondl, *Sweet Invention*, 209. New writing on Renaissance cooking and literature include Joan Fitzpatrick, *Food in Shakespeare*; David Goldstein, *Eating and Ethics in Shakespeare's England*; *Culinary Shakespeare*, ed. David Goldstein and Amy Tigner; and Wendy Wall, *Recipes for Thought*.

4. Flandrin, *Arranging the Meal*, 104. On banqueting in and as Renaissance theater, see Meads, *Banqueting Set Forth*.

The analogy with drama is immediate and compelling. If the main courses in the classical meal constitute a series of scenes that flow imperceptibly into each other, dessert is dinner's final act, and even its epilogue, a demarcated episode that both reasserts and reflects on the meal's dramatic character as an unfolding sequence of offerings. Dessert's special disclosures include the appearing of *foods* in their capacity to delight as well as to nourish; the appearing of *guests* in the risky performance of personhood; the appearing of *labor* in its capacity to confect, support, and inhabit worlds; the appearing of *things* as haptic bearers of multiple affordances; and the appearing of *ambience* as a cloud of sound, aroma, and light. Through its always-incipient pastoralism, which casts architecture as landscape architecture, dessert also brings into visibility the relationship of these diverse actors in every scene of commensality.

These forms of appearing in the drama of the meal gather and mingle under the canopy of dwelling, those routines of living that address our creaturely needs for shelter, sustenance, and sociability. The dessert course contributes to the arts of dwelling by curating moments of digestive reflection that link space, time, labor, leisure, and seasonality in potent bundles of fruit, sugar, nuts, dairy, pastry, and spice. Dessert as *desservi*, I argue, occasions an environmental and phenomenological engagement with food as part of a larger scene composed of biotechnical confabulations and affordances; it is precisely dessert's invitations to affiliation and acknowledgment, moreover, which have been largely occluded in our era of industrial sweets. When every meal has become a haven for rogue sugars and fats, what I am calling "room for dessert"—the act of clearing that precedes and solicits appearing—is disappearing. In this final chapter, I look at the emergence of the dessert course in the seventeenth century and then suggest its relevance to the final acts of *The Winter's Tale*. Whereas Marina's leafy shelter wove *Pericles* into the soft architecture of Sukkot, Perdita's Whitsun whitpot affiliates her sheep-shearing hospitality with the Jewish dairy festival of Shavuot and its translation into the Christian pastorals of Pentecost.

Cooking, Dwelling, Thinking: Renaissance Dessert Scenography

In the European cookbook tradition, architecture provides both setting and metaphor of the meal. One of the earliest cookbooks to appear in print (1475) was Platina's *On Right Pleasure and Good Health*; written by the first librarian for the new Vatican Library, Platina's interests stem from his vast knowledge of classical texts rather than from hands-on experience in the kitchen. Drawing on a classical topos, he presents the proper siting of one's estate as a condition of eating well: "A civilized and intelligent man should choose, in the city as well as in the country, the place most advantageous for the time of year, pleasant, delightful, charming where he may build, where he may devote his efforts to farming, where he may relax with his artistic interests, where he may, in sum, commune with the gods themselves."[5] Anticipating Heidegger's fourfold composition of *Wohnen* (dwelling), Platina's humanist ideal defines the man who dwells well as a creature who lives in harmony with the elements, especially air and earth; as a landowner who enjoys some proximity to the labors of husbandry; and as a scholar-poet whose environmental attunements imply an immanent theology: "he may, in sum, commune with the gods themselves."

Platina identifies the "third" or fruit course with the act of digestion:

> If it happens that you have eaten meat, either roasted or boiled according to the time of year, eat either apples or sour pears. Some, among whom is Nicander, in an amazing way approve the radish, derived from *radices* [roots], because, taken after food, it helps digestion, reduces phlegm by penetrating to the depths of the stomach, holds

5. Platina, *On Right Pleasure and Good Health*, 105. The editor suggests as a source for this passage Pietro de'Crescenzi's "On Choosing a Place to Live" (52–53).

> down the vapors from rising to the head, and purges the kidney and bladder. . . . A bit of very hard cheese is thought to seal the stomach and stop vapors from seeking the head and brain. Also it easily takes away squeamishness arising from too fat or sweet a meal. The more refined tables eat anise and coriander rolled in sugar as a remedy for mouth and head; the common people, fennel; all, chestnuts, whose force is cold and dry. . . . Taken with sugar or honey, they are thought to reduce phlegm. In addition, the eating of quince, pomegranate, especially the sour, and of all things that are astringent, like pulse and pistachios, is not frowned upon. Either almonds or hazelnuts or other nuts ought to be eaten after fish because they are thought to repress the cold and damp force of fish with their dryness.[6]

Platina's third course includes fruits, nuts, and cheese as well as candied seeds and spices. The service was not exclusively sweet (just try serving radishes for dessert!). Focusing on the digestive properties of foods, Platina presents this course as part of a sequence, with some types of "fruit" more appropriately following certain types of "meat." Digestion is understood primarily as a physiological property, but the separation of these foods into a third and final course demarcates a space-time for digestion in its more reflective and ruminative senses. Finally, Platina's third course at once differentiates the social classes and is modest and inclusive in its dietary aims: the wealthy eat candied spices, "the common people" take their anise in the form of fennel, and everyone eats chestnuts. Although Platina writes from a position of educated privilege, the foodscape of the third course encompasses a comprehensive social and biotechnical scene composed of many foods and eaters.

Sugar cultivation began in India, where sweet dishes are bound up with creation myths, votive offerings, and festival observances.[7] Arab cuisine borrowed sugar from India and added

6. Platina, *On Right Pleasure*, 463.

7. On cosmic cooking processes (the chemistry-cuisine-creation continuum), see Ian Grant, "The Chemical Paradigm." On sugar, gender, and the slave trade in the early modern period, see Kim Hall, "Culinary Spaces, Colonial Spaces." The classic study of sugar remains Mintz, *Sweetness and Power*.

key ingredients to the Indian repertoire, a marriage that in turn had an immense impact on medieval European cookery; Platina's "anise and coriander rolled in sugar" manifests the Hindu-Arab-European exchange of flavors and ingredients, like the candied anise served in Indian restaurants today. (Wherever sugar, rice, saffron, almonds, jellies, rose and orange water, and ices as well as artichokes, spinach, and eggplants appear on European tables, the Indo-Muslim influence is in evidence.)[8] Sugar does not dominate Platina's table, which is given over rather to a mix of fresh and preserved fruits and nuts. Candying and conserving allows perishable foods to be eaten later in the year; rather than being *un*-seasonal, however, such densely flavored essences seem rather to capture and transfer seasonality as such, along with the human art and effort required to transmit it. The jellies and marmalades of the Renaissance pantry are culinary memory banks that store and display both flavor and labor in their luminous liquefactions.[9] Heidegger converges with housekeeping in Platina's third course, which participates in acts of "keeping" and "preserving" that acknowledge our mortal habitation between air and earth.

Whereas Platina's *De Honesta Voluptate et Valetudine* is a humanist tract written by a scholar-librarian, Bartolomeo Scappi's *L'arte et prudenza d'un maestro cuoco* (1570) transmits the experience of a master chef who ran the kitchens for three cardinals and two popes. He begins his massive study of food and food practices by comparing his craft to that of the architect:

> It is necessary, therefore, insofar as my many years of experience have taught me, that a skilled and competent Master Cook, wishing to have a good beginning, a better middle, and a best ending, and always to derive honour from his work, should do as a wise Architect,

8. Krondl, *Sweet Invention*, 115–18; see also Ken Albala, *Cooking in Europe, 1250–1750*, 1–3.

9. On preservation and the Renaissance kitchen, see Wendy Wall, *Staging Domesticity*, 18–42, and *Recipes for Thought*, 167–208; and Spurling, *Elinor Fettiplace's Receipt Book*.

> who, following his careful design, lays out a firm foundation and on it presents to the world useful and marvelous buildings. The design of the Master Cook must be the fine and dependable method produced by experience, of which he should have acquired such knowledge that he could serve rather in the Office of the Steward than the Steward should serve as Cook. And he should strive to satisfy unusual, diverse tastes with delicate dishes. Not least, the dishes should be tasty and agreeable to the palate as well as pleasant and delightful to the eye with their pretty colours and appetizing appearance. The first foundation upon which he will set his main base must be his understanding of and experience with various kinds of foodstuffs.[10]

Scappi's comparison of cooking with architecture parallels the bids for professional acknowledgment made by many artisans striving to enhance their crafts with the prestige of design. Architecture is more than an analogy for Scappi, however: his book is distinguished by its detailed engravings of kitchen spaces and kitchen implements, images that document the architectural conditions of food service, including cooking in the field for a household constantly on the diplomatic move. Design enters Scappi's text both as an intellectual discourse furthering a planner's attitude toward the overall structure of the meal and as the comportment of an artisan-technician responding to the taskscapes of work and labor.

Like Platina, Scappi is attentive to the mise-en-scène of the meal:

> You should be aware of the seasons of the year, for you have seen quite well how felicitously Reverend Don Francisco has had [the table] set in springtime in cheerful locations that are sheltered from the breeze, in summer in airy, shaded places where there is lots of bubbling water, in the fall in a temperate location with an eastern exposure rather than northern, and in winter in rooms decorated with a variety of tapestries, sculptures, and paintings to please guests; and always has the table of a length proportionate to its width, so

10. Scappi, *Opera: L'arte et prudenza d'un maestro cuoco*, 99.

> that the attendants can set out and remove courses easily and those who are serving food or drink can move around freely and without inconvenience to their lords.[11]

Scappi treats meals as mobile events that accommodate seasonal shifts in order to enhance the pleasures and meanings of commensality. The affordances of the setting include temperature and ambience ("airy, shaded place," "bubbling water"). Scappi also pays attention to the affordances of furniture: a properly proportioned table facilitates the effortless movement of domestic labor, a service choreography staged for the benefit of the "lords," but calculated from the perspective of a *maestro cuoco* in charge of a large household staff. Design functions in Scappi's text as both a template for professionalization and as a more embedded and implicit ecology of tacit knowledge and local uses. The title of Scappi's book, "L'arte et prudenza d'un maestro cuoco," captures these two senses, with *arte* evoking the formal discourses of *disegno* and *prudenza* naming the vernacular virtues of dwelling.

Writing a hundred years after Platina, Scappi gives more detail than his forbearer regarding the rhythms of the emerging dessert course. The Italian service alternated between *cucina* and *credenza*, between the warm meals overseen by the cook and the cold dishes supervised by the *scalco*, the pantler or steward. The *scalco*, as Scappi makes clear with some irritation in his opening remarks on architecture, supervised the cook and the whole household staff. Because the preserved fruits and candied spices of the *credenza* course belonged to the pantry and not the kitchen, dessert recipes are largely neglected in the great Renaissance cookbooks of France and Italy, which focused on the *cucina*. Remnants of this practice remain in the accommodation of store-bought or guest-provided desserts at the end of a home-cooked feast. In the Italian service, a *credenza* course always ended the meal, although there were cold courses throughout; the *credenza* that began the meal was called the *antipasto*, and the *credenza* at the end was the *postpasto*. A *collazione* was

11. Scappi, *Opera*, 381.

a meal consisting exclusively of *credenza* dishes, both sweet and savory, and could be enjoyed in different parts of the house or estate; sometimes the *collazione* included a dramatic performance or entertainment.[12] Scappi records a "collation at the end of August in a vineyard after Vespers" and another *collazione* "arranged at the end of May on a Friday in Trastavere in a garden."[13] At the latter party, the table was adorned with "diverse flowers and foliage" and *la credenza*—referring to the sideboard that held the dishes as well as to the food arrayed upon it—was furnished with silver, gold, glass, and majolica vessels, along with a suite of sugar statues depicting Diana with nymphs. In Scappi's text, the *postpasto* is marked by standing up from the table, washing hands with water and white napkins, and then enjoying a final service of "sweet fresh fennel," candied fruits, seeds, and spices (perhaps in a separate room).[14] The action of *desservi* resonates in these gestures of rising, cleansing, and removing as well as in the pastoral character of the *credenza* course. *Postpasto* is Renaissance Italian for dessert.

Scappi's papal spreads far outspend Platina's frugal humanist dietary, but both texts radiate a sense of pastoral and dramaturgical responsiveness to time and locale. In Platina's and Scappi's environmentally attuned works, dessert erects its own fourfold; as such, dessert is indeed a branch of architecture, understood not mimetically (desserts look like buildings) but existentially: dessert participates in the work of dwelling by bidding the conditions of habitation to appear.

Neither Platina's nor Scappi's architectural musings specifically concern dessert, which was still emerging as a separate course in the Renaissance; indeed it is the tempo of that emergence that concerns me here. The French word *dessert* was used infrequently in England (and never by Shakespeare) until the later seventeenth century. Instead, the word "banquet" or "bankett" often

12. E.g., ibid., 408.
13. Ibid., 385–86.
14. Ibid., 396.

referred to a festive course of cold or sweet dishes eaten in a separate location, after the clearing of the main hall, equivalent to the Italian *collazione*. Under Elizabeth, the banqueting course was often eaten in a "withdrawing room" (the root of "drawing room"), or in separate structures that were architecturally distinct from the main house.[15] Sometimes banqueting houses—dessert rooms—were built on the roof, like the "little domed banqueting turrets" at Longleat, each housing six guests at most.[16] Banqueting houses could also be garden pavilions located a short walk away from the great house, perhaps connected by a gallery. The temporary character and pastoral decor of Renaissance banqueting houses associated dessert with acts of retreat that built social and environmental relationships in a place apart.

Prior to the Restoration, English cookbooks were far more workmanlike than the splendid productions of Platina and Scappi. Figure 4 shows the frontispiece of what may be the first English dessert cookbook, from 1653.[17] The book promises to teach the art of candying and preserving and the creation of "Sugar-works," the kinds of fanciful sculptures that Scappi served up on his *credenza*. The author also offers recipes for baked goods (pies, biscuits, cakes, tarts, fritters), the wet desserts still favored by the English (puddings, syrups, leaches, broths, snow), and banqueting confections like marzipan. Throughout the book, food and medicinal recipes lie side by side; a few items are designated as "banqueting stuff," such as marigolds preserved "in Spanish Candy."[18] Hugh Plat's 1602 *Delights for Ladies, to adorn their Persons, Tables, closets and distillatories* is also a protodessert cookbook, thanks to its emphasis on the conservation of fruits and flowers and its focus on the arts of the pantry rather than

15. Fumerton, *Cultural Aesthetics*, 112. See also C. Wilson, ed., *Banquetting Stuffe*, 2, 12, 55.

16. Fumerton, *Cultural Aesthetics*, 114.

17. Anonymous, *A Book of Fruits and Flowers* (1653).

18. "Cut in Wedges before it be through cold, gild it, and so you may box it, and keep it all the year. It is a fine sort of Banquetting stuffe" (27). Here "banquetting" refers to the dessert course or dessert party.

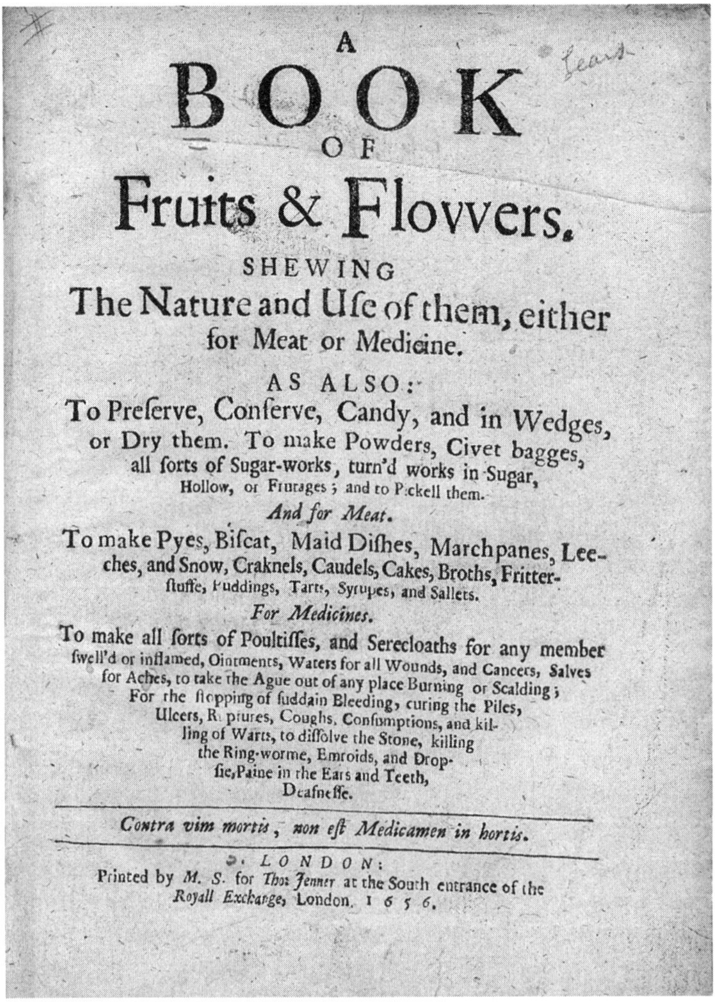

A
BOOK
OF
Fruits & Flovvers.
SHEWING
The Nature and Uſe of them, either
for Meat or Medicine.
AS ALSO:
To Preſerve, Conſerve, Candy, and in Wedges,
or Dry them. To make Powders, Civet bagges,
all ſorts of Sugar-works, turn'd works in Sugar,
Hollow, or Frutages; and to Pickell them.
And for Meat.
To make Pyes, Biſcat, Maid Diſhes, Marchpanes, Lee-
ches, and Snow, Craknels, Caudels, Cakes, Broths, Fritter-
ſtuffe, Puddings, Tarts, Syrupes, and Sallets.
For Medicines.
To make all ſorts of Poultiſſes, and Serecloaths for any member
ſwell'd or inflamed, Ointments, Waters for all Wounds, and Cancers, Salves
for Aches, to take the Ague out of any place Burning or Scalding;
For the ſtopping of ſuddain Bleeding, curing the Piles,
Ulcers, Ruptures, Coughs, Conſumptions, and kil-
ling of Warts, to diſſolve the Stone, killing
the Ring-worme, Emroids, and Drop-
ſie, Paine in the Ears and Teeth,
Deafneſſe.

Contra vim mortis, non eſt Medicamen in hortis.

LONDON:
Printed by *M. S.* for *Tho: Jenner* at the South entrance of the
Royall Exchange, London. 1656.

FIGURE 4. Title page from *A Book of Fruits and Flowers* (1656). Photograph: Library of the Arnold Arboretum, Harvard University, Cambridge, Massachusetts.

the kitchen. Addressing a range of concoctions and activities that are both more and less than dessert in the modern sense, these compilations reveal the multiple scenes of life—from the culinary to the medicinal to the cosmetic—to which fruited foods contributed their sociable sweetness.

Robert May's *The Accomplish't Cook*, published in the wake of the Civil War and its disruptions to traditional elite hospitality, begins with a loving description of a piece of extravagant food theater that culminates in a banqueting course. Under the heading "Triumphs and Trophies in Cookery, to be used at Festival Times, as Twelfth Day, &c.," this representative anecdote, not a recipe but rather a memorial reconstruction, includes a ship made out of pasteboard loaded with gun powder, pies pulsing with live frogs and birds, a pastry stag that bleeds claret when an arrow is removed from his side, and egg shells filled with rose water for the ladies to throw at each other ("to sweeten the stinck of the [gun] powder"). As the spectacle comes to a conclusion,

> candles are lighted, and a Banquet brought in, the musick sounds, and every one with much delight and content rehearses their actions in the former passages. These were formerly the delights of the Nobility, before good House-keeping had left *England*, and the Sword really acted that which was only counterfeited in such honest and laudable Exercises as these.

The banquet enters here as a separate service that crowns and reflects upon the food folly that has preceded it; dedicated to "rehearsing" the actions of the triumph, the banqueting course comes with its own ambience, provided by candles and music that diffuse and extend the levity released by the pastry pyrotechnics.

May's dessert tableau is a nostalgic homage to the Caroline court; the goal of his book, however, is not to recreate that world, but rather to translate royalist skills and values into postwar cooking projects for smaller householders living "some distance from Towns or Villages."[19] Given its aspirational character, May's

19. "In the contrivance of these my Labours, I have so managed them for the general good, that those whose Purses cannot reach to the cost of rich Dishes, I have descended to their meaner Expences, that they may give, though upon a sudden Treatment, to their Kindred, Friends, Allies, and Acquaintance, a handsome and relishing entertainment in all Seasons of the year, though at some distance from Towns or Villages" (*Accomplish't Cook*, preface).

recipes are more elaborate and decorative than those that appear in many English cookbooks, including patterns for cut crusts that release steam and reveal the fruited fillings beneath. Although May's pastry templates take us further than other cookbooks of the period into the design of dessert, he does not reveal the architectural secrets lauded in the prefatory poem by James Parry, who praises May as one "Who can in Paste erect, of finest flour, / A compleat Fort, a Castle, or a Tower." May's bills of fare, moreover, do not include any specific prescription for a third course or dessert service; his menus are restricted to two courses, perhaps because his book, following the French and Italian cookbook tradition, concerns the kitchen and not the pantry.[20]

Also writing after the English Civil War, Hannah Woolley gives us more sense of dessert in modest circumstances. Both widowhood and poor health seem to have led Woolley into writing as a livelihood, and she markets her book as a means of assisting women who have been displaced by the war. Toward the end of *The Queen-Like Closet*—the title and frontispiece themselves an architectural rendition of culinary knowledge (figure 2)—Woolley instructs her readers in the art of serving sweets to guests:

> Serve three or four small dishes also with Sweet-meats, such are most in season, with Vine Leaves and Flowers between the Dishes and the Plates, two wet Sweet-meats, and two dry, two of one colour, and two of another, or all of several colours. Also a Dish of Jellies of several colours in one Dish, if such be required.[21]

Woolley brightens her table with loose leaves and flowers from the garden, and the sweet offerings themselves compose a still

20. May, *The Accomplish't Cook* features recipes for quince pie with *fleur de lis* crust (225) and marchpane garnished with "pretty conceits" (253). "Triumphs and Trophies in Cookery": prefatory; not paginated.

21. Woolley, *The Queen-Like Closet*, 341–43. On the writings and career of Hannah Woolley, see Goldstein, "Woolley's Mouse" and "Recipes for Living." On Woolley's instructions for letter-writing, see Summit, "Hannah Wolley, the Oxinden Letters, and Household Epistolary Practice." I write about Woolley and Arendt in "Thinking with Things."

life arranged with a painterly attention to color, texture, and contrast. In her seasonal menus, Woolley does not use the word "dessert," but she presents the traditional "Third Course" in a manner similar to Platina and in a rhythm clearly linked to the action of *desservi*. Woolley's dessert service is typographically and choreographically distinct from the main menu, a separation marked by the act of clearing: "After these are *taken away*, then *serve in* your Cheese and Fruit" (328; emphasis added). Platina's modest dietary converges here with Woolley's English sense of thrift.[22] At the end of the *Closet*, however, Woolley gives her imagination over to a sugar-work fantasia, a garden of candied fruits and marzipan animals arranged in a basket as a portable landscape suitable for presentation as a gift. This nested scene is Woolley's counteroffer to May's "Triumphs and Trophies."

All of these authors, in different ways and to varying degrees, treat dessert as a kind of culinary landscape architecture. The clearing marked by the simple presentation of fruits and cheeses harbors within its horticultural parameters the promise of more spectacular forms of appearing, confections that transport the pastoral theme into a key that showcases the cook's skill and ingenuity. Its ingredients gathered from the orchard, the dairy, and the pantry, dessert is kissing cousin to the picnic, each dedicated to indoor-outdoor continua defined by portable foods arranged on fields of fabric. From Platina to Woolley, the Renaissance dessert course manifests a commensal flow between clearing and appearing, between the minimalist pastoral of simple foods and the virtuoso pastoral of the higher confectionary arts. At once nature preserve and theme park, dessert as a form of dwelling insistently folds human inventiveness into the *genius loci* that hosts it.

To clear the table completely is to reset the evening, to allow for a new beginning. (Dessert means that there is still time to land a flirtation or retract an insult.) Dessert is the "beginning of the end," but it is a beginning nonetheless; as such, dessert participates in what Agamben calls the messianic "time that

22. On thrift, see Jessica Rosenberg, "A Digression to Hospitality."

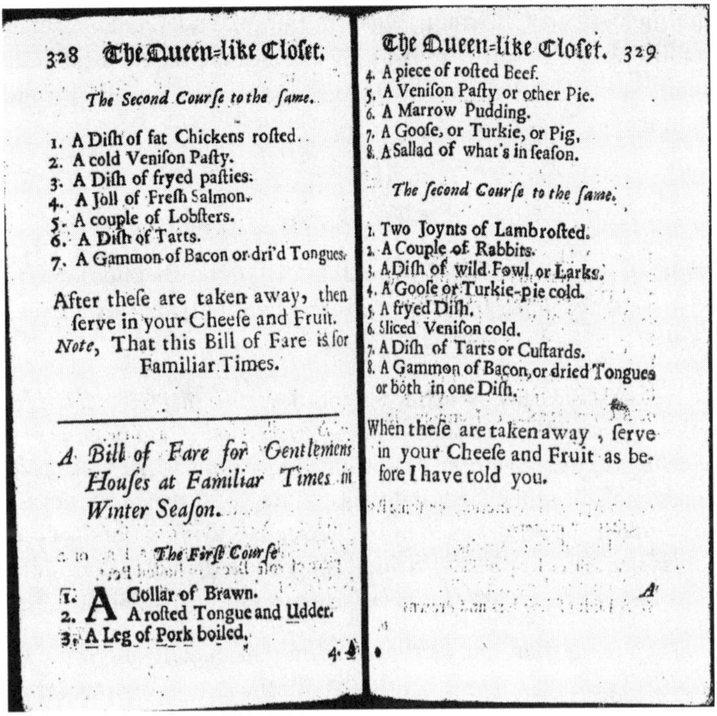

328 The Queen-like Cloſet.

The Second Courſe to the ſame.

1. A Diſh of fat Chickens roſted.
2. A cold Veniſon Paſty.
3. A Diſh of fryed paſties.
4. A Joll of Freſh Salmon.
5. A couple of Lobſters.
6. A Diſh of Tarts.
7. A Gammon of Bacon or dri'd Tongues.

After theſe are taken away, then ſerve in your Cheeſe and Fruit. *Note*, That this Bill of Fare is for Familiar Times.

A Bill of Fare for Gentlemens Houſes at Familiar Times in Winter Seaſon.

The Firſt Courſe.

1. A Collar of Brawn.
2. A roſted Tongue and Udder.
3. A Leg of Pork boiled.

The Queen-like Cloſet. 329

4. A piece of roſted Beef.
5. A Veniſon Paſty or other Pie.
6. A Marrow Pudding.
7. A Gooſe, or Turkie, or Pig.
8. A Sallad of what's in ſeaſon.

The ſecond Courſe to the ſame.

1. Two Joynts of Lamb roſted.
2. A Couple of Rabbits.
3. A Diſh of wild Fowl, or Larks.
4. A Gooſe or Turkie-pie cold.
5. A fryed Diſh.
6. Sliced Veniſon cold.
7. A Diſh of Tarts or Cuſtards.
8. A Gammon of Bacon, or dried Tongues or both in one Diſh.

When theſe are taken away, ſerve in your Cheeſe and Fruit as before I have told you.

FIGURE 5. Hannah Woolley, *The Queen-Like Closet* (1681), 328–29. Photograph: Reproduced by permission of the Huntington Library, San Marino, California.

remains."[23] Sweet foods are associated in many traditions with divine favor and a taste of heaven; the gradual exclusion of meat and the increasing celebration of fruit associate the landscape of the dessert table with the Garden of Eden. If Woolley's elaborate dessert basket is a representation of paradise, her modest sharing of foliage and jellies on the daily table is Edenic in its own way. The most minimalist dessert is also the most messianic: the *afikomen* (derived from the Greek word for dessert) is the piece of matzah split in half at the beginning of the Passover seder and then reconstituted at its end as an image of redemption. Even

23. Agamben, *The Time That Remains.*

the melding of Christian, Muslim, Hindu, and Greco-Roman traditions in the soft comfort zones of dessert seems messianic, an unexpected ingathering of peoples and cuisines around a common table set up outdoors.

The Winter's Tale *as Dessert Course*

In act 4, scene 3, of *The Winter's Tale*, the young shepherd enters with a shopping list from his stepsister Perdita larded with sweet foods:

> Let me see, what am I to buy for our sheep-shearing feast? *(He takes out a paper)* Three pounds of sugar, five pound of currants, rice—what will this sister of mine do with rice? But my father hath made her mistress of the feast, and she lays it on. . . . I must have saffron to colour the warden pies; mace; dates, none, that's out of my note; nutmegs, seven; a race or two of ginger, but that I may beg; four pound of prunes, and as many raisins o'th' sun. (4.3.35–48)[24]

The young man knows that Perdita will make warden pie (a pastry of pears), but he is not sure about the rice: "What will that sister of mine do with rice?" The inclusion of the more costly rice may signal the wealth of Perdita's adoptive family and their willingness to share their surplus and reward the labor of their workers in the sheep-shearing celebration. Joan Fitzpatrick observes that the feast appears to be vegetarian and that many of the items on the shopping list, including rice, are imported luxury items.[25]

A pudding seems to be in order: the sugar, raisins, and spices on the shepherd's list show up frequently in Renaissance recipes for whitpot, a dried fruit and dairy pudding featured in country diets in the western parts of England. Perdita's appellation as the "queen of curds and cream" (4.4.161) identifies her as the "Whitpot queen" of those Whitsun pastorals that she uses to mark her

24. Citations from *The Winter's Tale* are taken from the Oxford edition, ed. Stephen Orgel.

25. Fitzpatrick, *Food in Shakespeare*, 77.

reticent retreat from her own festive exuberance (4.4.133–35).[26] The young shepherd's shopping list and Perdita's Whitsun reference release a fragrant cloud of ingredients and controversies, including the dairy menus and holiday actions of Pentecostal celebration; the binding of Jewish, Christian, and agrarian calendars around the post-Paschal feast; and the debate within a divided Christendom about the propriety of Whitsuntide.

The Christian holiday of Pentecost celebrates the descent of the Holy Spirit into the community of the faithful (Acts 2:1–4). It is based on the Jewish Shavuot or Festival of Weeks that falls fifty days after the second day of Passover and commemorates the giving of the law at Sinai. From early on, the rabbis conceived of the covenant at Sinai as a marriage ceremony, in which God wedded Israel through the *ketubah* or marriage contract of the Decalogue.[27] Some synagogues dress the Torah up in white cloths and flowers and then wed her to the congregation.[28] Marriage and courtship imagery (including darker strains involving adultery, idolatry, and jealousy) runs through its liturgy, accompanied by the annual reading of the pastoral romance the Book of Ruth.[29] Christian Pentecost participates in the whirl created by Shavuot's God-revealing, community-building, and eschaton-hungry vectors. Flowing out of this sublime funnel into Christian history, Pentecost repeats and renews Shavuot's dedication to transcription and translation: both holidays commemorate the reconstitution of a mixed multitude of survivors from a traumatic event (Exodus, Easter) into a cohesive social body (Israel, church). Above and beyond any typological calculus, at stake in the two holidays

26. Orgel, 177n.

27. Kirby, *Ephesians*, 99.

28. On the Book of Ruth, Shavuot, and wedding imagery, see, e.g., Holdredge, *Veda and Torah*, 338; and Bloch, *Jewish Customs and Ceremonies*, 249–50. In some versions of the metaphor, Israel is the bride, God the groom, and the Torah the marriage contract; in other versions, the groom Israel marries the bride Torah. In the mystical tradition, Shavuot is also imagined as the marriage between the oral Torah and the written Torah (Ariel, *Kabbalah*, 169).

29. Kirby, *Ephesians*.

is shared testimony to a living word whose corporate significations are transmitted through acts of worship, interpretation, and faithful citizenship.

The Winter's Tale's Pentecostal calendaring occurs in the wake of Perdita's lyric florilegia to Florizel and her companions. Flushed by the forwardness of her own performance, Perdita retreats back into her more characteristic reserve:

> Come, take your flowers;
> Methinks I play as I have seen them do
> In Whitsun pastorals—sure this robe of mine
> Does change my disposition. (4.4.132–35)

Phebe Jensen argues that Perdita's distrust of masquerade indicates her temperamental affinity with her father's severe iconoclasm, an attitude corrected when the girl later kneels before the seeming statue of her mother: Perdita's "distaste for the popish ceremonies of 'Whitsun' is overcome, as she herself enthusiastically deploys the language of Marian worship, addressing the statue as 'Lady' and 'Dear queen.'"[30] Arguing for a Whitsuntide setting, Michael Bristol suggests that "the Lenten movement of time has already been completed" when the pastoral sequence opens, revealing an almanac world supported by "wakes, fairs, and bearbaiting."[31] Although these and other critics suggest the relevance of Whitsun to act 4's festive performativity, none of them lingers on Pentecost as a biblical holiday carried over from Judaism into Christianity. Set within the burgeoning world of creation while commemorating acts of revelation with the power to constitute and motivate human communities, Pentecost mediates between dwelling as creaturely routine and environmen-

30. Jensen, "Horn-Pipes," 304. She cites Michael O'Connell making a similar point: "If the scene for the moment fully associates theatricality with idolatry, Shakespeare does not counter, but embraces the charge" (*The Idolatrous Eye*, 141).

31. Bristol, "In Search of the Bear," 162, 163. See also François Laroque, who proposes a close connection between "the customs involving the fashions of popular and rural communities and the pastoral comedies that were traditionally performed at this time of year" (*Shakespeare's Festive World*, 137).

tal engagement (Heidegger) and drama as scene of significant speech and covenantal action (Arendt).

Religious conservatives intent on maintaining Whitsun observance were more likely to assert the antiquity of the holiday, including the continuities between the Jewish feast and its Christian translation. Edmund Reeve defended the traditional observance of Pentecost against Puritan reformers in 1635:

> See with what fervency God hath prescribed the *Whitsun-feast* to be kept for the rejoicing together of the whole body of a people, which belong each to other; in Deuter. 16.9.11.12. It is a matter greatly considerable to hear discret old folke relate, what justnesse, charitablenesse, and friendlinesse among neighbours was, when the said feast was godlily solemnized: how little viciousnesse, drunkenesse, whoredome, maliciousness, theft, & other enormities were then. Moreover, in keeping of the *Wakes,* our forefathers not only expressed every yeere a gratefull remembrance and thankesgiving unto God for their Churches builded, but also would unto that their said feast invite their friends of the Parishes round about or neere them, and then when their neighbours *Wakes* were, they were invited again. Thus the whole land feasted each other unto an unutterable co-servation of unity & godly love.[32]

In a tract dedicated to defending the use of "lawful sports,"[33] Reeve nostalgically recalls the acts of reciprocal hospitality manifested in the Whitsun wakes and the corporate cohesion it promised ("the whole body of a people, which belong each other"). He goes on to defend mixed-sex dancing, citing Jeremiah: "Then shall the virgin rejoice in the daunce, both young men and old together."[34] Leah Marcus notes that for cultural conservatives like

32. Edmund Reeve, *The Communion Book Catechisme Explained*, 9; 104.

33. See ibid., frontispiece: "Wherein also are explaned sundry of the highest points in divinity, and matter greatly considerable in these present times. In speciall there is demonstrated, that his most excellent Majesties declaration to his subjects, concerning lawfull sports to be used, doth tend unto a very great encrease of true godlinesse throng-hout [*sic*] the whole kingdome."

34. Ibid., 105.

Reeve, "the mirth of the maying season" embodied in Whitsuntide "*was* sacramental in the sense that it was an outward manifestation of the descent of the Holy Spirit."[35]

Reformers objecting to the pagan penumbra and secular pleasures of Whitsun games often called attention to the Jewish origins of the feast in order to discredit its idolatrous Catholic observance. Calvin reminds us that the Jewish law is "a deade letter"[36] and asserts the difference between the Jewish and the Christian dispensations: "So then let us mark that the holy Ghost was not sent unto us, to the ende that these figures should continue still: but to shewe that we differ from the people of olde time." Yet just as Deuteronomy remains part of scripture, so Pentecost retains some value for Calvin: "But nowe the ceremonie of this feast is no longer in vse, and yet the trueth thereof abideth with vs still."[37] Since the ceremonies of the law were not founded in vain, "now let us learne to rejoice in the presence of our God, and to make other folks partakers of our mirth." Honoring the original function of the Jewish holiday as well as marking Christianity's difference from it, Calvin warns against too strenuous a celebration of Pentecost, but also finds fault with too "precise" a rejection of this occasion for collective "mirth."

In the medieval calendar, the day before Pentecost was a fast day with dairy.[38] Milk-based meals were traditional at Whitsuntide in Ireland and Germany as well as England; dairy dishes, including rice puddings, are also favored by the Jews at Shavuot, a fact noted by at least one seventeenth-century commentator.[39] "Cake and pudding" could be wielded by religious conservatives

35. Leah S. Marcus, *Politics of Mirth*, 157.

36. Calvin, *Sermons on Deuteronomy*, 610.

37. Ibid., 608.

38. Winter, "The Low Countries," 209.

39. Cooper, *Eat and Be Satisfied*, 119. Lancelot Addison, writing in 1675, notes, "[The Jews'] entertainments likewise are at this time very plain and frugal . . . But still white meats, and confection of milks, are their prime Delicacies. And this sort of Viand is at this time made use, of, out of no less mystery, than that by its colour and dulcour, they might be remember'd of the purity and delightfulness of the Law" (*The Present State of the Jews*, 176).

as symbols of the world being lost,[40] while also providing fodder for anti-Catholic food fights. Thus Stephen Batman derided the pope for being borne by his deacons in "the maner of carrying Whytepot Queenes, in Westerne Maygames," a line frequently cited in conjunction with Camillo's ode to Perdita as "queen of curds and cream."[41]

As a sweet food capable of transport to outdoor and offsite settings (although also served warm from oven or bain-marie), whitpot may have gradually migrated from a generalized supper dish to a part of dessert considered as a distinct course and specialized menu.[42] Warden pies, which will be featured along with whitpot on Perdita's sweet menu, appear in Gervase Markham's instructions for the banqueting course. Although whitpot is often made with "manchet" (white bread), it sometimes features the more exotic and costly rice, as in this upscale recipe by Robert May:

> Take a quart of sweet cream, boil it, and put to it two ounces of picked rice, some beaten mace, ginger, cinamon, and sugar, let these steep in it till it be cold, and strain into it eight yolks of eggs and but two whites; then put in two ounces of clean washed and picked cur-

40. Jensen, "Singing Psalms to Horn-Pipes," citing Nicholas Breton (1602): "When men would meet on Sundayes at the Church, / With true deuotion, not for fashion sake . . . When Cake and Pudding was no simple feast" (290).

41. Batman, *The Golden Booke*, 30. Orgel cites Batman and the New Shakespeare editors (1807) on white-pot and white-pot queens. Antiquarian Thomas Dudley Fosbroke associated Maid Marian and the Queen of May with the "White-pot Queen" (*Encyclopedia of Antiquities*, 581). Fosbroke notes that "the Irish kept the feast with milk food, as among the Hebrews." Francis Douce also connected Maid Marian and the white-pot queen (*Illustrations of Shakespeare*, 479). Alfred Noyes's retro-Elizabethan poems speak of "A white-pot custard for my white-pot queen," and even gives an ingredient list: "A white-pot Mermaid custard, with a crust, / Lashings of cream, eggs, apple-pulse and spice, / A little sugar and manchet bread" (*Collected Poems*, 343).

42. In his dietary of 1683, Everard Maynwaring advises against eating white-pot and other spicy compounds after meat, suggesting that white-pot was being served at the end of the meal (*The methods and means of enjoying health, vigour and long life*, 79). In the 1694 translation of Rabelais's *Pantagruel*, white-pot is listed along with other traditional digestives (raisins, dates, chestnuts and walnuts, and filberts as well as parsnips and artichokes) in a lengthy list of foods eaten by Pantagruel after the fish course on fast days (*Pantagruel's Voyage*, 238).

> rans, and some salt, stir all well together, and bake it in paste, earthen pan, dish or deep bason; being baked, trim it with some sugar, and comfits of orange, cinamon or white biskets.[43]

Here are the Clown's sugar, rice, ginger, and currants. When Perdita notes that "our feasts / In every mess have folly, and the feeders / Digest it with a custom" (4.4.10–12), she grants to the license of holiday a dessert-like metabolic function, insofar as festive dress-up and foolery allow revelers to swallow and incorporate theatricality into the routines of dwelling. Perdita's pudding melds Jewish, Christian, Muslim, Hindu, and Hellenistic traditions in the heady spices of a homely dish shared by laborers, small landowners, disguised royalty, and itinerant urbanites. Her Whitsun whitpot is a messianic gathering of flavors and faiths around a table open to the heavens, shadowed by a sense of dispensations in conflict with each other.

If the sheep-shearing festival occurs in the rustic picnic clearing implied by Whitsun pastorals, the statue scene at the end of the play evokes the banqueting houses of higher Renaissance dessert practice. Announcing the existence of Hermione's statue "in the keeping of Paulina," the Third Gentleman confides that the royal party "with all greediness of affection" have gone to Paulina's lodgings, where "they intend to sup" (5.2.100–101), implying the kind of lighter meal or "banquet" that Lucentio, for example, provides as an after-dinner party to the wedding guests in act 5 of *Taming of the Shrew*.[44] Paulina keeps the statue in a "removed house," an outbuilding that resembles a Renaissance banqueting house. *The Winter's Tale* was performed at the Ban-

43. Robert May, *The Accomplish't Cook*, 282. May's recipe is very close to Markham's in *The English House-wife* (1631). Some white-pot recipes feature rose water, a classic Hindu-Muslim ingredient. See Cooper, "How to make a White pot," 122. His white-pot is served warm. Not all white-pots are lacto-vegetarian; Nicolas Lémery suggests adding "the brawn of a Capon" to the mix (*Modern Curiosities*, 188). Hannah Woolley adds sliced marrow (*The accomplished ladys delight*, 118).

44. "Feast with the best, and welcome to my house. / My banket is to close our stomachs up / After our great good cheer" (*Taming of the Shrew*, 5.2.8–10). Note the reference to closing the stomach, a commonplace of dessert theory.

queting House at Whitehall in 1611, a setting that would on that occasion have associated the play as a whole with the specialized space-time of dessert. While the statue scene itself is marked by a sense of courtly spectacle, Shakespeare's emphasis on the rhythm of withdrawal keeps in play the existential function of clearing that gives dessert its dramatic character as well as its intimacy. Thus Leontes speaks of a journey through spaces of removal:

> Your gallery
> Have we passed through, not without much content
> In many singularities, but we saw not
> That which my daughter came to look upon,
> The statue of her mother. (5.3.10–14)

The wandering syntax of his plea enacts the effortful action of *desservi* as retreat to a space apart in search of a messianic "time of refreshing" (Acts 3:19) that takes place in the "time that remains."

When Leontes finally sees Hermione, his language shimmers with the haptic offerings of dessert: "this affliction has a taste as sweet / As any cordial comfort" (5.3.76–77). Cordials—distilled beverages often combining fruits, spices, sugar, or honey tempered with bitter herbs like wormwood and rue—were a key component of the dessert course thanks to their restorative virtues.[45] Paulina describes the king's visit to her "poor house" as a "surplus of your grace which never / My life may last to answer" (5.3.6–8), but the true surplus is hers to manage, not his to give. The pouring of grace in act 5 is "cordial" in the intoxicating, convivial, and gustatory resonances of the word, even to the point of retaining a rueful edge of bitterness in the hesitations and remembrances of the play's final recognitions. Leontes exclaims upon touching Hermione:

45. In Plat, see, e.g., "Spirit of Hony" (13), "Spirit of Herbs and Flowers" (17), and "Wine tasting of Wormwood, made speedily" (33). A similar image appears in *Pericles*: "It hath been sung at festivals, / On ember eves and holy ales / And lords and ladies in their lives / Have read it for restoratives" (Gower's Chorus, 1.0.5–8).

Oh, she's warm!
If this be magic, let it be an art
Lawful as eating. (5.3.109–11)

Leontes's enigmatic phrase distills the several properties of the dessert course, including its liturgical promise, its ritual dimensions, its healing gifts, and its aesthetic effects. The desire to reconcile nature, law, and art supports the movement of *The Winter's Tale* as a whole, which does not typologically replace the Old Testament with the New so much as tap their shared yearnings in a messianic art "lawful as eating." If dessert as a courtly practice appears elitist and exclusive, the environmental decor, seasonal attunement, pantry provisions, and increasingly lacto-vegetarian menu of dinner's final act composes a convivial scene dedicated to honoring interpersonal and environmental dependencies.

At Jewish tables the meal concludes with a special blessing, the *birkat hamazon*; dessert *is* a blessing after meals, the curatorial stewardship of earthly delights whose presentation and enjoyment affirms the sociable and creaturely conditions of life. The play's final "cordial comfort" is the blessing that Hermione pours out for Perdita. Her prayer speaks twice of preservation:

Tell me, mine own,
Where has thou been *preserved* . . .
. . . For thou shalt hear that I,
Knowing by Paulina that the oracle
Gave hope thou wast in being, have *preserved*
Myself to see the issue. (5.3.123–28)

Although Gillian Woods links preservation in this passage to embalming,[46] I smell a connection with the kitchen arts of preserving, a word featured in the titles of many recipe collections of the period.[47] The housekeeper puts up the offerings of spring and summer in the pantry for enjoyment during the long winter

46. Woods, *Shakespeare's Unreformed Fictions*, 191. Compare the spices that Pericles packs into Thaisa's bitumened coffin.

47. *A Book of Fruits and Flowers*, frontispiece.

months, conserving what Wendy Wall calls "things in need of duration."[48] Hermione asks the gods to "pour out" an aqua vitae distilled from the first fruits of a childbirth lost, the sweetness of the present restoration tempered with the rosemary and rue of grace and remembrance (4.4.74–76). Hermione's blessing allows us to digest the folly of the play (its fantastic improbabilities) with the virtues of a custom (the act of benediction) without making us swallow more than is palatable (a forced forgiveness). Like a good *panna cotta*, Hermione's blessing is sweet, but not too sweet.

To eat cake is to refuse to live by bread alone. Dessert's original ties to seasonality, in the form of both fresh and preserved fruits, resonate with elements of the slow food, locavore, urban farming, and community-supported agriculture movements. In an age in which sugar threatens to saturate every meal in a neo-medieval influx of deregulated sweetness, I proffer "room for dessert" as a design resource for renewing our collective relationships to cooking and eating and to the spaces dedicated to sustenance and commensality. "Room for dessert" might also offer a model for the humanities. It is something of a cliché to speak of the arts and humanities as lovely but superfluous add-ons in a period of limited resources. Rather than simply defending humanities as meat and potatoes, however, which would mean emphasizing the instrumental benefits of our fields at the expense of the reflective and aesthetic capacities that we have historically cultivated, we might also link the proverbial "icing on the cake" to the social, digestive, and renewing function of dessert considered in its full rhythmic and spatial unfolding. The humanities permit a clearing—the establishment of spaces for free discussion and for the bringing into visibility of overlooked or unconsidered phenomena from everyday experience, from past periods of history, and from unfamiliar cultures and comportments. These clearings allow for rumination and reflection; they can also gather us for future action and make us attentive to the environments in

48. Wall, "Just a Spoonful of Sugar," 160.

which action occurs. In other words, like the dessert course, the humanities can help us learn how to rezone spaces, reorganize scripts and services, and reoccupy forgotten forms of life so that our settings for work and for dwelling afford more opportunities for acknowledgment, creativity, and action.

Epilogue

Fight Call

Christopher Sly: Is not a comonty a Christmas gambold, or a tumbling-trick?
Page: No, my good lord, it is more pleasing stuff.
Christopher Sly: What, household stuff?
Page: It is a kind of history.
«*The Taming of the Shrew*, Induction, 2.137–41[1]»

Sly thinks comedies are a matter of village sport: a Christmas gambol ("an energetic or exaggerated leap or bound made by a horse"[2]) or a tumbling trick, like the jigs that ended Elizabethan plays with a splash of music and dance. Sly then imagines that comedy might involve "household stuff," naming the continuum between domesticity and dramaturgy that I have gathered here under the dwelling perspective. The Page instructs Sly that comedy is "a kind of history," a humanist form that eschews rustic sports for the narrative coherence and fictive world-building of drama. The ensuing play provides it all, integrating popular gaming with humanist learning in settings laden with joint-stools, Turkey cushions, pewter and brass, and a dessert course or two.[3]

1. Cited from *The Riverside Shakespeare*.

2. "Gambol," *OED*, 1.

3. Lesley Wade Soule, "Tumbling Tricks: Presentational Structure and 'The Taming of the Shrew,'" 164. On *Shrew* and household stuff, see Natasha Korda, *Shakespeare's*

To "tumble" is "to fall in a helpless way, as from stumbling or violence" (*OED*, II.3a); it is also to "dance with posturing, balancing, contortions, and the like; to perform as an acrobat" (*OED*, I.1). A tumbling trick orchestrates—or perhaps *tames*—the horror of free fall into the delight of dance, while the Page's "kind of history" subordinates acrobatic kinesis to dramatic mimesis. Tumbling tricks are the essence of stage combat, which uses athletic cooperation to create the fiction of fighting, heightening the impact of the "kind of history" that drama provides. I witnessed my first fight call during dress rehearsals for *The Comedy of Errors*, staged at UC Irvine in the summer of 2011. Half an hour before curtain time, the stage manager called the actors to run through every scene that involved fighting, tumbling, or dances with lifts—any routine that might endanger actors or audience. A fight call resembles a movie trailer: all the action bits happen in sequence, played before your eyes in triplicate, first in slow motion, then at half speed, and then at full tilt. Fight call leaves the actors limber, loose, and ready to go, while the lucky observer gets to see exactly how the falls are faked and the slaps kept happy. Bam! Kapow! Not.

In a production of *Shrew* at UC Irvine in 2017, director Beth Lopes brilliantly integrated a fistfight between Kate and Petruchio into act 4, scene 5's "I say it is the moon" routine. Their mock-heroic *aristea*, in which great warriors prove their arête in face-to-face combat, ends in a draw, with the spouses lying spent on the ground and laughingly acknowledging the spunk and skill of the other. When the dialogue resumes, they have become partners in a social dance of verbal wit and comic redescription. Cued by guitar chords in keeping with the 1980s setting, what looked like a domestic assault happening in real time was actually a dance unfolding in rehearsed time. In scenes like these, the actors learn

---

Domestic Economies; and Julia Lupton, *Thinking with Shakespeare*, 25–67. Sly is served "conserves" (preserved fruit) (Induction, 2.3), and the final "banquet" following the wedding ceremony and presented in Lucentio's rented quarters would have been a light repast (Oxford *Shrew*, 221n).

to rely on each other and their muscle memory to take each other through to a safe and smooth finish. Specially trained fight choreographers work with the actors to create the illusion of spontaneous physical violence, and the fight call takes all the partners in the routine through its constituent parts. Physical theater, in which actors use the push and pull of their bodies to compose actions and tableaux with minimal recourse to props or scenography, elaborates tumbling tricks into an independent form of drama. In her moving adaptations of Ovid's *Metamorphoses* and Homer's *Odyssey*, my colleague Annie Loui, a student of Jerzy Grotowski, uses bodies in movement to build ships, monsters, storms, and palaces.[4]

Stage combat and physical theater visualize the taking apart and putting together that animates all sorts of intellectual and creative work, from chemistry to choreography. When I decide to cook from a recipe, the deliberate staging of ingredients boosts my speed and confidence on those other evenings when I compose meals directly from the fridge. Religious practice can also be a form of physical theater. When I pray with others, light Sabbath candles, or make a Passover seder, I am not replacing everyday experience with something mystical or otherworldly. Instead, I am using liturgy to decompose and recompose the blur of normal reality in order to live more fluently. The seven days of creation are neither fact nor fiction. Instead, they are a fight call for the world and a recipe for the creative process. Divide, organize, and assemble; constellate, animate, and populate; rest and repeat.

Tumbling tricks and stage combat require trust as well as training. Many of Annie Loui's exercises for the physical actor are designed to enhance cooperation among the players; her "trust-nod" exercise, for example, requires attentive watching and silent signaling as members of the ensemble exchange places in a circle: "After several rounds you will find that the actors respond

4. Annie Loui, *The Physical Actor: Exercises for Action and Awareness.*

more quickly, having learned that vigilant attentiveness to the action makes them more successful participants."[5] In exercises such as "waterfall" and "push-me, pull-me," pairs of players learn "to manipulate and control the flow of weight and momentum of another person." The two "sharers in the endeavor" shift between "responsive and active roles" in the orchestration of movements that Loui compares to "a good conversation."[6] "Trust" and "courage" are recurrent words in Loui's manual. The trust at stake is interpersonal, but it is also environmental, involving the actor's responsiveness to the affordances of the space. Many exercises developed in contact improvisation and physical theater have been adapted for civilian team-building, from boardrooms to summer camps. In the classic "trust fall," which has become a cliché of the organizational management repertoire, participants risk falling backward because they trust that others will catch them, a trust built upon the covenantal rhythm of taking turns.

Some trust exercises involve a blindfolded partner giving herself over to guidance by another, who must then submit to the same deprivation and dependency. Edgar's leading of the blinded Gloucester to Dover is an early form of physical theater, built out of children's games like blind man's bluff, hide-and-seek, and peekaboo. Such games alter perceptual experience in order to initiate new relationships to the environment and to one's partners in play. Although many readers fault Edgar for not revealing himself to his father, I see the long walk to Dover as a trust-building sojourn that establishes a rapport between the blind man and his guide by retuning sensory knowledge and soliciting interpersonal dependency. The time of the journey allows for rehab and repair, in which Gloucester learns to see feelingly: that is, to walk with his partner through the blinded landscape and to enter into a middle zone of anticipatory and partial recognition of his son. Smelling his way to Dover, Gloucester trusts the beggar to lead him to the cliff, but he may also trust Edgar to prevent real

5. Ibid., 41.
6. Ibid., 92,

harm. In the words of cognitive literary historian Hannah Chapelle Wojciehowski, Shakespeare is a "sensory-motor artist" who draws on both actor and audience experiences of recomposed vitality in order to build new stories out of Christmas gambols and tumbling tricks.[7]

Trust exercises develop the environmental aspects of trust in tandem with its social valences. We are speaking of trust in environmental terms when we talk about "trusting our senses" or "trusting a chair" or "not trusting the weather." The Nurse weans Juliet while leaning against a dovehouse wall, an evocative environment of trust that supports separation, a kind of controlled betrayal. *Macbeth* depicts sleep as a delicate ecology of bedtime prayers, drugged possets, posted guards, and soft furnishings, which together induce the recipient to fall into a slumber; in *Shrew*, Petruchio takes aim at that same sleep ecology when he plans to "fling the pillow, there the bolster, / This way the coverlet, another way the sheets" in order to keep his bride awake all night (4.1.188–90). The 2015 film *Room* takes its title from the terrible shed whose bleak familiarity allows mother and child to build trust and eventually exercise courage. Hospitality constitutes at once a liturgy, a dramaturgy, and a scenography of trust and risk. Defining trust as an "anticipatory affect," philosopher Sverre Raffnsøe explores trust as "a resolve to bear an experienced risk by confiding in the new and unknown."[8] As a transactional virtue, trust becomes a gift to the other person, who, rising to the call for courage and care requested of him, enters into a ramifying covenant based on reciprocity and the generation of a new interpersonal surplus that in turn fortifies the social body.[9]

Every act of theater is an exercise of courage as well as trust, precisely because actors can forget lines or drop their partners,

7. See Hannah Chapelle Wojciehowski on Shakespeare as "a sensory-motor artist"; she interprets "games of childhood through the lens of embodied cognition, in order to analyse the 'vitality effects'" of the statue scene in *The Winter's Tale*. "Statues That Move: Vitality Effects in *The Winter's Tale*."

8. Sverre Raffnsøe, "Beyond Rule: Trust and Power as Capacities."

9. Ibid., 234.

audiences can laugh or sneeze at the wrong moment, and sound and lighting can fail. Such lapses flare into existential anxiety around identity, embodiment, and exposure, for the audience as well as the actors, and manifest the same risks that afflict speech in daily life. In Sonnet 23, Shakespeare connects the vocation of the actor with the virtue of courage:

> As an imperfect actor on the stage, who with his fear is put
> besides his part,
> Or some fierce thing replete with too much rage,
> Whose strength's abundance weakens his own heart.

The actor overcome by fear and unable to speak his lines is like "some fierce thing" whose upsurge of anger "weakens his own heart," rendering him unable to do anything at all. "Heart" here names not love but courage, *cour-age*, the pulse of appearance and withdrawal, speaking and listening, entrance and exit, that composes theater as an art of action that belongs to life. Courage = *courage* = heart = art. Courage involves trust: an element of faith in the goodwill and receptiveness of the interlocutor and the framework of the speech situation, whose contingencies must be real enough to afford a new act but reliable enough to allow that act to meet with a meaningful response, even if it is rejection or critique.

As we have seen, Hannah Arendt defines courage as the act of "leaving one's private place and showing who one is, disclosing and exposing one's self." Transferred from the battlefield to the polis, for Arendt courage is a quintessentially humanist virtue that concerns the nature of public speech, for both official state actors and for para-citizens—Arendt's trio of "women, slaves and barbarians"—who were excluded from Greek public life. The humanities, I'd like to suggest, *cultivate courage* in *environments of trust*. At stake here are not only major acts of outspokenness—students becoming activists or occupiers—but also the modest efforts at self-disclosure that humanities instructors solicit every day from freshmen and nonmajors, students of color, and underresourced and first-generation college-goers. These are the Arendtian "women, slaves, and barbarians" whose presence makes every university a *public university*, a space that tests our ability to mutually appear to and recognize each other. Current debates about safe spaces and microaggressions speak as much to a betrayal of trust on the part of university institutions as to a failure of courage by those demanding new protections; meanwhile, students who organize in favor of such measures are themselves exercising courage as communicative capacity. Microaggression is the reverse of stage combat; in fight choreography, what appears to be violence is actually a dance, while in microaggression, what appears to be ordinary speech is in fact hurtful action. The challenge confronting universities right now is how to build environments of trust in which speech can be exercised with more awareness of inequities in empowerment, self-confidence, and belonging in order to reclaim the person-disclosing capacities of speech from acknowledgment-denying habits of privilege. The current term "campus climate" is an evocatively ambient word that locates the possibilities of speech in virtue ecologies that distribute and require trust unevenly, leading to disturbances in courage.

Niklaus Luhmann writes that "the basis of all trust is the presentation of the individual self as a social identity which builds itself up through interaction and which corresponds to its environment."[10] Luhmann indicates here the dramatic character of trust in its social (interpersonal) and environmental (systems) dimension, whose conjunction can be thickened to accommodate differentials in status and power. All literature, but especially dramatic literature, enacts the risk and new birth of self-disclosure through speech in relation to others. *Reading* literature requires that we participate in that disclosure as witnesses to it: imagining, attending, judging, recognizing, empathizing, admitting, allowing. *Teaching* literature transforms that witnessing into something more fully dialogic, requiring greater responsiveness on the parts of both instructors and students. In practicing that

10. Luhmann, *Trust and Power*, 62.

witnessing in the disciplined space of the classroom, conceived as both a physical setting and a communicative climate, the partners in learning develop but also disclose—develop precisely through disclosing—aspects of their own mental functioning. Teaching literature is an art of *encouragement*: of bringing out and exercising human capacities for principled self-disclosure. Understanding and protecting that dynamic may help us get at the heart (*cour-age*) of what animates both literary education and live performance. In future work, I want to mount a defense of the humanities that would reconvene the critical and creative skills needed for meaningful employment and active citizenship within a framework of virtues, including trust, courage, judgment, attention, resilience, fidelity, and respect. Virtues are transactional and interpersonal, requiring the cooperation of partners and the presence of witnesses gathered in settings shaped by their own affordances and constraints. And virtues reveal their transactional rhythms and situational dependencies in the copresence and counterbalance of classroom work. Reading literature collectively can allow us to reflect on virtue practices in a manner that is historically and politically attuned to the uneven sharing of capability, in order to engage virtue not as fossilized ideology but as renewable resource.[11]

In *The Human Condition*, Arendt notes the unexpected proximity between political action and the affective labors of the healer, the flute player, the clergyman, and the housekeeper:

> Aristotle, in his political philosophy, is still well aware of what is at stake in politics, namely, no less than the *ergon tou anthrōpou* (the "work of man" *qua* man), and if he defined this "work" as "to live well" (*eu zēn*), he clearly meant that "work" here is no work product but exists only in its sheer actuality. This specifically human achievement lies altogether outside the category of means and ends; the "work of man" is no end because the means to achieve it—the virtues, or *aretai*—are not qualities which may or may not be actualized, but are themselves "actualities." . . . It was precisely these occupations—

11. See Martha Nussbaum, *Creating Capabilities: The Human Development Approach*.

> healing, flute-playing, play-acting—which furnished ancient thinking with examples for the highest and greatest activities of man. (206–7)

Here Arendt draws together not only political action, drama, and music in the temporality of performance, but also the "menial services" of housework and the healing arts of the physician, whose efforts refresh place and person without producing tangible objects. The work of teaching and administration, which aim to create and curate spaces for others to appear and flourish, could easily be added to the list. Arendt associates this cluster of activities that extend from the *oikos* to the polis with the virtuality of virtue, which is realized in and as its performance. In John Kiess's helpful gloss, "the virtues are not simply tools that help us arrive at happiness, but are themselves a tangible taste of happiness."[12]

Shrew convenes tumbling tricks, household stuff, and humanist storytelling in order to test the transformations and occlusions of affect, impact, status, and power that accompany the search for speech. *Shrew* also mobilizes a remarkable range of virtues—human, animal, and environmental; civic and domestic; literary and musical—that contribute their potentialities to both the drama of dwelling and the art of theater. In Shakespearean drama, the physical enskillment implied by "taming" and pursued in sports, husbandry, and dance is wedded with the humanist arts of literary and musical education explored in the tutorials of *Shrew*'s romantic subplot. In the scene at Dover, Edgar and Gloucester cocreate a risky trust exercise that swirls the new visual technology of perspective with the sensory experiments inherent in children's games into a powerful vortex of virtuality with the capacity to both heal and kill. The action at Dover Cliff draws on the roots of Shakespearean drama in game, ritual, prayer, and passion play in a manner that offers them up to us as living resources for theater and life. *The Taming of the Shrew* and *King Lear* enter the region of arête from comic and tragic

12. *Hannah Arendt and Theology*, 173.

doors, but they animate a stage space whose existential stakes are not micromanaged by the rules of genre. In Shakespeare's plays, especially in his later works, but already in *Shrew*'s testing of comic decorum, genre allows the unknown to be released and encountered within the bounds of the known. In the words of Paul Kottman, "formal rules for storytelling are no help for a body of drama . . . that has to solve for itself, again and again with each new play and performance, what a drama *is* and what it might become."[13] Ultimately, received forms cannot explain the enterprise of plays that test the interdependence of human emotions, virtuous capacities, and environmental *données*. It is in this sense that Shakespeare's dwelling perspective provides designs for the theater of life.

13. Paul A. Kottman, "Why Think about Shakespearean Tragedy Today?," 245.

Acknowledgments

A book on dwelling begins and ends at home. To my *beschert*, Kenneth Reinhard, I owe my education in loving and living as well as my late-coming passion for the joys of performance. To our children, Hannah, Isabel, Lucy, and Eliot, I owe my sense of messianic time. My mother, Mary Jane Lupton, led the way into professing English and continues to inspire me with her willingness to take on new academic projects in retirement, as well as her adventures in *ecclesia*. My father, Bill Lupton, is a DIY architect; Ken Baldwin continues to teach me about housing; and Lauren Carter understands the arts of healing. I am sorry not to be able to share this book with my inspiring and endlessly supportive father-in-law, Frank Reinhard.

My sister, Ellen Lupton, has been teaching me about design since our early childhood in Richard Scarry's Busytown. Colby Gordon's thinking about place and other stuff colors many pages of this book, which could not have been completed without his intensive feedback during a crisis of confidence. This book is dedicated to Ellen and to Colby.

My colleagues at the University of California, Irvine (UCI), especially Jonathan Alexander, Elizabeth Allen, Vivian Folkenflik, Robert Folkenflik, Daniel Gross, Jayne Lewis, Jack Miles, and Jane O. Newman, have been supports and inspirations. The Department of Drama invited me into their most intimate workings by allowing me to serve as dramaturg for New Swan Shakespeare Festival; special thanks to Eli Simon, Robert Cohen, Annie Loui, Ian Munro, and the many talented actors, designers, and stage crew who have welcomed me as a participant-observer.

I had the pleasure of collaborating with Lowell Gallagher, James Kearney, and Sean Keilen in the formation of w/Shakespeare, a multicampus research group funded by the University of California Humanities Research Institute (2011 to 2013). The w/Shakespeare group hosted a range of conversations whose fruits are partly gathered in this book, including several opportunities to learn from the amazing Bruce Smith; a two-day seminar on *Romeo and Juliet*; and a set of events at the Clark Library on Shakespeare between performance and philosophy from 2016 to 2017.

Eric Santner and Pam Pascoe have been intellectual friends and supporters of a rare sort, as have Graham Hammill, Paul Kottman, and Jerry Christensen.

This work was conducted in the context of institutions and communities that have sustained me, including the women and men of Congregation B'nai Israel, Tarbut V'Torah Community Day School, and University Hills; the leadership and membership of the Shakespeare Association of America; my colleagues at UCI, which has been my intellectual home since 1989; and the Departments of English and Drama, the Group for the Study of Early Cultures, the UCI Shakespeare Center, and Humanities Core, which have given me numerous and extraordinary occasions for growth and meaningful exchange during the course of writing this book. I would also like to thank my many community reading partners for their insights and support, especially Kirk Davis Jr., who assisted with copyediting on my end; CeCe Sloan, an indefatigable community-builder; and Marilyn Sutton, who generously funded a research assistant, the amazing Laura Hatch, when I really needed help.

At the School of Criticism and Theory in 2013, I taught a seminar titled "Dwelling | Telling | Selling: Contemporary Design Topographies"; many thanks to Amanda Anderson, Ian Baucom, Jane Bennett, Jenny Williams, and my seminar participants.

From 2013 to 2014, a Guggenheim Fellowship allowed me concentrated time on this project.

My graduate students at UCI have contributed immeasurably to the development of this project. I would like to call out for special thanks Peter Cibula, Tracy Cummings, Chris Dearner, Chris Foley, Letty Garcia, Laura Hatch, Sheiba Kian Kaufman, Daniel Keegan, Donovan Sherman, Robin Stewart, Shaina Trapedo, Jeffrey Wilson, and Alexandra Zobel. Chris Dearner assisted with proofreading and the index.

Other scholars whose work has touched me deeply during this period include Tommy Anderson, Sarah Beckwith, Sanford Buddick, Joseph Campana, Paul Cefalu, Brian Cummings, Kevin Curran, Drew Daniel, Maria Devlin, Hugh Grady, Margreta de Grazia, David Goldstein, Hugh Grady, Richard Halpern, Peter Holland, Bonnie Honig, Sean Keilen, Lloyd Kermode, Mary Jo Kietzman, James Kuzner, William Junker, Naomi Liebler, Unhae Lingis, Randall Martin, Benjamin Parris, Björn Quiring, Sverre Raffnsøe, Matthew J. Smith, Ellen Spolsky, Peter Stallybrass, Joseph Sterrett, Richard Strier, Garrett Sullivan, Viola Timm, Lynn Tribble, Henry Turner, Jennifer Waldron, and W. B. Worthen.

I delivered portions of this project at many venues, including meetings of the Modern Language Association, the Shakespeare Association of America, the Renaissance Society of America, and the World Shakespeare Congress; the University of California campuses at Santa Barbara and Berkeley, as well as at Irvine; New York University; Rice University; University of Pennsylvania; University of Utah; the California State University at Long Beach; Harvard University; and Johns Hopkins University.

The anonymous readers for the University of Chicago Press provided invaluable advice at two stages of the writing process, and Alan Thomas delivered some astute style directives that will continue to shape my writing for years to come. Mark Reschke provided careful and sensitive copyediting.

Shakespeare Dwelling has been built iteratively and in response to a range of invitations to think and play with others. Thus portions of some chapters have appeared in print over the period of the book's composition.

Elements of chapter 1 appeared in "Making Room, Affording Hospitality: Environments of Entertainment in *Romeo and Juliet*," *Journal of Medieval and Early Modern Studies* 43, no. 1 (2013): 145–72.

Elements of chapter 2 appeared in "Shakespearean Softscapes: Hospitality, Phenomenology, Design," in *The Return of Theory in Early Modern English Studies*, vol. 2, ed. Paul Cefalu, Gary Kuchar, and Bryan Reynolds, 143–64 (Basingstoke: Palgrave Macmillan, 2014), reproduced with permission of Palgrave Macmillan; and "*Macbeth*'s Martlets: Shakespearean Phenomenologies of Hospitality," *Criticism* 54, no. 3 (Summer 2012): 365–76, published by Wayne State University Press.

A version of chapter 3 was published as "Shakespeare Dwelling: *Pericles* and the Affordances of Action," *Shakespeare and the Urgency of Now*, ed. Hugh Grady and Cary DiPietro, 60–82 (Basingstoke: Palgrave Macmillan, 2013); reproduced with permission of Palgrave Macmillan.

A version of chapter 5 was published as "Room for Dessert: Sugared Shakespeare and the Dramaturgy of Dwelling," in *Culinary Shakespeare: Staging Food and Drink in Early Modern England*, ed. David B. Goldstein and Amy L. Tigner, 199–224 (Pittsburgh: Duquesne University Press, 2016).

I wrote several concept pieces that helped establish the terrain of this book, including "Hospitality," which appeared in *Early Modern Theatricality*, ed. Henry S. Turner (Oxford: Oxford University Press, 2013), 423–41; and "Dwelling," which appeared in the *Cambridge Companion to Literature and Religion*, ed. Susan M. Felch, 86–102 (Cambridge: Cambridge University Press, 2016). My thanks to Henry Turner and Susan Felch for their encouragement and feedback.

Bibliography

Abbot, George. *An Exposition upon the prophet Ionah*. London: Richard Field, 1600.

Adams, Thomas. *The Sacrifice of Thankfulnesse: A Sermon preached at Pauls Crosse, the third of December, being the first Adventuall Sunday, anno 1615*. London, 1616.

Addison, Lancelot. *The Present State of the Jews (more particularly relating to those in Barbary), wherein is contained an exact account of their customs, secular and religious*. London, 1675.

Adrichem, Christiaan van. *A brief description of Hierusalem and of the suburbs thereof.* Translated by Thomas Tymme. London, 1595.

Aesop. *Esops fables*. London: Thomas Man, 1617.

Affinati, Giacomo. *The dumbe diuine speaker*. London: R. Bradock for William Leake, 1605.

Agamben, Giorgio. *Profanations*. Translated by Jeff Fort. New York: Zone Books, 2007.

———. *The Time That Remains: A Commentary on the Letter to the Romans*. Translated by Patricia Dailey. Stanford, CA: Stanford University Press, 2005.

Agnon, S. Y. *Present at Sinai: The Giving of the Law*. Translated by Michael Swirsky. Philadelphia: Jewish Publication Society, 1994.

Agrippa, Henry Cornelius. *Three Books of Occult Philosophy*. London: RW for Gregory Moule, 1651.

Ahmed, Sara. *Queer Phenomenology: Orientations, Objects, Others*. Durham, NC: Duke University Press, 2006.

Ainsworth, Henry. *Annotations upon the five bookes of Moses*. London: John Bellamie, 1627.

Albala, Ken. *Cooking in Europe, 1250–1650*. Westport, CT: Greenwood Press, 2006.

Albright, Daniel. *Musicking Shakespeare: A Conflict of Theatres*. Rochester, NY: University of Rochester Press, 2007.

Anderson, Judith M. "Working Imagination in the Early Modern Period: Donne's Secular and Religious Lyrics and Shakespeare's Hamlet, Macbeth, and Leontes." In *Shakespeare and Donne: Generic Hybrids and the Cultural Imaginary*, edited by Judith H. Anderson and Jennifer C. Vaught, 185–219. New York: Fordham University Press, 2013.

Andreoli, Ilaria. "Ovid's 'Meta-metamorphosis': Book Illustration and the Circulation of Erotic Iconographical Patterns." In *Shakespeare's Erotic Mythology and Ovidian Renaissance Culture*, edited by Agnès Lafont, 19–39. Farnham: Ashgate, 2013.

Andrewes, Lancelot. *XCVI Sermons*. London: George Miller for Richard Badger, 1629.

Anonymous. *A Book of Fruits and Flowers, shewing the Nature and use of them, either for Meat or Medicine. As Also: To Preserve, Conserve, Candy, and in Wedges, or Dry Them*. London: Thomas Jenner, 1653.

Appadurai, Arjun. "Modernity at Large." In *Design Studies: A Reader*, edited by Hazel Clark and David Brody, 421–25. Oxford: Berg, 2009.

Appelbaum, Robert. "'Standing to the Wall': The Pressures of Masculinity in *Romeo and Juliet*." *Shakespeare Quarterly* 48, no. 3 (Autumn 1997): 251–72.

Arbery, Glenn C. "The Displaced Nativity in Cymbeline." In *Shakespeare's Last Plays: Essays in Literature and Politics*, edited by Stephen W. Smith and Travis Curtright, 157–78. Lanham, MD: Lexington Books, 2002.

Archer, Bruce. "The Three Rs." In *A Framework for Design and Design Education*. Warwickshire: Design and Technology Association, 2005.

Arendt, Hannah. "The Crisis in Culture: Its Social and Its Political Significance." In *Between Past and Future: Eight Exercises in Political Thought*, 197–226. New York: Viking, 1968.

———. "The Crisis in Education." In *Between Past and Future: Eight Exercises in Political Thought*, 173–96. New York: Viking, 1968.

———. *The Human Condition*. 2nd ed. Chicago: University of Chicago Press, 1958.

———. *Love and St. Augustine*. Edited by Joanna Vechiarelli Scott and Judith Chelius Stark. Chicago: University of Chicago Press, 1996.

———. *The Origins of Totalitarianism*. New York: Harcourt and Brace, 1978.

Ariel, David S. *Kabbalah: The Mystic Quest in Judaism*. Lanham, MD: Rowman and Littlefield, 2005.

Armstrong, Karen, ed. *Tongues of Fire: An Anthology of Religious and Poetic Experience*. London: Puffin Books, 1987.

Arvidsson, Adam. *Brands: Meaning and Value in Media Culture*. New York: Routledge, 2006.

Astington, John. *English Court Theatre, 1558–1642*. Cambridge: Cambridge University Press, 1999.

Auerbach, Erich. "Figura." In *Time, History, and Literature: Selected Essays of Erich Auerbach*, edited by James I. Porter and translated by Jane O. Newman, 65–113. Princeton, NJ: Princeton University Press, 2014.

———. *Mimesis: The Representation of Reality in Western Literature*. Translated by Willard R. Trask. Princeton, NJ: Princeton University Press, 1953.

Badiou, Alain. *Rhapsody for the Theatre*. Edited and translated by Bruno Bosteels. London: Verso, 2013.

Ballantyne, Andrew. *Architecture Theory: A Reader in Philosophy and Culture*. London: Continuum, 2005.

Ballantyne, Andrew, and Chris L. Smith, eds. *Architecture in the Space of Flows*. London: Routledge, 2011.

Balmori, Diana. *A Landscape Manifesto*. New Haven, CT: Yale University Press, 2010.

Balmori, Diana, and Joel Sanders. *Groundwork: Between Landscape and Architecture*. New York: Random House, 2011.

Barba, Eugenio. *On Directing and Dramaturgy: Burning the House*. Translated by Judy Barba. London: Routledge, 2010.

Barkan, Leonard. "Making Pictures Speak: Renaissance Art, Elizabethan Literature, Modern Scholarship." *Renaissance Quarterly* 48, no. 2 (Summer 1995): 326–51.

Barrow, Henry. *A Brief Discourse of the False Churche*. London, 1591.

Bataille, Georges. *The Accursed Share*. Vol. 1, *Consumption*. Translated by Robert Hurley. Cambridge, MA: Zone Books, 1992.

Bate, Jonathan. *The Song of the Earth*. Cambridge, MA: Harvard University Press, 2000.

Batman, Stephen. *Batman vppon Bartholome His Booke De proprietatibus rerum*. London: Thomas East, 1582.

———. *The Golden Booke of the Leaden Goddes*. London, 1577.

Baucom, Ian. "History 4°: Postcolonial Method and Anthropocene Time." *Cambridge Journal of Postcolonial Literary Inquiry* 1, no. 1 (March 2014): 123–42.

Baxter, Nathaniel. *Sir Philip Syndeys Ourania, that is, Endimions song and tragedie, containing all philosophie*. London: Ed. Allde for Edward White, 1606.

B. E. *A New Dictionary of the Canting Crew*. London, 1699.

Beacham, Richard C. *Adolphe Appia: Theater Artist*. Cambridge: Cambridge University Press, 1987.

Beckwith, Sarah. *Shakespeare and the Grammar of Forgiveness*. Ithaca, NY: Cornell University Press, 2011.

Belsey, Catherine. "Ekphrasis in *Lucrece* and Beyond." *Shakespeare Quarterly* 63, no. 2 (Summer 2012): 175–98.

Benjamin, Walter. *Illuminations*. Edited by Hannah Arendt. Translated by Harry Zohn. New York: Schocken Books, 1968.

Benyosef, Simcha H. *Living the Kabbalah: A Guide to the Sabbath and Festivals in the Teachings of Rabbi Rafael Moshe Luria*. New York: Continuum, 2006.

Bennett, Jane. "Thing-Power." In *Political Matter: Technoscience, Democracy, and Public Life*, edited by Bruce Braun and Sarah J. Whatmore, 35–62. Minneapolis: University of Minnesota Press, 2010.

———. "Vegetal Life and OntoSympathy." Paper delivered at the School for Criticism and Theory, Cornell University, 2013.

———. *Vibrant Matter: A Political Ecology of Things*. Durham, NC: Duke University Press, 2010.

Bennett, Susan. *Theatre Audiences: A Theory of Production and Reception*. 2nd ed. New York: Routledge, 1997.

Berensmeyer, Ingo. "Shakespeare and Media Ecology: Beyond Historicism and Presentism." *Poetics Today* 35, no. 4 (2014): 515–38.

Berger, Harry, Jr. *A Fury in the Words: Love and Embarrassment in Shakespeare's Venice*. New York: Fordham, 2013.

———. *Making Trifles of Terrors: Redistributing Complicities in Shakespeare*. Edited by Peter Erickson. Stanford, CA: Stanford University Press, 1997.

Berlant, Lauren. *Cruel Optimism*. Durham, NC: Duke University Press, 2011.

Berman, Louis A. *The Akedah: The Binding of Isaac*. Northvale, NJ: Aaronson Books, 1997.

Bernstein, Susan. *Housing Problems: Writing and Architecture in Goethe, Walpole, Freud, and Heidegger*. Stanford, CA: Stanford University Press, 2008.

Berry, Philippa. "Between Idolatry and Astrology: Modes of Temporal Repetition in *Romeo and Juliet*." In *A Feminist Companion to Shakespeare*, edited by Dympna Callaghan, 358–72. Malden, MA: Blackwell, 2000.

Betteridge, Tom. *Literature and Politics in the English Reformation*. Manchester: University of Manchester Press, 2004.

———. "Writing Faithfully in a Post-Confessional World." In *Late Shakespeare, 1608–1613*, edited by Andrew J. Power and Rory Loughnane, 225–42. Cambridge: Cambridge University Press, 2013.

Bevington, David. *This Wide and Universal Theater: Shakespeare in Performance, Then and Now*. Chicago: University of Chicago Press, 2007.

———. "Tragedy in Shakespeare's Career." In *The Cambridge Companion to Shakespearean Tragedy*, edited by Claire McEachern, 51–70. 2nd ed. New York: Cambridge University Press, 2013.

Bèze, Théodore. *Sermons upon the three chapters of the canticle of canticles*. London: Joseph Barnes, 1587.

Bicks, Caroline. "Backsliding at Ephesus: Shakespeare's Diana and the Churching of Women." In *Pericles: Critical Essays*, edited by David Skeele, 205–27. New York: Garland, 2000.

Blau, Herbert. *The Dubious Spectacle: Extremities of Theater, 1976–2000*. Minneapolis: University of Minnesota Press, 2000.

Bloch, Abraham P. *The Biblical and Historical Background of Jewish Customs and Ceremonies*. New York: KTAV Publishing House, 1980.

Blumenberg, Hans. *Shipwreck with Spectator: Paradigm of a Metaphor for Existence*. Translated by Stephen Rendall. Cambridge, MA: MIT Press, 1997.

Boccaccio, Giovanni. *The Decameron*. Translated by G. H. McWilliam. London: Penguin, 1972.

Bodin, Jean. *Colloquium of the Seven about Secrets of the Sublime*. Translated and edited by Marion Leathers Kuntz. University Park: Pennsylvania State University Press, 2008.

Botwinick, Aryeh. "Shakespeare in Advance of Hobbes: Pathways to the Modernization of the European Psyche as Charted in *The Merchant of Venice*." *Telos* 153 (2010): 132–59.

Bradbrook, M. C. *The Living Monument: Shakespeare and the Theatre of His Time*. Cambridge: Cambridge University Press, 1976.

Bradley, A. C. *Shakespearean Tragedy*. New York: Merdian Books, 1955.

Bratich, Jack. "The Digital Touch: Craft-Work as Immaterial Labour and Ontological Accumulation," *ephemera* 10, no. 3/4 (2010): 303–18.

Brickner, David. *Christ in the Feast of Pentecost*. New York: Moody Publishers, 2008.

Bristol, Michael. "In Search of the Bear: Spatiotemporal Form and the Heterogeneity of Economies in *The Winter's Tale*." *Shakespeare Quarterly* 42, no. 2 (Summer 1991): 145–67.

———. "Macbeth the Philosopher." *New Literary History* 42, no. 4 (Autumn 2011): 641–62.

Brooks, Cleanth. *The Well Wrought Urn*. New York: Harcourt Brace, 1947.

Brooks, Mary M. *English Embroideries of the Sixteenth and Seventeenth Centuries in the Collection of the Ashmolean Museum*. London: Jonathan Horne, 2004.

Brown, Carolyn E. "Juliet's Taming of Romeo." *Studies in English Literature, 1500–1900* 36, no. 2 (Spring 1996): 333–55.

Bruckner, Lynne. "'Consuming means, soon preys upon itself': Political Expedience and Environmental Degradation in *Richard II*." In *Shakespeare and the Urgency of Now*, edited by Cary DiPietro and Hugh Grady, 126–47. New York: Palgrave MacMillan, 2013.

Bruckner, Lynne, and Daniel Brayton, eds. *Ecocritical Shakespeare*. Burlington, VT: Ashgate, 2011.

Bryant, Levi. *The Democracy of Objects*. Ann Arbor, MI: Open Humanities Press, 2011.

Burdick, Anne, Johanna Drucker, Peter Lunenfeld, Todd Presner, and Jeffrey Schnapp. *Digital_Humanities*. Cambridge, MA: MIT Press, 2012.

Budick, Sanford. "The Emergence of Oedipus' Blessing: Evoking Wolfgang Iser." *Partial Answers: Journal of Literature and the History of Ideas* 7, no. 2 (January 2009): 63–85.

———. "King Lear and Secular Benediction: The Language of Tragic Community in *King Lear*." In *Religious Diversity and Early Modern*

English Texts: Catholic, Judaic, Feminist, and Secular Dimensions, edited by Arthur F. Marotti and Chanita Goodblatt, 330–52. Detroit: Wayne State University Press, 2013.

Calvin, John. *Sermons of M. John Calvin upon the Fifth Book of Moses Called Deuteronomie.* Translated by Arthur Golding. London, 1583.

Campana, Joseph. "Spenser's Inhumanity." *Spenser Studies* 30 (2015): 277–99.

———. "The Traffic in Children: Shipwrecked Shakespeare, Precarious Pericles." In *Childhood, Education, and the Stage in Early Modern Europe*. Edited by Richard Preiss and Deanne Williams, 37–57. Cambridge: Cambridge University Press, 2017.

Campana, Joseph, and Scott Maisano, eds. *Renaissance Posthumanism.* New York: Fordham University Press, 2016.

Campbell, Stephen J. "Giorgione's *Tempest*, *Studiolo* Culture, and the Renaissance Lucretius." *Renaissance Quarterly* 56, no. 2 (Summer 2003): 299–332.

Campbell, Thomas. *Henry VIII and the Art of Majesty: Tapestries at the Tudor Court.* New Haven, CT: Yale University Press, 2007.

Campi, Emido, and Joseph C. McLelland, eds. *Commentary on the Nichomachean Ethics*. Kirksville, MO: Truman State University, 2006.

Cantarella, Eva. *Bisexuality in the Ancient World.* Translated by Cormac O Cuileanain. New Haven, CT: Yale University Press, 1992.

Carpenter, Eugene E., and Philip W. Comfort. *Holman Treasury of Key Bible Words*. Nashville: Broadman and Holman, 2000.

Carroll, William C., ed. *Macbeth: Texts and Contexts*. New York: Bedford, 1999.

Carruthers, Mary. "Mystery of the Bed Chamber: Mnemotechnic and Vision in Chaucer's *Book of the Dutchess*." In *The Rhetorical Poetics of the Middle Ages*, edited by J. M. Hill and D. Sinnreich-Levi, 67–87. Madison, NJ: Fairleigh Dickinson University Press, 2000.

Cicero. *The First book of Tullies Offices*. London: Thomas Man, 1616.

Cohen, A., ed. *The Twelve Prophets*. Soncino Hebrew-English Bible. London: Soncino Press, 1994.

Cohen, Jeffrey Jerome, ed. *Animal, Vegetable, Mineral: Ethics and Objects*. Washington, DC: punctum books/Oliphaunt Books, 2012.

Cohen, Jeffrey Jerome, and Julian Yates, eds. *Object Oriented Environs*. Earth: punctum books, 2016.

Cole, Mary Hill. *The Portable Queen: Elizabeth I and the Politics of Ceremony*. Amherst: University of Massachusetts Press, 1999.

Coolidge, John. *The Pauline Renaissance: Puritanism and the Bible*. Oxford: Clarendon Press, 1970.

Cooper, John. *Eat and Be Satisfied: A Social History of Jewish Food*. Northvale, NJ: Jason Aaronson, 1993.

Cooper, Joseph. *The Art of Cookery refin'd and augmented*. London, 1654.

Cormack, Braden. "Decision, Possession: The Time of Law in *The Winter's* Tale and the Sonnets." In *Shakespeare and the Law*, edited by Cormack, Richard Strier, and Martha Nussbaum, 44–71. Chicago: University of Chicago Press, 2013.

———. *A Power to Do Justice: Jurisdiction, English Literature, and the Rise of Common Law, 1509–1625*. Chicago: University of Chicago Press, 2007.

———. "Shakespeare's Other Sovereignty: On Particularity and Violence in *The Winter's Tale* and the Sonnets." *Shakespeare Quarterly* 62, no. 4 (Winter 2011): 485–513.

Cosgrove, Denis. *Social Formation and Symbolic Landscape*. Madison: University of Wisconsin Press, 1984.

Cova, Bernard, Robert V. Kozinets, and Avi Shankar, eds. *Consumer Tribes*. Amsterdam: Elsevier, 2007.

Cummings, Brian. *Mortal Thoughts: Religion, Secularity and Identity in Shakespeare and Early Modern Culture*. Oxford: Oxford University Press, 2013.

Curran, Kevin. "Feeling Criminal in *Macbeth*." *Criticism* 54, no. 3 (Summer 2012): 391–401.

Csíkszentmihályi, Mihály, and Isabella Selega Csíkszentmihályi, eds. *Optimal Experience: Psychological Studies of Flow in Consciousness*. Cambridge: Cambridge University Press, 1988.

Daniel, Drew. "All Sound Is Queer." *The Wire* 33, no. 3 (2011): 43–46.

———. *The Melancholy Assemblage: Affect and Epistemology in the English Renaissance*. New York: Fordham University Press, 2013.

Dargis, Manohla. "This Is How the End Begins (Lars von Trier's *Melancholia*)." *New York Times*, December 30, 2011. http://www.nytimes.com/2012/01/01/movies/awardsseason/manohla-dargis-looks-at-the-overture-to-melancholia.html?_r=0. Accessed November 20, 2013.

Davidson, Clifford. *Festivals and Plays in Late Medieval Britain*. Farnham, Surrey: Ashgate, 2007.

Davies, W. D. *Paul and Rabbinic Judaism: Some Rabbinic Elements in Pauline Theology*. Philadelphia: Fortress Press, 1980.

Day, Richard. *A Booke of Christian Prayers*. London: John Day, 1578.

Dean, Jodi. *Blog Theory: Feedback and Capture in the Circuits of the Drive*. Cambridge: Polity Press, 2010.

———. *Democracy and Other Neoliberal Fantasies: Communicative Capitalism and Left Politics*. Durham, NC: Duke University Press, 2009.

Dearner, Christopher. "'The Art of Our Necessities Is Strange': Accommodation, Affordances, and Thing Power on the Heath in *King Lear*." Master's essay, University of California, Irvine, 2012.

Degenhardt, Jane Hwang. "Seduction, Resistance, and Redemption." In *Islamic Conversion and Christian Resistance on the Early Modern Stage*, 1–31. Edinburgh: Edinburgh University Press, 2010.

de Granada, Luis. *A paradise of prayers*. London, 1614.

Derrida, Jacques. *Of Hospitality*. Translated by Rachel Bowlby. Stanford, CA: Stanford University Press, 2000.

———. *Spectres of Marx*. New York: Routledge, 1994.

Dessen, Allen, and Leslie Thomson. *Dictionary of Stage Directions, 1580–1642*. Cambridge: Cambridge University Press, 1999.

de Vries, Hent. "Introduction." In *Political Theologies: Public Religions in a Post-Secular World*. New York: Fordham University Press, 2006.

Dewey, John. "Interest and Effort in Education." In *The Middle Works of John Dewey, 1899–1924*, edited by Ralph Ross, 151–98. Carbondale: University of Southern Illinois Press, 1979.

Diehl, Huston. "'Does Not the Stone Rebuke Me?': The Pauline Rebuke and Paulina's Lawful Magic in the Winter's Tale." In *Shakespeare and the Cultures of Performance*, edited by Paul Yachnin et al., 69–82. Aldershot: Ashgate, 2008.

Dolan, Frances E. "Gender and the 'Lost' Spaces of Catholicism." *Journal of Interdisciplinary History* 33, no. 4 (Spring 2002): 641–65.

———. "Hermione's Ghost: Catholicism, the Feminine, and the Undead in Early Modern Studies." In *The Impact of Feminism on Early Modern Studies*, edited by Dympna Callaghan, 214–37. New York: Palgrave, 2007.

Douce, Francis. *Illustrations of Shakespeare, and of Ancient Manners*. 2 vols. London, 1807.

Drayton, Michael. *The barrons wars in the raigne of Edward the second. With Englands heroicall epistles*. London, 1603.

Drucker, Johanna. *Graphesis: Visual Forms of Knowledge Production*. Cambridge, MA: Harvard University Press, 2014.

Dubrow, Heather. *Shakespeare and Domestic Loss*. Cambridge: Cambridge University Press, 1999.

Duckert, Lowell. "Exit, Pursued by a Polar Bear (More to Follow)." *Upstart: A Journal of English Renaissance Studies* (June 24, 2013). https://upstart.sites.clemson.edu/Essays/exit-pursued-by-a-polar-bear/exit-pursued-by-a-polar-bear.xhtml.

Duncan, Helga L. "'Here at the Fringe of the Forest': Staging Sacred Space in *As You Like It*." *Journal of Medieval and Early Modern Studies* 43, no. 1 (Winter 2013): 121–44.

Duncan-Jones, Katherine. *Shakespeare: An Ungentle Life*. London: Methuen/Arden, 2010.

Dyson, J. P. "The Structural Function of the Banquet Scene in *Macbeth*." *Shakespeare Quarterly* 14, no. 4 (Autumn 1963): 369–78.

Easterling, Keller. *Organization Space: Landscapes, Highways, and Houses in America*. Cambridge, MA: MIT Press, 1999.

Egan Gabriel. *Green Shakespeare: From Ecopolitics to Ecocriticism*. London: Routledge, 2006.

Elam, Keir. *The Semiotics of Theatre and Drama*. 2nd ed. New York: Taylor and Francis, 2005.

Elyot, Thomas. *The dictionary of syr Thomas Eliot knight*. London: Thomas Berthelet, 1538.

Engle, Lars. "Pragmatism." In *The Oxford Handbook Of Shakespeare*, edited by Arthur F. Kinney, 641–62. New York: Oxford University Press, 2012.

Epstein, Louis M. *The Jewish Marriage Contract: A Study in the Status of Women in Jewish Law*. New York: Jewish Theological Seminary of America, 1927.

Ewert, Kevin. "Colm Feore." In *The Routledge Companion to Actors' Shakespeare*, edited by John Russell Brown Abingdon, 49–62. Oxon: Routledge: 2012.

Feldman, Emmanuel. *The Shul without a Clock*. Jerusalem: Feldheim Publishers, 2001.

Félix, Joseph. *Notre Dame du Cenacle: Our Lady of the Cenacle, or of the Retreat*. New York: Lafayette Press, 1896.

Feuer, Lois. "Hired for Mischief: Masterless Men in *Macbeth*." In *Macbeth: New Critical Essays*, edited by Nick Moschovakis, 151–62. New York: Routledge, 2008.

Finkelstein, Richard. "*Pericles*, Paul, and Protestantism." *Comparative Drama* 442 (Summer 2010): 101–29.

Fiorenza, Elisabeth Schüssler. *But She Said: Feminist Practices of Biblical Interpretation*. Boston: Beacon Press, 1992.

———. *In Memory of Her: A Feminist Theological Reconstruction of Christian Origins*. New York: Crossroads, 1983.

Fitzherbert, John. *The boke of husbandry*. London: Thomas Berthelet, 1540.

Fitzpatrick, Joan. *Food in Shakespeare: Early Modern Dietaries and the Plays*. Aldershot: Ashgate, 2007.

Flandrin, Jean-Louis. *Arranging the Meal: A History of Table Service in France*. Translated by Julie E. Johnson with Sylvie and Antonio Roder. Berkeley: University of California Press, 2007.

Floyd-Wilson, Mary. *Occult Knowledge, Science, and Gender on the Shakespearean Stage*. Cambridge: Cambridge University Press, 2013.

Fosbroke, Thomas Dudley. *Encyclopedia of Antiquities*. Vol. 2. London: John Nicols, 1825.

Fradenburg, Aranye. *Staying Alive: A Survival Manual for the Liberal Arts*. Brooklyn, NY: punctum books, 2013.

Fraiman, Susan. "Shelter Writing: Desperate Housekeeping from *Crusoe* to *Queer Eye*." *New Literary History* 37, no. 2 (Summer 2006): 341–59.

Frank, Marcie, Jonathan Goldberg, and Karen Newman, eds. *This Distracted Globe: Worldmaking in Early Modern Literature*. New York: Fordham University Press, 2016.

Fraser, Antonia. *A History of Toys*. Frankfurt-am-Main: Delacorte Press, 1966.

Freedman, H., and Maurice Simon, eds. *Midrash Rabbah*. 3rd ed. 10 vols. London: Soncino, 1983.

Friedman, John Block. *Orpheus in the Middle Ages*. Syracuse, NY: Syracuse University Press, 2000.

Frye, Susan. *Pens and Needles: Women's Textualities in Early Modern England*. Philadelphia: University of Pennsylvania Press, 2010.

Fumerton, Patricia. *Cultural Aesthetics: Renaissance Literature and the Practice of Social Ornament*. Chicago: University of Chicago Press, 1991.

Gallagher, Lowell. "'This Seal'd up Oracle': Ambivalent Nostalgia in *The Winter's Tale*." *Exemplaria* 7, no. 2 (1995): 455–98.

Garber, Marjorie. *Shakespeare after All*. New York: Anchor Books, 2004.

Geller, Lila. "*Cymbeline* and the Imagery of Covenant Theology." *Studies in English Literature, 1500–1900* 20, no. 2 (1980): 241–55.

Gibson, James J. "Ambulatory Vision and Knowledge of One's Habitat," February 21, 1979, for a lecture at UCSD. From the papers of James J. Gibson, Division of Rare and Manuscript Collections, Carl A. Kroch Library, Cornell University. Box 5, Folder 76, 14/23/1832.

———. *The Ecological Approach to Visual Perception*. New York: Taylor and Francis, 1986.

———. "General Purpose of 'Building,'" notes from 1972. Division of Rare and Manuscript Collections, Carl A. Kroch Library, Cornell University. Box 5, Folder 24, 14/23/1832.

———. *Reasons for Realism: Selected Essays of James J. Gibson*. Edited by Edward Reed and Rebecca Jones. Hillsdale, NJ: Lawrence Erlbaum Associates, 1982.

Gilders, William K. "Sacrifice in Ancient Israel." *Society of Biblical Literature*, http://www.sbl-site.org/assets/pdfs/TBv2i5_Gilders2.pdf. Accessed October 31, 2013.

Gladwell, Malcolm. "The Coolhunt." *New Yorker*, March 17, 1997. http://gladwell.com/the-coolhunt/. Accessed August 5, 2017.

Goddard, Harold. *The Meaning of Shakespeare*. Vol. 2. Chicago: University of Chicago Press, 1951.

Goldstein, David. *Eating and Ethics in Shakespeare's England*. Cambridge: Cambridge University Press, 2013.

———. "Recipes for Living: Martha Stewart and the New American Subject." In *Ordinary Lifestyles: Popular Media, Consumption and Taste Cultures*, edited by David Bell and Joanne Hollows, 47–62. London: Open University Press, 2005.

———. "Woolley's Mouse: Early Modern Recipe Books and the Uses of Nature." In *Ecofeminist Approaches to Early Modernity*, edited by Jennifer Munroe and Rebecca Laroche, 105–28. New York: Palgrave Macmillan, 2011.

Goldstein, David S., and Amy L. Tigner, eds. *Culinary Shakespeare*. Pittsburgh: Duquesne University Press, 2015.

Googe, Barnaby. *Four Bookes of Husbandry*. London: Richard Watkins, 1577.

Gopnik, Blake. "Rarely One for Sugarcoating: Kara Walker Creates a Confection at the Domino Refinery." *New York Times*, April 25, 2014. Accessed July 17, 2015.

Gordon, Colby. "Bread God, Blood God: Wonderhosts and Early Encounters with Secularization." *Genre* 44, no. 2 (Summer 2011): 105–28.

———. "Shakespearean Futurism: Utopia and Landscapes in Renaissance Drama." Dissertation, University of California, Irvine, 2013.

———. "Shakespearean Futurity: Soft Cities in *Antony and Cleopatra*." *postmedieval* 6, no. 4 (2015): 429–38.

Gottlieb, Susannah Young-ah. *Regions of Sorrow: Anxiety and Messianism in Hannah Arendt and W. H. Auden*. Stanford, CA: Stanford University Press, 2003.

Gower, John. *Confessio Amantis*. Edited by Russell A. Peck. Vol. 1. Kalamazoo, MI: Medieval Institute Publications, 2000.

Grady, Hugh. *Impure Aesthetics*. Cambridge: Cambridge University Press, 2009.

———. "*Timon of Athens*: The Dialectic of Usury, Nihilism, and Art." In *A Companion to Shakespeare's Works: The Tragedies*, edited by R. Dutton and J. Howard, 430–51. Malden, MA: Blackwell, 2003.

Grant, Ian. "The Chemical Paradigm." *Collapse* 7 (2011): 39–82.

Granville-Barker, Harley. *Prefaces to Shakespeare*. Princeton, NJ: Princeton University Press, 1974.

Grassl, Wolfgang. "The Reality of Brands: Towards an Ontology of Marketing." *American Journal of Economics and Sociology* 58, no. 2 (1999): 313–59.

Graves, Robert B. *Lighting the Shakespearean Stage, 1567–1642*. Carbondale: Southern Illinois University Press, 1999.

Green, Barbara. *Jonah's Journeys*. Collegeville, MN: Liturgical Press, 2005.

Green, Jeffrey Edward. *The Eyes of the People: Democracy in the Age of Spectatorship*. Oxford: Oxford University Press, 2010.

Greene, Roland. *Five Words: Critical Semantics in the Age of Shakespeare*. Chicago: University of Chicago Press, 2013.

Gritz, Sharon Hodgin. *Paul, Women Teachers, and the Mother Goddess at Ephesus*. Lanham, MD: University Press of America, 1991.

Gwalther, Rudolf. *An hundred, threescore and fiftene homelyes or sermons, vppon the Actes of the Apostles, written by Saint Luke*. London, 1572.

Hall, Edward T. *The Hidden Dimension*. New York: Anchor Books, 1982.

Hall, Kim F. "Culinary Spaces, Colonial Spaces: The Gendering of Sugar in the Seventeenth Century." In *Feminist Readings of Early Modern Culture: Emerging Subjects*, edited by Valerie Traub, M. Lindsay Kaplan, and Dympna Callaghan, 168–90. Cambridge: Cambridge University Press, 1996.

Halpern, Richard. "Theater and Democratic Thought: Arendt to Rancière." *Critical Inquiry* 37, no. 3 (Spring 2011): 545–72.

Hamlin, Hannibal. *The Bible in Shakespeare*. Oxford: Oxford University Press, 2013.

Hammill, Graham. *The Mosaic Constitution: Political Theology and Imagination from Machiavelli to Milton*. Chicago: University of Chicago Press, 2012.

———. "The Spirit of Europe: Political Theology from Shakespeare to Spinoza." Unpublished essay.

Hansell, Peter and Jean. *Dovecotes*. London: Shire Library, 2008.

Hardt, Michael. "Affective Labour." *boundary 2* 26, no. 2 (Summer 1999): 89–100.

Harlan, Susan. "'Certain condolements, certain vails': Staging Rusty Armour in Shakespeare's *Pericles*." *Early Theater* 11, no. 2 (2008): 129–40.

Harmon, Graham. *The Quadruple Object*. Washington, DC: Zero Books, 2011.

———. *Tool-Being: Heidegger and the Metaphysics of Objects*. Peru, IL: Open Court, 2002.

Harries, Karsten. *The Ethical Function of Architecture*. Cambridge, MA: MIT Press, 1997.

Harris, Jonathan Gil. "Shakespeare's Hair: Staging the Object of Material Culture." *Shakespeare Quarterly* 52 (2001): 479–91.

———. *Untimely Matter in the Time of Shakespeare*. Philadelphia: University of Pennsylvania Press, 2009.

Harris, Jonathan Gil, and Natasha Korda, eds., *Staged Properties in Early Modern English Drama*. Cambridge: Cambridge University Press, 2002.

Harris, Rachel Lee. "Michael Fassbender and the Robes of Royalty." *New York Times*, December 16, 2015. Accessed December 17, 2015.

Hart, Trevor. "Conversation after Pentecost? Theological Musings on the Hermeneutic Motion." *Literature and Theology* 28, no. 2 (June 2014): 164–78.

Hartley, Andrew James. "Sinead Cusack." In *The Routledge Companion to Actors' Shakespeare*, edited by John Russell Brown, 15–26. New York: Routledge, 2012.

Hartson, H. Rex. "Cognitive, Physical, Sensory, and Functional Affordances in Interaction Design." *Behaviour and Information Technology*, 2003. http://courses.cs.vt.edu/~cs5714/fall2003/Affordances,%20as%20appeared.pdf. Accessed September 2, 2013.

Hawkes, Terence, ed. *Twentieth Century Interpretations of Macbeth*. Englewood Cliffs, NJ: Prentice-Hall, 1977.

Heal, Felicity. *Hospitality in Early Modern England*. Oxford: Oxford University Press, 1990.

Hecker, Joel. *Mystical Bodies, Mystical Meals: Eating and Embodiment in Medieval Kabbalah*. Detroit: Wayne State University Press, 2005.

Heffernan, James. *Hospitality and Treachery in Western Literature*. New Haven, CT: Yale University Press, 2014.

Heft, Harry. "Affordances and the Body: An Intentional Analysis of Gibson's Ecological Approach to Visual Perception." *Journal for the Theory of Social Behaviour* 19, no. 1 (1989): 1–30.

———. "Affordances, Dynamic Experience, and the Challenge of Reification." *Ecological Psychology* 15, no. 2 (2003): 149–80.

———. "Ecological Psychology and Religious Meaning: Strange Bedfellows?" *Religion, Brain and Behavior* (2013): 1–4.

———. *Ecological Psychology in Context: James Gibson, Roger Barker, and the Legacy of William James's Radical Empiricism*. New York: Taylor and Francis, 2001.

Heidegger, Martin. "Building Dwelling Thinking." In *Poetry, Language, Thought*, translated by Albert Hofstadter, 143–59. New York: Harper and Row, 1971.

———. "The Thing." In *Poetry, Language, Thought*, translated by Albert Hofstadter, 161–84. New York: Harper and Row, 1971.

Helfer, Rebecca. *Spenser's Ruins and the Art of Recollection*. Toronto: University of Toronto Press, 2013.

Henderson, Diana E. *Passion Made Public: Elizabethan Lyric, Gender, and Performance*. Urbana: University of Illinois Press, 1995.

Henslowe's Diary. Edited by R. A. Foakes. New York: Cambridge University Press, 2002.

Herman, David. "Re-Minding Modernism." In *The Emergence of Mind: Representations of Consciousness in Narrative Discourses in English*, edited by David Herman, 243–72. Lincoln: University of Nebraska Press, 2011.

Herodotus. *The Famous History of Herodotus*. New York: AMS Press, 1967.

Herrick, Robert. *Hesperides*. London, 1648.

Heylyn, Peter. *Mikrokosmos: A Little Description of the Great World*. Oxford: William Turner, 1639.

———. *Respondet Petrus*. London, 1658.

Heywood, Thomas. *Gynaikeion; or, Nine books of various history Concerninge women*. London: Adam Islip, 1624.

Heyworth, G. G. "Missing and Mending: *Romeo and Juliet* at Play in the Romance Chronotope." *Yearbook of English Studies* 30 (2000): 5–20.

Hochschild, Arlie. *The Managed Heart: Commercialization of Human Feeling*. Berkeley: University of California Press, 2012.

Hoffman, Christine. "Much Ado about Planking." In *Object Oriented Environs*, edited by Jeffrey Jerome Cohen and Julian Yates, 35–46. Earth: punctum books, 2016.

Holdredge, Barbara A. *Veda and Torah: Transcending the Textuality of Scripture*. Albany: State University of New York Press, 1996.

Holinshed, Raphael. *The first volume of the chronicles of England, Scotland, and Ireland*. London, 1577.

Honig, Bonnie. "Antigone in Context(s): Humanism and the Political Stakes of the Ethical Turn." Seminar for the School of Criticism and Theory, Cornell University, Summer 2010.

———. "Antigone's Laments, Creon's Grief: Mourning, Membership, and the Politics of Exception." *Political Theory* 37, no. 1 (February 2009): 5–43.

———. "The Laws of the Sabbath (Poetry): Arendt, Heine, and the Politics of Debt." *UC Irvine Law Review* 5 (2015): 463–82.

———. "'Out Like a Lion': *Melancholia* with Euripides and Winnicott." In *Politics, Theory, and Film: Critical Encounters with Lars von Trier*, edited by Honig and Lori J. Marso, 356–88. Oxford: Oxford University Press, 2016.

———. "The Politics of Public Things: Neoliberalism and the Routine of Privatization." *No Foundations* 10 (2013): 59–76.

———. *Public Things: Democracy in Disrepair*. New York: Fordham University Press, 2017.

———. "Resilience." *Political Concepts: A Critical Lexicon* 3, no. 4 (Fall 2015): 1–5.

———. "What Kind of a Thing Is Land? Hannah Arendt's Object Relations; or, The Jewish Unconscious of Arendt's Most 'Greek' Text." *Political Theory* 44, no. 3 (2016): 307–36.

Hopkins, Lisa. "Household Words: *Macbeth* and the Failure of Spectacle." *Shakespeare Survey* 50 (1997): 101–10. Reprinted in *Shakespeare and Language*, edited by Catherine M. S. Alexander. Cambridge: Cambridge University Press, 2004.

———. "'The Shores of Mortality': *Pericles*'s Greece of the Mind." In *Pericles: Critical Essays*, edited by David Skeele, 228–37. New York: Garland, 2000.

Hussain, Nasser, and Austin Sarat, eds. *Forgiveness, Mercy, and Clemency*. Stanford, CA: Stanford University Press, 2007.

Ichikawa, Mariko. *Shakespearean Entrances*. Houndmills: Palgrave Macmillan, 2002.

———. *The Shakespearean Stage Space*. Cambridge: Cambridge University Press, 2013.

Idel, Moshe. *Messianic Mystics*. New Haven, CT: Yale University Press, 1998.

Ingold, Tim. *The Perception of the Environment: Essays on Livelihood, Dwelling and Skill*. New York: Psychology Press, 2000.

———. "The Temporality of the Landscape." *World Archaeology* 25, no. 2 (October 1993): 152–74.

Jackson, Ken. "'Grace to Boot': St. Paul, Messianic Time, and Shakespeare's *The Winter's Tale*." In *The Return of Theory in Early Modern English Studies*, edited by Paul Cefalu and Bryan Reynolds, 199–201. New York: Palgrave Macmillan, 2011.

———. *Shakespeare and Abraham*. Notre Dame, IN: University of Notre Dame Press, 2015.

Jeanneret, Michel. *A Feast of Words: Banquets and Table Talk in the Renaissance*. Translated by Jeremy Whitely and Emma Hughes. Chicago: University of Chicago Press, 1991.

Jenkins, Willis. *Ecologies of Grace: Environmental Ethics and Christian Theology*. Oxford: Oxford University Press, 2008.

Jensen, Phebe. *Religion and Revelry in Shakespeare's Festive World*. Cambridge: Cambridge University Press, 2009.

———. "Singing Psalms to Horn-Pipes: Festivity, Iconoclasm, and Catholicism in *The Winter's Tale*." *Shakespeare Quarterly* 55, no. 3 (Autumn 2004): 279–306.

Johnson, Samuel. "Number 168." Saturday, October 26, 1750, *The Rambler*. In *The Works of Samuel Johnson*, edited by Arthur Murphy. Vol. 1. New York: George Dearborn, 1834.

Jones, Ann Rosalind, and Peter Stallybrass. *Renaissance Clothing and the Materials of Memory*. Cambridge: Cambridge University Press, 2000.

Juan, Rose Marie. "The Court Lady's Dilemma: Isabella d'Este and Art Collecting in the Renaissance." *Oxford Art Journal* 14, no. 1 (1991): 67–78.

Kahn, Victoria. "Political Theology and Liberal Culture: Strauss, Schmitt, Spinoza, and Arendt." In *Political Theology and Early Modernity*, edited by Graham Hammill and Julia Reinhard Lupton, 23–47. Chicago: University of Chicago Press, 2012.

Kathman, David. "Grocers, Goldsmiths, and Drapers: Freemen and Apprentices in the Elizabethan Theater." *Shakespeare Quarterly* 55, no. 1 (Spring 2004): 1–49.

Kaufman, Eleanor. "The Saturday of Messianic Time (Agamben and Badiou on the Apostle Paul)." *South Atlantic Quarterly* 107. no. 1 (Winter 2008): 37–54.

Kaufman, Shieba Kian. "The Hospitable Globe: Persia and the Early Modern Stage." Dissertation, University of California, Irvine, 2016.

Kavka, Martin. *Jewish Messianism and the History of Philosophy*. Cambridge: Cambridge University Press, 2004.

Keegan, Daniel. "The Prophetic Stage." Dissertation, Department of Drama, University of California, Irvine, 2013.

Kemsley, Roderick, and Christopher Platt. *Dwelling with Architecture*. London: Routledge, 2012.

Kent, Keri Wyatt. *Deeper into the Word: Reflections on One Hundred Words from the Old Testament*. Bloomington, MN: Bethany House Publishers, 2011.

Kernan, Alvin B. *Shakespeare, the King's Playwright: Theater in the Stuart Court*. New Haven, CT: Yale University Press, 1997.

Kerridge, Richard. "An Ecocritic's *Macbeth*." In *Ecocritical Shakespeare*, edited by Lynne Bruckner and Dan Brayton, 193–210. Farnham: Ashgate, 2011.

Kiess, John. *Hannah Arendt and Theology*. London: Bloomsbury, 2016.

Kietzman, Mary Jo. "Performing Biblical Stories in *Titus Andronicus* and *The Merchant of Venice*." *ELH*, forthcoming.

Kinney, Arthur R., ed. *The Oxford Handbook of Shakespeare*. Oxford: Oxford University Press, 2013.

Kirby, John C. *Ephesians: Baptism and Pentecost*. Montreal: McGill University Press, 1968.

Klingmann, Anna. *Brandscapes: Architecture in the Experience Economy*. Cambridge, MA: MIT Press, 2007.

Knapp, James A. *Image Ethics in Shakespeare and Spenser*. New York: Palgrave Macmillan, 2013.

Kneidel, Gregory. *Rethinking the Turn to Religion in Early Modern English Literature*. London: Palgrave Macmillan, 2008.

Knight, Douglas H. *The Eschatological Economy: Time and the Hospitality of God*. Grand Rapids, MI: Eerdmans 2006.

Knight, G. Wilson. *Imperial Theme*. London: Methuen, 1931; 1951.

———. "The Writing of *Pericles*." In *Pericles: Critical Essays*, edited by David Skeele, 78–113. New York: Garland Publishing, 2000.

Knights, L. C. "Macbeth." In *Twentieth Century Interpretations of Macbeth*, edited by Terence Hawkes, 83–106. Englewood Cliffs, NJ: Prentice-Hall, 1977.

Kompridis, Nicholas. "Recognition and Receptivity: Forms of Normative Response in the Lives of the Animals We Are." *New Literary History* 44, no. 1 (Winter 2013): 1–24.

Korda, Natasha. *Labors Lost: Women's Work and the Early Modern Stage*. Philadelphia: University of Pennsylvania Press, 2011.

———. *Shakespeare's Domestic Economies: Gender and Property in Early Modern England*. Philadelphia: University of Pennsylvania Press, 2002.

Kott, Jan. *Shakespeare Our Contemporary*. New York: Norton, 1974.

Kottman, Paul. "Defying the Stars: Tragic Love as the Struggle for Freedom in *Romeo and Juliet*." *Shakespeare Quarterly* 63, no. 1 (Spring 2012): 1–38.

———. "Introduction." In *Philosophers on Shakespeare*, edited by Paul Kottman, 1–17. Stanford, CA: Stanford University Press, 2009.

———. *A Politics of the Scene*. Stanford, CA: Stanford University Press, 2008.

———. "What Is Shakespearean Tragedy?" In *Oxford Handbook of Shakespearean Tragedy*, edited by David Schalkwyk and Michael Neill, 3–18. Oxford: Oxford University Press, 2016.

———. "Why Think about Shakespearean Tragedy Today?" In

Cambridge Companion to Shakespearean Tragedy, edited by Claire McEachern. Cambridge: Cambridge University Press, 2013.

Kouak, Theodore F. "Homo Faber, Action Hero Manqué." *Shakespeare Quarterly* 66, no. 4 (2015): 409–39.

Krondl, Michael. *Sweet Invention: A History of Dessert*. Chicago: Chicago Review Press, 2011.

Kunin, Aaron. "Marlowe's Footstools." In *This Distracted Globe: Worldmaking in Early Modern Literature*, edited by Marcie Frank, Jonathan Goldberg, and Karen Newman, 64–78. New York: Fordham University Press, 2016.

Lafont, Agnès. "Political Uses of Erotic Power in an Elizabethan Mythological Programme: "Dangerous Interactions with Diana in Hardwick Hall." In *Shakespeare's Erotic Mythology and Ovidian Renaissance Culture*, edited by Agnès Lafont, 41–57. Farnham: Ashgate, 2013.

———, ed. *Shakespeare's Erotic Mythology and Ovidian Renaissance Culture*. Farnham: Ashgate, 2013.

Lander, Bonnie. "Interpreting the Person: Tradition, Conflict, and *Cymbeline*'s Innogen." *Shakespeare Quarterly* 59, no. 2 (Summer 2008): 156–84.

Laroque, François. "The Hybridity of Popular Culture in *The Winter's Tale*." *Sillages Critiques* 13 (2011): 1–11.

———. *Shakespeare's Festive World: Elizabethan Seasonal Entertainment*. Cambridge: Cambridge University Press, 1991.

Latour, Bruno. "From Realpolitik to Dingpolitik." In *Making Things Public: Atmospheres of Democracy*, 14–44. Cambridge, MA: MIT Press, 2005.

———. *Pandora's Hope: Essays on the Reality of Science Studies*. Cambridge, MA: Harvard University Press, 1999.

———. *Reassembling the Social: An Introduction to Actor-Network Theory*. Oxford: Oxford University Press, 2005.

Lawson, Bryan. *The Language of Space*. Oxford: Architectural Press, 2001.

Lazzarato, Maurizio. "Immaterial Labour." In *Radical Thought in Italy: A Potential Politics*, edited by Paolo Virno and Michael Hardt, 133–50. Minneapolis: University of Minnesota Press, 1996.

Leatherbarrow, David. "Breathing Walls." In *Architecture Oriented Otherwise*, 21–42. New York: Princeton Architectural Press, 2009.

———. "Topographical Premises." *Journal of Architectural Education* 57, no. 3 (2004): 70–73.

Lémery, Nicolas. *Modern Curiosities of art and nature extracted out of the cabinets of the most eminent personages of the French court*. London, 1685.

Levey, Santina M. *Elizabethan Treasures: The Hardwick Hall Textiles*. London: National Trust, 1998.

———. *The Embroideries at Hardwick Hall: A Catalogue*. London: National Trust, 2008.

———, ed. *Of Household Stuff: The 1601 Inventories of Bess of Hardwick*. London: National Trust, 2001.

Levinas, Emmanuel. "The Dwelling." In *Totality and Infinity*, translated by Alphonso Lingis. Pittsburgh: Duquesne University Press, 1969.

Levine, Caroline. *Forms: Whole, Rhythm, Hierarchy, Network*. Princeton, NJ: Princeton University Press, 2015.

Lewis, Jayne. *Air's Appearance: Literary Atmosphere in British Fiction, 1660–1794*. Chicago: University of Chicago Press, 2012.

Liebler, Naomi Conn. "'There is no world without Verona's walls': The City in Romeo and Juliet." In *A Companion to Shakespeare's Works*, vol. 1, ed. Richard Dutton and Jean E. Howard, 303–18. Malden, MA: Blackwell, 2003.

Ligouri, Saint Alphonsus Ligouri. "Prayer Before Sleep." *CatholiCity*, http://www.catholicity.com/prayer/prayer-before-sleep.html. Accessed November 11, 2013.

Lin, Ingrid. "Evaluating a Servicescape: The Effect of Cognition and Emotion." *Hospitality Management* 23 (2004): 163–78.

Lin, Tao. *Shoplifting from American Apparel*. Brooklyn, NY: Melville House, 2009.

Lingis, Unhae. "Love and Death: *Discordia Concors* in *Romeo and Juliet*." Manuscript.

Lok, Henry. *Ecclesiastes, otherwise called The preacher, with Sundrie Sonnets*. London, 1597.

Loui, Annie. *The Physical Actor: Exercises for Action and Awareness*. New York: Routledge, 2009.

Low, Setha M., and Denise Lawrence-Zúñiga, eds. *The Anthropology of Space and Place*. New York: Blackwell, 2003.

Lowrance, Brian. "'Modern Ecstasy': *Macbeth* and the Meaning of the Political." *English Literary History* 79, no. 4 (Winter 2012): 823–49.

Luhmann, Niklaus. *Trust and Power*. Chichester: John Wiley, 1973.

Lundgren, Svante. *Particularism and Universalism in Modern Jewish Thought*. Binghamton: SUNY Binghamton Press, 2001.

Lunenfeld, Peter. *User*. Cambridge, MA: MIT Press, 2005.

Lupton, Ellen. "The Designer as Producer." In *The Education of a Graphic Designer*, edited by Steven Heller, 159–62. New York: Allworth Press, 1998.

Lupton, Julia Reinhard. *Afterlives of the Saints: Hagiography, Typology and Secular Literature*. Stanford, CA: Stanford University Press, 1996.

———. *Citizen-Saints: Shakespeare and Political Theology*. Chicago: University of Chicago Press, 2005.

———. "Creature Caliban." *Shakespeare Quarterly* 51, no. 1 (Spring 2000): 1–23.

———. "Hospitality." In *Early Modern Theatricality*, edited by Henry S. Turner, 423–41. Oxford: Oxford University Press, 2013.

———. "Judging Forgiveness: Hannah Arendt, W. H. Auden, and *The Winter's Tale*." *New Literary History* 45 (2014): 641–63.

———. "Pauline Edifications: Staging the Sovereign Softscape in Renaissance England." In *Political Theology and Early Modernity*, edited by Graham Hammill and Julia Reinhard Lupton, 210–37. Chicago: University of Chicago Press, 2012.

———. "Room for Dessert: Sugared Shakespeare and the Dramaturgy of Dwelling." In *Culinary Shakespeare*, edited by David Goldstein and Amy Tigner, 199–224. Pittsburgh: Duquesne University Press, 2016.

———. "Shakespearean Softscapes: Hospitality, Phenomenology, Design." In *The Return of Theory in Early Modern English Studies*, vol. 2, edited by Paul Cefalu, Gary Kuchar, and Bryan Reynolds, 143–64. New York: Palgrave Macmillan, 2014.

———. "Soft Res Publica: On the Assembly and Disassembly of Courtly Space." *Republics of Letters* 2, no. 2 (June 1, 2011), http://rofl.stanford.edu/node/96. Accessed July 22, 2017.

———. "The Taming of the Shrew; or, Arendt in Italy." *Law, Culture and the Humanities* 8, no. 1 (2012): 1–16.

———. "Thinking with Things: From Hannah Woolley to Hannah Arendt." *postmedieval* 3, no. 1 (2012): 1–17.

Lynch, Kevin. *The Image of the City*. Cambridge, MA: MIT Press, 1960.

Maccoy, Peter. *Essentials of Stage Management*. London: Methuen, 2004.

MacFaul, Tom. *Problem Fathers in Shakespeare and Renaissance Drama*. Cambridge: Cambridge University Press, 2013.

MacGeorge, A. *Flags: Some Account of Their History and Uses*. London: Blackie and Son, 1881.

MacIntrye, Alidsair. *After Virtue*. 2nd ed. Notre Dame, IN: University of Notre Dame Press, 1984.

Maguire, Laurie. "The Girls from Ephesus." In *The Comedy of Errors: Critical Essays*, edited by Robert S. Miola, 355–92. New York: Routledge, 2001.

Maier, J. R. A., and G. M. Faidel, "An Affordance-Based Approach to Architectural Theory, Design and Practice." *Design Studies* 30 (2009): 393–414.

Maimonides. *Ethical Writings of Maimonides*. Edited by Raymond L. Weiss with Charles Butterworth. New York: Dover Publications, 1975.

Mansfield, Howard. *Dwelling in Possibility: Searching for the Soul of Shelter*. Peterborough, NH: Bauhan Publishing, 2013.

Marcus, Leah. *The Politics of Mirth: Jonson, Herrick, Milton, Marvell, and the Defense of Old Holiday Pastimes*. Chicago: University of Chicago Press, 1986.

Markell, Patchen. "Arendt's Work: On the Architecture of *The Human Condition*." *College Literature* 38, no. 1 (Winter 2011): 16–44.

Markham, Gervase. *Cheape and Good Husbandry*. London, 1614.

———. *Countrey Contentments in Two Books*. London: J.B. for R. Jackson, 1615.

———. *The English House-wife*. London, 1631.

———. *A health to the gentlemanly profession of servingmen; or, The servingmens comforts*. London, 1598.

Martin, Randall. "Rediscovering Artemis in *The Comedy of Errors*." In *Shakespeare and the Mediterranean*, edited by Thom Clayton et al., 363–79. Newark: University of Delaware Press, 2004.

———. *Shakespeare and Ecology*. New York: Oxford University Press, 2015.

———. "Shakespearean Biography, Biblical Allusion and Early Modern Practices of Reading Scripture." *Shakespeare Survey* 63 (2011): 212–24.

Marx, Steven. *Shakespeare and the Bible*. Oxford: Oxford University Press, 2000.

Mason, Pamela. "Sunshine in *Macbeth*." In *Macbeth: New Critical Essays*, edited by Nick Moschovakis, 335–49. New York: Routledge, 2008.

Matz, Robert. "'Who Is Speaking Here?' Shakespeare's Sonnets, Modern Authorship, and the Contemporary University." In *This Distracted Globe: Worldmaking in Early Modern Literature*, edited by Marcie Frank, Jonathan Goldberg, and Karen Newman, 81–99. New York: Fordham University Press, 2016.

Maxwell, John. *The Mirrour of Religious Men*. London: E. White, 1611.

May, Robert. *The Accomplish't Cook*. London, 1660.

Maynwaringe, Everard. *The methods and means of enjoying health, vigour and long life*. London, 1683.

McCarthy, Mary. "General Macbeth." In *Twentieth-Century Interpretations of Macbeth*, edited by Terence Hawkes, 126–27. Englewood Cliffs, NJ: Prentice-Hall, 1977.

McCoy, Richard. *Faith in Shakespeare*. Oxford: Oxford University Press, 2013.

McDermott, Ryan, trans. and ed. "The Ordinary Gloss on Jonah." *PMLA* 128, no. 2 (2013): 424–38.

McEachern, Claire, ed. *Cambridge Guide to Shakespearean Tragedy*. Cambridge: Cambridge University Press, 2013.

———. "Religion and Shakespearean Tragedy." In *Cambridge Guide to Shakespearean Tragedy*, edited by Claire McEachern, 89–109. Cambridge: Cambridge University Press, 2013.

McKinney, Joslin, and Philip Butterworth. *The Cambridge Introduction to Scenography*. Cambridge: Cambridge University Press, 2009.

McNulty, Tracy. *Wrestling with the Angel: Experiments in Symbolic Life*. New York: Columbia University Press, 2014.

McWhorter, Ladelle, and Gail Stenstad. *Heidegger and the Earth: Essays in Environmental Philosophy*. Toronto: University of Toronto Press, 2009.

Meads, Chris. *Banqueting Set Forth: Banqueting in English Renaissance Drama*. Manchester: Manchester University Press, 2001.

Meillassoux, Quentin. *After Finitude: An Essay on the Necessity of Contingency*. Translated by Ray Brassier. New York: Continuum, 2008.

Mentz, Steven. *At the Bottom of Shakespeare's Ocean*. London: Bloomsbury, 2009.

———. *Shipwreck Modernity: Ecologies of Globalization, 1550–1719*. Minneapolis: University of Minnesota Press, 2015.

Merleau-Ponty, Maurice. *Phenomenology of Perception*. Translated by Colin Smith. London: Routledge, 1961.

Meyler, Bernadette. "Theaters of Pardoning: Sovereignty and Judgment from Shakespeare to Kant." Dissertation, University of California, Irvine, 2006.

Middleton, Thomas. *A Courtly Masque: The device called the world tost at tennis*. London, 1620.

Miller, Abbott. *Design and Content*. New York: Princeton Architectural Press, 2014.

Milton, John. *John Milton: Complete Poems and Major Prose*. Edited by Merritt Y. Hughes. Upper Saddle River, NJ: Prentice-Hall, 1957.

Mintz, Sidney W. *Sweetness and Power: The Place of Sugar in Modern History*. New York: Viking Penguin, 1986.

Misztal, Barbara. *Trust in Modern Societies: The Search for the Bases of Social Order*. New York: Polity Press, 1988.

Mitchell-Buck, Heather S. "Maintaining the Realm: City, Commonwealth, and Crown in Chester's Midsummer Plays." In *The Chester Cycle, 1555–1575*, edited by Jessica Dell, David Klausner, and Helen Ostovich, 179–92. Farnham: Ashgate, 2013.

Moffet, Robin. "*Cymbeline* and the Nativity." *Shakespeare Quarterly* 13, no. 2 (Spring 1962): 207–18.

Morton, Timothy. *Ecology without Nature*. Cambridge, MA: Harvard University Press, 2007.

———. "Here Comes Everything: The Promise of Object-Oriented Ontology." *Qui Parle* 19, no. 2 (Spring/Summer 2011): 163–90.

———. *Hyperobjects: Philosophy and Ecology after the End of the World*. Minneapolis: University of Minnesota Press, 2013.

———. "An Object-Oriented Defense of Poetry." *New Literary History* 43 (2012): 205–24.

Moschovakis, Nicholas, ed. *Macbeth: New Critical Essays*. New York: Routledge, 2008.

Muehlebach, Andrea. "On Affective Labor in Post-Fordist Italy." *Cultural Anthropology* 26, no. 1 (2011): 59–82.

Muir, Kenneth. *Shakespeare's Sources: Comedies and Tragedies*. New York: Routledge, 1961.

Muir, Lynette. *The Biblical Drama of Medieval Europe*. Cambridge: Cambridge University Press, 1995.

Murphy-O'Connor, Jerome. *St. Paul's Ephesus: Texts and Archaeology*. Collegeville, MN: Liturgical Press, 2008.

Muniz, Albert M., Jr., and Thomas C. O'Guinn. "Brand Community." *Journal of Consumer Research* 27, no. 4 (March 2001): 412–32.

Munro, Ian. "*Romeo and Juliet*: Performance History." In *Romeo and Juliet: A Critical Reader*, edited by Julia Reinhard Lupton, 53–78. London: Bloomsbury Arden Shakespeare, 2016.

Nardizzi, Vin. *Wooden O's: Shakespeare's Theatres and England's Trees*. Toronto: University of Toronto Press, 2013.

Nevo, Ruth. "Tragic Form in *Romeo and Juliet*." *Studies in English Literature, 1500–1900* 9, no. 2 (Spring 1969): 241–58.

Ngai, Sianne. *Our Aesthetic Categories*. Cambridge, MA: Harvard University Press, 2012.

Nirenberg, David. *Anti-Judaism: The Western Tradition*. New York: Norton, 2013.

Norberg-Schulz, Christian. *The Concept of Dwelling*. New York: Rizzoli, 1985.

———. *Genius Loci: Towards a Phenomenology of Architecture*. New York: Rizzoli, 1991.

———. "The Phenomenon of Place." In *The Urban Design Reader*, edited by Michael Larice and Elizabeth Macdonald, 276–77. 2nd ed. New York: Routledge, 2013.

Norman, Donald. *The Design of Everyday Things*. New York: Basic Books, 2013.

Noschka, Michael. "Thinking Hospitably with *Timon of Athens*: Towards an Ethics of Stewardship." In *Shakespeare and Hospitality*, edited by David Goldstein and Julia Reinhard Lupton, 242–64. New York: Routledge, 2016.

Novenson, Matthew V. *Christ among the Messiahs: Christ Language in Paul and Messiah Language in Ancient Judaism*. Oxford: Oxford University Press, 2012.

Noyes, Alfred. *Collected Poems*. 2 vols. New York: Frederick Stokes, 1913.

Nunn, Trevor, dir. *Macbeth*. Video. London: Thames Television, 1978.

Nussbaum, Martha. *Creating Capabilities: The Human Development Approach*. Cambridge, MA: Belknap Press, 2011.

———. *Political Emotions: Why Love Matters for Justice*. Cambridge, MA: Belknap Press, 2015.

Nye, Joseph, Jr. *Soft Power: The Means to Succeed in World Politics*. New York: Perseus Books, 2004.

O'Connell, Michael. *The Idolatrous Eye: Iconoclasm and Theater in Early-Modern England*. New York: Oxford University Press, 2000.

Oldridge, Darren. "Something of the Night." In *Staging the Superstitions of Early Modern Europe*, edited by Verena Theile and Andrew D. McCarthy, xv–xxiii. Farnham: Ashgate, 2013.

Olson, Lois. "Pietro de Cresenczi: The Founder of Modern Agronomy." *Agricultural History* 18, no. 1 (1944): 35–40.

Olson, Rebecca. "Before the Arras: Textile Description and Innogen's Translation in *Cymbeline*." *Modern Philology* 108, no. 1 (August 2010): 45–64.

Orlin, Lena Cowlin. *Private Matters and Public Culture in Post-Reformation England*. Ithaca, NY: Cornell University Press, 1994.

Ovid. *Heroides and Amores*. Translated by Grant Showerman. Cambridge, MA: Harvard University Press, 1958.

———. *Tristia. Ex Ponto*. Translated by A. L. Wheeler. Cambridge, MA: Harvard University Press, 1959.

Paavolainen, Teemu. "From Props to Affordances: An Ecological Approach to Theatrical Objects." *Theatre Symposium* 18 (2010): 116–34.

———. *Theatre/Ecology/Cognition: Theorizing Performer-Object Interaction in Grotowski, Kantor, and Meyerhold*. New York: Palgrave MacMillan 2012.

Palfrey, Simon. "Formaction." In *Twenty-First Century Approaches to Theatricality*, edited by Henry S. Turner. Oxford: Oxford University Press, 2014.

———. *Shakespeare's Possible Worlds*. Cambridge: University of Cambridge Press, 2014.

Palmer, Darryl. *Hospitable Performances: Dramatic Genre and Cultural Practices in Early Modern England*. West Lafayette, IN: Purdue University Press, 1992.

Panofsky, Erwin. *Early Netherlandish Painting*. New York: Harper and Row, 1970.

Park, Sejin. *Pentecost and Sinai: The Festival of Weeks as a Celebration of the Sinai Event*. New York: T and T Clark International, 2008.

Parker, Patricia. *Shakespeare from the Margins: Language, Culture, Context*. Chicago: University of Chicago Press, 1996.

Parris, Benjamin. "'The body is with the king, but the king is not with the body': Sovereign Sleep in *Hamlet* and *Macbeth*." *Shakespeare Studies* 40 (2012): 102–42.

———. "'Watching to banish Care': Sleep and Insomnia in Book I of *The Faerie Queene*." *Modern Philology* 113, no. 3 (November 2015): 151–77.

Pask, Kevin. *The Fairy Way of Writing: Shakespeare to Tolkien*. Baltimore: Johns Hopkins University Press, 2013.

Paster, Gail Kern. *Humoring the Body: Emotions and the Shakespearean Stage*. Chicago: University of Chicago Press, 2004.

Pearl Poet. *Complete Works of the Pearl Poet*. Translated and edited by Casey Finch. Berkeley: University of California Press, 1993.

Phiston, William. *The Schoole of Good Manners*. London, 1595.

Picciotto, Joanna. *Labors of Innocence in Early Modern England*. Cambridge, MA: Harvard University Press, 2010.

Pine, R. Joseph, II, and James H. Gilmore. *The Experience Economy*. 2nd ed. Cambridge, MA: Harvard Business Press, 2011.

Plat, Hugh. *Delightes for Ladies, to adorn their Persons, Tables, closets, and Distillatories: with Beauties, banquets, perfumes and Waters*. London: H. L., 1608.

Platina. *On Right Pleasure and Good Health*. Edited and translated by Mary Ella Milham. Tempe, AZ: Medieval and Renaissance Texts and Studies, 1998.

Pocock, J. G. A. *The Machiavellian Moment: Florentine Political Thought and the Atlantic Republican Tradition*. 2nd ed. Princeton, NJ: Princeton University Press, 2003.

Polanyi, Michael. *Personal Knowledge: Towards a Post-Critical Philosophy*. Chicago: University of Chicago Press, 2015.

Poletto, Marco, and Claudia Pasquero. *Systemic Architecture: Operating Manual for the Self-Organizing City*. London: Routledge, 2012.

Poole, Kristin. *Supernatural Environments in Shakespeare's England: Spaces of Demonism, Divinity, and Drama*. Cambridge: Cambridge University Press, 2011.

Porsdam, Helle. *Civil to Human Rights: Dialogues on Law and Humanities in the United States*. Cheltenham: Edward Elgar Publishing Limited, 2009.

Potter, Lois. *The Life of William Shakespeare: A Critical Biography*. Malden, MA: Wiley-Blackwell, 2012.

Praz, Mario. *An Illustrated History of Furnishing from the Renaissance to the 20th Century*. New York: George Brazillier, 1964.

Quiring, Björn. *Shakespeare's Curse: The Aporias of Ritual Exclusion in Early Modern Royal Drama*. New York: Routledge, 2014.

Rabelais, François. *Pantagruel's Voyage*. Translated by Mr. Motteux. London, 1694.

Raffnsøe, Sverre. "Beyond Rule: Trust and Power as Capacities." *Journal of Political Power* 6, no. 2 (2013): 241–60.

Rapaport, Herman. "The Phenomenology of Spenserian Ekphrasis." In *Murray Krieger and Contemporary Critical Theory*, edited by Bruce Henrickson, 157–82. New York: Columbia University Press, 1986.

Rashi. *Chumash with Rashi's Commentary*. Edited by A. M. Silberman. 5 vols. Jerusalem: Feldheim, 1934.

Rayner, Alice. "Rude Mechanicals and the *Specters of Marx*." *Theatre Journal* 54, no. 4 (December 2002): 535–54.

Reeve, Edmund. *The Communion Book Catechisme Explained*. London, 1635.

Relihan, Constance C. "Liminal Geography: *Pericles* and the Politics of Place." *Philological Quarterly* 71, no. 3 (Summer 1993): 281–300.

Reuther, Rosemary Radford, and Herman J. Reuther. *The Wrath of Jonah: The Crisis of Religious Nationalism in the Israeli-Palestinian Conflict*. 2nd ed. Minneapolis: Fortress Press, 2002.

Richardson, Catherine. *Domestic Life and Domestic Tragedy in Early Modern England: The Material Life of the Household*. Manchester: Manchester University Press, 2006.

R. M. *An exercise for a Christian Family*. London, 1585.

Roberts, Sasha. "'Let me the curtains draw': The Dramatic and Symbolic Properties of the Bed in Shakespeare." In *Staged Properties in Early Modern English Drama*, edited by Jonathan Gil Harris and Natasha Korda, 153–74. Cambridge: Cambridge University Press, 2002.

Robertson, Lisa. *Occasional Work and Seven Walks from the Office for Soft Architecture*. 3rd ed. Astoria, OR: Clear Cut Press, 2011.

Rosenberg, Jessica. "A Digression to Hospitality: Thrift and Christmastime in Shakespeare and in the Literature of Husbandry." In *Shakespeare and Hospitality: Ethics, Politics, and Exchange*, edited by Julia Reinhard Lupton and David Goldstein, 39–66. New York: Routledge, 2016.

Rosenzweig, Franz. *The Star of Redemption*. Translated by Barbara Galli. Madison: University of Wisconsin Press, 2005.

Rowland, C. C., and Christophe R. A. Morray-Jones. *The Mystery of God: Early Jewish Mysticism and the New Testament*. Leiden: Brill, 2009.

Rutter, Carol Chillington. "Simon Russell Beale." In *The Routledge Companion to Actors' Shakespeare*, edited by John Russell Brown. New York: Routledge, 2013.

Rykwert, Joseph. *On Adam's House in Paradise: The Idea of the Primitive Hut in Architectural History*. Cambridge, MA: MIT Press, 1981.

Salter, Chris. *Entangled: Technology and the Transformation of Performance*. Cambridge, MA: MIT Press, 2010.

Sanders, E. P. *Paul, the Law, and the Jewish People*. Philadelphia: Fortress Press, 1983.

Sanders, John. "Affordances: An Ecological Approach to First Philosophy." In *Perspectives on Embodiment: The Intersections of Nature and Culture*, edited by Gail Weiss and Honi Fern Haber, 121–42. New York: Routledge, 1999.

Santner, Eric. *On Creaturely Life: Rilke, Benjamin, Sebald*. Chicago: University of Chicago Press, 2006.

———. *The Weight of All Flesh*. Oxford: Oxford University Press, 2016.

Sarna, Nahum M. *The JPS Torah Commentary: Five Volumes*. Philadelphia: Jewish Publication Society, 1989–91.

Scappi, Bartolomeo. *Opera: L'arte et prudenza d'un maestro cuoco*. Translated by Terence Scully. Toronto: University of Toronto Press, 2008.

Scarry, Elaine. *The Body in Pain: The Making and Unmaking of the World*. New York: Oxford University Press, 1985.

Scharr, Adam. *Heidegger for Architects*. New York: Routledge, 2007.

Schmitt, Bernd, and Alex Simonson. *Marketing Aesthetics: The Strategic Management of Brands, Identity, and Image*. New York: Simon and Schuster, 1997.

Schoenbaum, S. *William Shakespeare: A Compact Documentary Life*. Rev. ed. New York: Oxford University Press, 1987.

Scholem, Gershom. *The Messianic Idea in Judaism: And Other Essays on Jewish Spirituality*. 2nd ed. New York: Random House, 1995.

Schwartz, Howard. *Tree of Souls: The Mythology of Judaism*. Oxford: Oxford University Press, 2004.

Sellers, E., ed. *The Elder Pliny's Chapters on the History of Art*. Translated by K. Jex-Blake. London: Macmillan, 1896.

Seneca. "Hercules Furens." In *Tragedies I*, translated by Frank Justus Miller. Cambridge: Loeb Classics, 1979.

Shakespeare, William. *As You Like It*. Edited by David Bevington. New York: Broadview, 2012.

———. *The Comedy of Errors*. In *The Riverside Shakespeare*, edited by G. Blakemore Evans. 2nd ed. New York: Houghton Mifflin, 1997.

———. *The Comedy of Errors*. Edited by Charles Whitworth. Oxford: Oxford University Press, 2002.

———. *Cymbeline*. Edited by Roger Warren. Oxford: Oxford University Press, 1998.

———. *Julius Caesar*. In *The Riverside Shakespeare*, edited by G. Blakemore Evans. 2nd ed. New York: Houghton Mifflin, 1997.

———. *Macbeth*. Edited by Nicholas Brooke. Oxford: Oxford University Press, 1990.

———. *A Midsummer Night's Dream*. In *The Riverside Shakespeare*, edited by G. Blakemore Evans. 2nd ed. New York: Houghton Mifflin, 1997.

———. *The Plays of William Shakespeare*. Edited by Samuel Johnson and George Steevens. Vol. 10. London: C. Bathurst, 1773.

———. *Romeo and Juliet*. Edited by Jill Levinson. Oxford: Oxford University Press, 2000.

———. *Romeo and Juliet*. Edited by Brian Gibbons. Walton-on-Thames: Nelson and Sons, 1997.

———. *Sonnets*. Edited by Stephen Booth. New Haven, CT: Yale University Press, 1977.

———. *The Taming of the Shrew*. In *The Riverside Shakespeare*, edited by G. Blakemore Evans. 2nd ed. New York: Houghton Mifflin, 1997.

———. *Venus and Adonis*. In *The Riverside Shakespeare*, edited by G. Blakemore Evans. 2nd ed. New York: Houghton Mifflin, 1997.

———. *The Winter's Tale*. Edited by Stephen Orgel. New York: Oxford University Press, 2008.

Shannon, Laurie. *The Accommodated Animal: Cosmopolity in Shakespearean Locales*. Chicago: University of Chicago Press, 2013.

———. "Poor, Bare, Forked: Animal Sovereignty, Human Negative

Exceptionalism, and the Natural History of *King Lear*." *Shakespeare Quarterly* 60, no. 2 (Summer 2009): 168–96.

Shaviro, Steven. *The Universe of Things: On Speculative Realism*. Minneapolis: University of Minnesota Press, 2014.

Shepphard, Geroald T., ed. *Annotated New Testament, 1602 Edition*. New York: Pilgrim Press, 1989.

Sherman, Donovan. *Second Death: Theatricalities of the Soul in Shakespeare*. Edinburgh: University of Edinburgh Press, 2017.

———. "'What More Remains?': Messianic Performance in *Richard II*." *Shakespeare Quarterly* 65, no. 1 (Spring 2014): 22–48.

Simmonds, Peggy Muñoz. *Myth, Emblem, and Music in Shakespeare's "Cymbeline."* Newark: University of Delaware Press, 1992.

Simmons, J. L. "Shakespeare's *Hamlet* and Familial Blessings: Historical Abruptions." *MLQ* 74, no. 4 (December 2013): 441–63.

Simon, Uriel, ed. *The JPS Bible Commentary: The Book of Jonah*. Philadelphia: Jewish Publication Society, 1999.

Slater, Ann Pasternak. "Petrarchanism Come True in *Romeo and Juliet*." In *Images of Shakespeare*, edited by Werner Habicht et al., 129–46. Cranbury, NJ: Associated University Presses, 1988.

Smith, Bruce. *The Acoustic World of Early Modern England: Attending to the O-Factor*. Chicago: University of Chicago Press, 1999.

———. *The Key of Green: Passion and Perception in Renaissance Culture*. Chicago: University of Chicago Press, 2009.

———. *Phenomenal Shakespeare*. Chichester: Wiley Blackwell, 2010.

Smith, Korydon, ed. *Introducing Architectural Theory: Debating a Discipline*. New York: Routledge, 2012.

Smith, Matthew. "Describing the Sense of Confession in Hamlet." In *The Return of Theory in Early Modern English Studies*, vol. 2, edited by Paul Cefalu, Gary Kuchar, and Bryan Reynolds, 149–65. New York: Palgrave Macmillan, 2014.

———. "Stage, Cathedral, Wagon, Street: Theatrical Belief in Early Modern England." Manuscript.

Sofer, Andrew. *Dark Matter: Invisibility in Drama, Theater, and Performance*. Ann Arbor: University of Michigan Press, 2013.

———. "Spectral Readings." *Theatre Journal* 64, no. 3 (October 2012): 323–36.

———. *The Stage Life of Props*. Ann Arbor: University of Michigan Press, 2003.

Soja, Edward. "In Different Spaces: Interpreting the Spatial Organization of Societies." In *Proceedings of the Third International Space Syntax Symposium*, Atlanta, 2001. http://www.ucl.ac.uk/bartlett/3sss/papers_pdf/s1_Soja.pdf. Accessed July 4, 2013.

Soule, Lesley Wade. "Tumbling Tricks: Presentational Structure and 'The Taming of the Shrew.'" *New Theatre Quarterly* 20, no. 2 (2004): 164–201.

Sousa, Geraldo U. de. *At Home in Shakespeare's Tragedies*. Farnham: Ashgate, 2011.

Spiegel, Shalom. *The Last Trial: On the Legends and Lore of the Akedah*. Woodstock, VT: Jewish Lights, 1993.

Spolsky, Ellen. "An Embodied View of Misunderstanding in *Macbeth*." *Poetics Today* 32, no. 3 (Fall 2011): 489–520.

———. *Word vs. Image: Cognitive Hunger in Shakespeare's England*. New York: Palgrave MacMillan, 2007.

Spurgeon, Carolyn. *Shakespeare's Imagery and What It Tells Us*. Cambridge: Cambridge University Press, 1935.

Spurling, Hilary. *Elinor Fettiplace's Receipt Book: English Country House Cooking*. London: Faber and Faber, 2011.

Stallybrass, Peter. "The Mystery of Walking." *Journal of Medieval and Early Modern Studies* 32, no. 3 (Fall 2002): 571–80.

Stanley, Thomas. *The History of Philosophy in Eight Parts*. Cambridge: Chadwyck-Healey, 1992.

States, Bert. *Great Reckonings in Little Rooms: On the Phenomenology of Theater*. Berkeley: University of California Press, 1985.

———. "The Horses of 'Macbeth.'" *Kenyon Review* 7, no. 2 (Spring 1985): 52–66.

Stead, Jennifer. "Bowers of Bliss: The Banqueting Setting." In *Banqueting Stuffe*, edited by C. Anne Wilson, 115–57. Edinburgh: Edinburgh University Press, 1991.

Sterrett, Joseph. *The Unheard Prayer: Religious Toleration in Shakespeare's Drama*. Leiden: Brill, 2013.

Strate, Lance. "Violence, Power, Technology, and Identity." Hannah Arendt Center Blog, December 7, 2011, http://www.hannaharendtcenter.org/?p=3103.

Strelan, Rick. *Paul, Artemis, and the Jews of Ephesus*. Berlin: Walter de Gruyter, 1996.

Sullivan, Garrett A. *Sleep, Romance and Human Embodiment: Vitality from Spenser to Milton*. Cambridge: Cambridge University Press, 2012.

Summerscale, Anne, ed. and trans. *Malvasi's Life of the Caracci: Commentary and Translation*. University Park: Pennsylvania State University Press, 2000.

Summit, Jennifer. "Hannah Woolley, the Oxinden Letters, and Household Epistolary Practice." In *Women, Property, and the Letters of the Law in Early Modern England*, edited by Margaret W. Ferguson, A. R. Buck, and Nancy Wright, 201–18. Toronto: University of Toronto Press, 2004.

Swaffield, Simon, ed., *Theory in Landscape Architecture: A Reader*. Philadelphia: University of Pennsylvania Press, 2002.

Swift, Daniel. *Shakespeare's Common Prayers: The Book of Common Prayer and the Elizabethan Age*. New York: Oxford University Press, 2012.

Tamari, Meir. *Truths Desired by God: An Excursion into the Weekly Haftarah*. Jerusalem: Geffen Books, 2011.

Targoff, Ramie. *Common Prayer: The Language of Public Devotion in Early Modern England*. Chicago: University of Chicago Press, 2001.

Taylor, Jeremy. *Eniatos*. London: Richard Royston, 1653.

Terranova, Tiziana. *Network Cultures: Politics for the Information Age*. London: Pluto Press, 2004.

Thacker, Eugene. *After Life*. Chicago: University of Chicago Press, 2010.

———. *In the Dust of This Planet: Horror of Philosophy*. Vol. 1. Washington, DC: Zero Books, 2010.

Thomson, Stephen. "The Adjective, My Daughter: Staging T. S. Eliot's 'Marina.'" *Yearbook of English Studies* 32 (2002): 110–26.

Thornton, Peter. *The Italian Renaissance Interior, 1400–1600*. New York: Abrams, 1991.

Tiffany, Daniel. *Infidel Poetics: Riddles, Nightlife, Substance*. Chicago: University of Chicago Press, 2009.

Tigner, Amy. "Eating with the Sidneys: Hospitality at Penshurst." Paper for Seminar on Shakespeare and Hospitality, convened by David Goldstein and Julia Reinhard Lupton, Shakespeare Association of America, Spring 2013.

Torsellino, Orazio. *The History of Our B. Lady of Loreto*. Ilkley: Scolar Press, 1976.

Trencsényi, Katalin, and Bernadette Cochrane, eds. *New Dramaturgy: International Perspectives on Theory and Practice*. London: Bloomsbury, 2014.

Trevisan, Sara. "The Impact of the Netherlandish Tradition on Poetry and Painting in Early Modern England." *Renaissance Quarterly* 66, no. 3 (Fall 2013): 866–903.

Tribble, Evelyn. *Cognition in the Globe: Attention and Memory in Shakespeare's Theatre*. New York: Palgrave MacMillan 2011.

Trivedi, Poonam, and Dennis Bartholomeusz. *India's Shakespeare: Translation, Interpretation, and Performance*. Newark: University of Delaware Press, 2005.

Turner, Harold W. *From Temple to Meeting House: The Phenomenology and Theology of Places of Worship*. The Hague: Walter de Gruyter, 1979.

Turner, Henry S. "Life Science: Rude Mechanicals, Human Mortals, Posthuman Shakespeare." *South Central Review* 26, nos. 1 & 2 (Winter and Spring 2009): 197–217.

———. *Shakespeare's Double Helix*. London: Continuum, 2008.

Tusser, Thomas. *Five Hundred Points of Good Husbandry*. London: Lackington, Allen, and Company, 1812.

Valls-Russell, Janice. "Erotic Perspectives: When Pyramus and Thisbe Meet Hero and Leander in *Romeo and Juliet*." In *Shakespeare's Erotic Mythology and Ovidian Renaissance Culture*, edited by Agnès Lafont, 77–91. Farnham: Ashgate, 2013.

Varriano, John. "At Supper with Leonardo." *Gastronomica* 8, no. 1 (Winter 2008): 75–79.

Vatter, Miguel. "Natality and Biopolitics in Hannah Arendt." *Revista de Ciencia Política* 26, no. 2 (2006): 137–59.

Virno, Paolo. "Virtuosity and Revolution: The Political Theory of Exodus." In *Radical Thought in Italy: A Potential Politics*, edited by Paolo Virno and Michael Hardt, 188–209. Minneapolis: University of Minnesota Press, 1996.

Vitruvius. "Ten Books of Architecture." In *Introducing Architectural Theory: Debating a Discipline*, edited by Korydon Smith, 313–18. New York: Routledge, 2012.

Waldheim, Charles, ed. *Landscape Urbanism Reader*. New York: Princeton Architectural Press, 2002.

Waldron, Jennifer. "Lavinia is Philomel." Paper for seminar "Object-Oriented Shakespeare," Shakespeare Association of America, Saint Louis, 2014.

Walker, D. P. "The Astral Body in Renaissance Medicine." *Journal of the Warburg and Courtauld Institutes* 21, no. 1/2 (1958): 119–33.

Walker, Jeremy, and Melinda Cooper. "Genealogies of Resilience: From Systems Ecology to the Political Economy of Crisis Adaptation." *Security Dialogue* 42, no. 2 (2011): 143–60.

Wall, Wendy. "Just a Spoonful of Sugar: Syrup and Domesticity in Early Modern England." *Modern Philology* 104, no. 2 (Fall 2006): 149–72.

———. "Literacy and the Domestic Arts." *Huntington Library Quarterly* 73, no. 3 (September 2010): 383–412.

———. *Recipes for Thought: Knowledge and Taste in the Early Modern Kitchen*. Philadelphia: University of Pennsylvania Press, 2016.

———. *Staging Domesticity: Household Work and English Identity in Early Modern Drama* Cambridge: Cambridge University Press, 2002.

Wallace, David Foster. "Mister Squishy." In *Oblivion*. New York: Back Bay Books, 2004.

Walsham, Alexandra. *The Reformation of the Landscape: Religion, Identity, and Memory in Early Modern Britain and Ireland*. Oxford: Oxford University Press, 2011.

Ware, Owen. "Dialectic of the Past/Disjuncture of the Future: Derrida and Benjamin on the Concept of Messianism." *Journal of Religious and Cultural Theory* 5, no. 2 (April 2004): 99–114.

Warthall, Mark A. "Unconcealment." In *A Companion to Heidegger*, edited by Hubert L. Dreyfus and Mark A. Warthall, 334–59. Malden, MA: Wiley Blackwell, 1993.

Watson, Robert. *Back to Nature: The Green and the Real in the Late Renaissance*. Philadelphia: University of Pennsylvania Press, 2006.

———. "The Ecology of Self in *Midsummer Night's Dream*." In *Ecocritical Shakespeare*, edited by Lynne Bruckner and Dan Brayton, 33–56. Farnham: Ashgate, 2011.

———. "'Thriftless Ambition,' Foolish Wishes, and the Tragedy of *Macbeth*." In *Macbeth*, edited by Harold Bloom. New York: Chelsea House, 2005.

Watson, Thomas. *Hekatompathia; or, Passionate centurie of love*. Gainesville, FL: Scholars' Facsimiles & Reprints, 1964.

Wehrs, Douglas. "Placing Human Constants within Literary History: Generic Revision and Affective Sociality in *The Winter's Tale* and *The Tempest*." *Poetics Today* 32, no. 3 (Fall 2011): 521–91.

Weigert, Laura. "Chambres d'amour: Tapestries of Love and the Texturing of Space." *Oxford Art Journal* 31, no. 3 (2008): 317–36.

Welker, Michael. *God the Spirit*. Minneapolis: Fortress Press, 1994.

Wells, James. "'To be thus is nothing': *Macbeth* and the Trials of

Dramatic Identity." In *Macbeth: New Critical Essays*, edited by Nick Moschovakis, 224–39. New York: Routledge, 2008.

Wells-Cole, Anthony. *Art and Decoration in Elizabethan and Jacobean England: The Influence of Continental Prints, 1558–1625*. New Haven, CT: Yale University Press, 1997.

Westra, Adam. Review, Hans Blumenberg, *Paradigms for a Metaphorology*. *Ithaque* 7 (Fall 2010): 119–29.

Wilcox, Helen, and Richard Todd, eds. *George Herbert: Sacred and Profane*. Amsterdam: VU University Press, 1995.

Wilder, Lena Perkins. *Shakespeare's Memory Theatre: Recollection, Properties, and Character*. Cambridge: Cambridge University Press, 2010.

Willet, Andrew. *Hexapla in Danielem*. Cambridge: Printed for Leonard Greene, 1610.

Williams, Philip. "The Rosemary Theme in *Romeo and Juliet*." *Modern Language Notes* 68, no. 6 (1953): 400–403.

Wilson, Anne C., ed. *Banquetting Stuffe*. Edinburgh: Edinburgh University Press, 1991.

Wilson, Luke. "The Fate of the Second Bird." In *Object Oriented Environs*, edited by Jeffrey Jerome Cohen and Julian Yates, 153–63. Earth: punctum books, 2016.

Wilson, Richard. *Secret Shakespeare: Studies in Theatre, Religion and Resistance*. Manchester: Manchester University Press, 2004.

Winiarski, Catherine. "'A world ransomed, or one destroyed': Romance and Messianism in *The Winter's Tale*." Paper presented at Renaissance Society of America, 2013.

Winnicott, D. W. *Playing and Reality*. Oxon: Routledge, 2005.

Winter, Johanna Maria van. "The Low Countries in the Fifteenth and Sixteenth Centuries." In *Regional Cuisines of Medieval Europe*, edited by Malitta Weiss Adamson, 197–211. New York: Routledge, 2002.

Witthoft, Bruccia. "Marriage Rituals and Marriage Chests in Quattrocento Florence." *Artibus et Historiae* 3, no. 5 (1982): 43–59.

Wojciehowski, Hannah Chapelle. "Statues That Move: Vitality Effects in *The Winter's Tale*." *Literature and Theology* 28, no. 3 (2014): s.

Womack, Peter. "Shakespeare and the Sea of Stories." *Journal of Medieval and Early Modern Studies* 29, no. 1 (Winter 1999): 169–87.

Woods, Gillian. *Shakespeare's Unreformed Fictions*. New York: Oxford University Press, 2013.

Woolley, Hannah. *The accomplished ladys delight in preserving, physic and cookery*. London, 1675.

———. *The Gentlewoman's Companion*. London, 1673.

———. *The Queen-Like Closet or Rich Cabinet*. 4th ed. London: R. Chisewel, 1681.

Worthen, W. B. *Drama between Poetry and Performance*. Malden, MA: Wiley-Blackwell, 2010.

Yates, Amanda. "Oceanic Spaces of Flow." In *Architecture in the Space of Flows*, edited by Andrew Ballantyne and Chris L. Smith, 63–80. New York: Routledge, 2012.

Yates, Frances. *Shakespeare's Last Plays: A New Approach*. London: Routledge, 1975.

Yates, Julian. *Error, Misuse, Failure: Object Lessons from the English Renaissance*. Minneapolis: University of Minnesota Press, 2003.

———. "Skin Merchants: Jack Cade's Futures and the Figural Politics of *Henry VI, Part III*." In *Go Figure: Energies, Forms, and Institutions in the Early Modern World*, edited by Judith H. Anderson and Joan Pong Linton, 149–70. New York: Fordham University Press, 2011.

———. "Towards a Theory of Agentive Drifts; Or, A Particular Fondness for Oranges circa 1597." *Parallax* 8, no. 1 (2002): 47–58.

———. "What Are 'Things' Saying in Renaissance Studies?" *Literature Compass* 3, no. 5 (2006): 992–1010.

Yiu, Mimi. *Architectural Involutions: Writing, Staging, and Building Space, c. 1435–1650*. Evanston, IL: Northwestern University Press, 2015.

Yong, Amos. *Hospitality and the Other: Pentecost, Christian Practices, and the Neighbor*. Maryknoll, NY: Orbis Books, 2008.

Zaleski, Philip, and Carol Zaleski. *Prayer: A History*. New York: Houghton Mifflin, 2005.

Zamir, Tzachi. *Acts: Theater, Philosophy, and the Performing Self*. Cambridge, MA: Harvard University Press, 2014.

Ziegler, Georgianna. "My Lady's Chamber: Female Space, Female Chastity in Shakespeare." *Textual Practice* (1990): 73–90.

Zim, Rivkah. "Stephan Batman." In *Oxford Dictionary of National Biography*. http://www.oxforddnb.com/view/article/1704.

Žižek, Slavoj, Eric Santner, and Kenneth Reinhard. *The Neighbor: Three Inquiries into Political Theology*. Chicago: University of Chicago Press, 2013.

Index